Economic Reform and Social Change in China

Economic growth in China has transformed both politics and society. Old orthodoxies are painfully being eroded in the drive for reform while new social and cultural tensions are coming to light. It has been argued that the cycles of reform and retreat since 1978 which culminated in the Tiananmen Square tragedy were induced by the tensions of the reform process. It is clear that the way in which China handles these issues in the future will have major implications for the next phase of the country's development.

The authors of this book analyse how reform has affected major groups in society such as urban workers, rural and urban cadres, the army, intellectuals and private entrepreneurs. They examine the interaction between old attitudes and new needs in areas such as education, policing and social control, rural administration and the status of women. What emerges is a broad insight into China's reform process which looks at both the enormous changes that have come about and the problems to follow.

This book will appeal to scholars and students of Chinese studies, development, politics and economics, and to those who have professional interests in China and its agenda for reform.

Andrew Watson is Professor of Asian Studies and Co-Director of the Chinese Economy Research Unit at the University of Adelaide, South Australia.

ECONOMIC REFORM AND SOCIAL CHANGE IN CHINA

Edited by
ANDREW WATSON

London and New York

First published 1992
by Routledge
11 New Fetter Lane, London EC4P 4EE

Simultaneously published in the USA and Canada
by Routledge
a division of Routledge, Chapman and Hall, Inc.
29 West 35th Street, New York, NY 10001

Typeset in Garamond by LaserScript Limited, Mitcham, Surrey
Printed and bound in Great Britain by
Biddles Ltd, Guildford and King's Lynn

British Library Cataloguing in Publication Data
A catalogue reference for this title is available from the British Library.
ISBN 0–415–06973–4

Library of Congress Cataloging in Publication Data
Economic reform and social change in China/edited by Andrew Watson.
p. cm.
Includes bibliographical references and index.
ISBN 0–415–06973–4
1. China – Economic policy – 1976– 2. China – Social policy.
3. China – Politics and government – 1976– I. Watson, Andrew, 1942–
HC427.92.E368 1992
303.4'2'095109048 – dc20 91-44804
CIP

CONTENTS

v

TABLES

CONTRIBUTORS

Sylvia Chan is Senior Lecturer in Chinese Studies at the Centre for Asian Studies of the University of Adelaide.

Michael Dutton is Lecturer in Politics in the Department of Political Science at the University of Melbourne.

Christopher Findlay is Associate Professor in the Department of Economics of the University of Adelaide, and Research Associate of the Australia–Japan Research Centre at the Australian National University. He is also co-Director of the Chinese Economy Research Unit at the University of Adelaide.

Tamara Jacka is Lecturer in Chinese Studies at Murdoch University.

Jiang Shu is a graduate of the International University of Japan, with a Masters in International Relations. While working on this project, he was a research assistant in the Department of Economics at the University of Adelaide.

Greg O'Leary is Senior Lecturer in Labour Studies at the University of Adelaide.

Andrew Watson is Professor of Asian Studies at the University of Adelaide and co-Director of the University's Chinese Economy Research Unit.

Dennis Woodward is Senior Lecturer in Politics at Monash University.

Susan Young is Tutor in Chinese Studies in the Centre for Asian Studies at the University of Adelaide. She is also a member of the University's Chinese Economy Research Unit.

Zhang Ning is Lecturer in Chinese Studies in the Centre for Asian Studies at the University of Adelaide.

ACKNOWLEDGEMENTS

This collection originated in a series of workshop and conference presentations held during 1989 and revised in the light of developments in China since the tragic events of that year. Various parts of the work were supported by grants from the Australian Research Council and the University of Adelaide. The authors are grateful for the critical comments of participants in the workshops and conferences, in particular from Barbara Bray, Peter Burns, Hsu Chiacheng, Bill Jenner, Peter Mayer, Li Qingzeng, Doug McEachern and Jonathan Unger.

ABBREVIATIONS

ACFTU	All-China Federation of Trade Unions
BR	*Beijing Review*
CCP	Chinese Communist Party
GMRB	*Guangming Ribao (Bright Daily)*
FNGZ	*Funü Gongzuo (Women's Work)*
FX	*Faxue (Legal Studies)*
FXYJ	*Faxue Yanjiu (Legal Research)*
JFJB	*Jiefangjun Bao (Liberation Army Daily)*
JJCK	*Jingji Cankao (Economic Reference News)*
JJRB	*Jingji Ribao (Economics Daily)*
JJYJ	*Jingji Yanjiu (Economic Research)*
JYYJ	*Jiaoyu Yanjiu (Educational Research)*
JYQBCK	*Jiaoyu Qingbao Cankao (Educational Information Reference News)*
NYJJWT	*Nongye Jingji Wenti (Problems in Agricultural Economics)*
NMRB	*Nongmin Ribao (Peasants' Daily)*
PLA	People's Liberation Army
PR	*Peking Review*
RMJY	*Renmin Jiaoyu (People's Education)*
RMRB	*Renmin Ribao (People's Daily)*
SWB	*Summary of World Broadcasts, Part 3, The Far East* (British Broadcasting Corporation)
ZGFN	*Zhongguo Funü (Chinese Women)*
ZGJYB	*Zhongguo Jiaoyu Bao (Chinese Education Daily)*
ZGNCJJ	*Zhongguo Nongcun Jingji (China's Rural Economy)*
ZGQN	*Zhongguo Qingnian (China's Youth)*

1

INTRODUCTION

Andrew Watson

The aim of this book is to explore the relationship between economic growth and social change, as experienced in the process of reform in China since 1978. During this time China has experienced the longest phase of sustained economic growth since the founding of the People's Republic. The real rate of growth between 1977 and 1986 was 9.2 per cent per year and in the years 1986 to 1988 slightly higher at 9.6 per cent.[1] At the same time, many of the social and institutional structures established in the preceding years have been modified or replaced, and there has been an explosion of debate, experimentation and innovation. The entire process has been characterized by *ad hoc* adjustments, pragmatic experiments, and lively analytical discussion.

Not surprisingly, a transformation of such magnitude and speed has given rise to a host of new issues. Rapid economic growth has brought equally rapid changes in the distribution of economic wealth and in the social and political relationships which that distribution embodies. It has transformed the balance between economic sectors and led to renewed debate over the distribution of wealth. It has also raised new questions about the relationships between Chinese society and the environment and between China and the rest of the world. The size and speed of such changes have thus presented major challenges to the established order. What are the political and social consequences of rapid growth? Can Chinese society bear the strains induced? How do institutions established to manage one type of economic system cope with an entirely new one? What further social and institutional adjustments are required to ensure continued economic development? Is there an incompatibility between economic trends and social and political structures such that the pace and nature of economic growth may become constrained or distorted? As the 1980s drew to a close, these were among the most hotly debated questions in China. The solutions will affect both how the Chinese economy continues to grow and the way Chinese society evolves.

Issues such as these have, of course, long been a major focus of the study of economic development. Writing in 1971, Albert Hirschman argued that

> At any one historical stage, the economy functions within a given political and institutional framework; on the basis of and owing to this framework, economic forces left to themselves can achieve some forward movement, but beyond a certain point further development becomes more difficult and eventually is held back by the unchanging political framework which, from a spur to progress turns into a 'fetter'; at that point political–institutional change is not only necessary to permit further advances, but is also highly likely to occur, because economic development will have generated some powerful social group with a vital stake in the needed change.[2]

Such arguments have a long history and share much ground with Marxist views on the relationship between economic forces on the one hand and political and social forces on the other, even though there is disagreement over whether the processes involved are revolutionary or evolutionary. Analysis of development therefore tends to focus on the relationship between economic, technical, social and political factors as growth takes place.[3] What happens in a society to call forth particular types of accumulation and investment, to change factor productivity, and to induce structural shifts in the relationship between different economic sectors? Can such events be explained purely in economic terms? What is the relative significance of technology in this process? Is technological change in a particular economic sector driven by endogenous or exogenous forces? What is the role of cultural, political and institutional adaptation in the face of changing economic relationships? Can such adaptation be managed in ways which facilitate the development and introduction of new technologies and managerial efficiencies, or is it primarily the product of conflict between old and new vested interests, involving disputes over economic and political power and over equity and the distribution of benefits? These questions have absorbed the energies of both those attempting to explain the evolution of economic and social systems and those consciously engaged in directing economic growth.

Exploring these issues also inevitably involves questions of causal linkages. Some perspectives emphasize the primacy of economic factors, while others stress the social and political dimensions. Clearly the economic parameters set limits on how a society can function, yet they are themselves conditioned by the set of institutions and values through which they are realized. Economic behaviour can be understood only in its social context. The two dimensions are part of a whole and causal linkages can be traced in both directions. It is thus difficult to establish the primacy of one set of factors over the other.

Within China, much of the intellectual ferment which has produced the reforms has focused precisely on this relationship between economic growth and its social context. Chinese scholars have debated the 'deep structure' or 'feudal' heritage of Chinese culture and the bearing that they might have on the country's recent history and current performance. They have addressed the Marxist view of the relationship between the superstructure and the economic base and considered whether the social relations of centralized planning and collective farming were too 'advanced' for the level of development of the forces of production, or conversely whether institutional and political changes are needed as a prerequisite for further economic growth and technical modernization. Liberal thinkers have blamed the authoritarian nature of the Chinese political and economic system on the 'feudal' past. By contrast, many within the Chinese Communist Party have been profoundly worried by the relaxation in controls over social behaviour brought about by the reforms, arguing that only a reassertion of party supremacy can guide further development. All these issues have been the subject of intense theoretical analysis. They have also had an immediate social significance as was graphically demonstrated by the events of May and June 1989. The political and economic stresses brought about by ten years of reform and the changing social relationships that it engendered resulted in a challenge to the authority of the Chinese Communist Party and created deep divisions within the political system. The way those divisions are resolved will, in turn, have major implications for the next phase of economic growth.

Reform in China is thus not simply a question of finding the right sequence of economic policy choices, such as deciding whether one kind of price reform should precede another, or whether enterprise autonomy is a precondition for price reform, or whether the balance in taxation between central and local governments should shift in one direction or the other. It encompasses the complete fabric of political, social and economic relationships. The Beijing massacre and the subsequent shifts in policies did nothing either to change this reality or to resolve the underlying tensions in the mix that now exists. Much of the previous orthodoxy is now untenable, and economic growth has created new demands and pressures. The failure of more conservative policies to stem the tide of change during 1989 and 1990 and the subsequent reassertion of the need for further reform provide strong evidence of this.

The chapters in this book set out to examine how various dimensions of this relationship between economic growth and social change were addressed in the course of China's reforms. By examining specific aspects of social, cultural, political and institutional change, they seek to explain both the effect economic development has had on those areas and the feedback from them into further economic change. By exploring how the momentum set in motion by the reforms evolved, they elucidate both the complexities of the underlying relationships and the options for the next phase of economic and social development in China.

THE CHINESE CONTEXT

Arguments over the relationship between economic growth, institutional structures and social attitudes in China can be traced back to the debate over the relationship between Chinese essence and foreign 'know-how', between *ti* and *yong*. The assumption has been that social and cultural forces are a prime constraint on economic growth and technical modernization. After 1949 this relationship remained a key concern of Mao Zedong. The introduction of centralized planning in the 1950s was a major effort to transform institutions in order to facilitate economic development. Mao's focus on social contradictions during the late 1950s and early 1960s reflected his belief that the consequences of the Soviet model were both hampering economic growth and creating a new and unwelcome set of social relationships. The Cultural Revolution posed the question of whether social and ideological factors were the key to economic growth and change, even though in reality it was often little more than an intense political and factional struggle. The nature of economic policies from the 1950s to 1978 was thus profoundly shaped by Mao's concern with this relationship. It led many to consider him as a 'voluntarist', or at least an opponent of a mechanical and deterministic Marxism which gives total primacy to the economic base.

By 1978, the challenges facing Chinese society were the product of three main factors: the social and institutional constraints of the bureaucratic distribution system and its values; the political factionalism of the Cultural Revolution; and the new relationships created by the economic growth which had occurred since 1949. Over the previous thirty years, significant growth had taken place, with concomitant changes in sectoral relationships, in levels of income, in levels of accumulation, in distribution of population, and in the economic relationship with the rest of the world. These developments raised the question of whether further innovation should take place in the established institutional and social system. And that, in turn, affected the vested political interests of the factions that had evolved through the Cultural Revolution. Economic factors such as the slow growth in the productivity of labour, the increasing costs of generating employment in the state sector, income inequalities between urban and rural areas and the changing balance of economic relationships between different regions were also forcing the pace of change. It was not surprising to find that early in the debate over the need for reform, Deng Xiaoping raised the question of whether advanced technology placed new demands on social institutions,[4] and the debates which preceded the reform decisions also saw social change as an essential element in economic development. Throughout the history of both modern China and the People's Republic, therefore, discussion of this relationship has been at the forefront of China's agenda for revolution and change.

THE ISSUES

The above discussion suggests the series of themes around which the chapters in this book have been constructed. One of the most fundamental is whether economic pluralism demands political, institutional, social and cultural pluralism. What, in other words, is the relationship between liberalization as an economic process and democratization as a political process? It might be argued (and has been within China) that a more market-oriented economy needs a more decentralized set of institutions, with more political pluralism and multipolarity in order to express and resolve the conflicting interests of different economic groups. On the other hand, it might also be argued (and, indeed, also has been within China) that the transition to the new set of institutions requires strong central authority to overcome any resistance from entrenched groups opposing change. In specific terms, the issue is whether the political institutions which accompanied the pre-reform economy correspond to the current economic reality, and, if not, how should they be rebuilt? By what mechanisms? And by whom? Such issues are, to varying degrees, addressed by all of the contributions to this collection.

A second theme is the changing position of different social groups, such as intellectuals, peasants, industrial managers, workers, cadres, teachers and the army. The reforms have transformed the distribution of economic benefits between them, with implications for their social power, prestige and influence. At the same time, the values placed on different types of behaviour have also changed. The selfish or illegal behaviour of one era has become the positive entrepreneurial behaviour of another and, as a consequence, this has even required a redefinition of the nature of crime and the appropriate punishment. All of these changes, in turn, feed into other spheres of social behaviour, affecting a wide range of phenomena from the self-image of intellectuals to the status of and attitudes towards women.

A third area of concern is the ideological justification of the reforms. This is fundamental for the legitimacy of the Communist Party and its social authority. Until Mao's death, legitimacy focused on revolutionary goals. Since the reforms, the achievement of economic modernization has replaced social transformation as the key aim of policy and as the demonstration of the correctness of party leadership. In the primary stage of socialism, the litmus paper to detect whether a policy or an institutional arrangement is appropriate is no longer whether it conforms to long-term revolutionary goals but whether it promotes the growth of the forces of production. Such a view implies that almost all the established features of contemporary Chinese society might be open to renewed scrutiny. The nature of ownership, the form and content of laws, and the structure of social authority might all be amended. Yet there is a tension between such economic pragmatism and the party's perception of itself and its role as the guardian of revolutionary change defined by established doctrine. At another level, that tension between practice and doctrine is also reflected in the generational changes taking place in the membership of the party and in its leadership.

A further set of issues revolves around the relationship between 'tradition' and 'change'. Here the focus is on the inertia of existing institutions, patterns of behaviour and attitudes. 'Tradition' is not only the product of long-standing cultural and social patterns within China which influence the way people behave and the way institutions and values evolve, but also embodies the traditions of post-1949 orthodoxy. It is a process whereby the existing helps define the parameters of the new. It is not a static set of attributes. The responses of the party and other social institutions to the challenges presented by the reforms have been shaped by the managerial mechanisms, administrative procedures and values which matured in another context. Innovations rarely come *ex nihilo* but have to be based on the resources available. Both the demand for change and the choices made are conditioned by the immediate past. The result is, inevitably, a mixture of constraints and contradictions. The party, for example, wants local initiative and central control. Urban residents demand greater economic freedom and higher incomes but are unwilling to relinquish the economic guarantees that the former system gave them. The conflicts created by such opposing trends add to the complexity of the social developments taking place. As these essays show, this tension between old and new is a major issue in the problems currently facing China.

Finally, another crucial issue is the relationship between the reforms and the reactions from outside of China. At the simplest level, a positive response to China's increased participation in world trade expressed through such things as an openness to China's products or a willingness to supply technology might strengthen the hand of reformers within the Chinese system. Conversely, the adoption of barriers to China's exports or a shift in terms of trade against China might give strength to those within China who see dependency on the world economy as a strategic weakness and a political retreat. Both responses are shaped by forces outside of China's control but bear on the options China has. Although these chapters do not directly examine the external dimension and its impact, the changing perception of China's position in the world has been a significant factor affecting the evolution of the reforms. It has also directly influenced the reform of the PLA.

Studying these themes in the Chinese context also has significance for another broad set of issues. China's reforms are an example of the general problems that confront all centrally-planned economies. They must be seen as part of a process of on-going debate over and destruction of socialist theory and practice as established by Lenin and Stalin. When they began in the late 1970s, China's reforms were in many ways in the forefront of this process. While Eastern Europe had long debated the need for change, it was China which took the lead in practice. The political and social tensions engendered in China ultimately led to the reaction of June 1989. By contrast, the changes in Europe and the Soviet Union since that time have led to the collapse of the Stalinist political system, while the new economic system is yet to evolve. Why has the path of change become so diverse? And what factors have led China in a different direction? These chapters throw light on the extent to which China's policies are the product of a particular set of cultural and institutional patterns and the extent to which they can provide insights into the general problems of development and change in socialist countries.

THE STUDIES

The chapters in this book do not attempt to cover all of the multitude of issues that could be studied in this framework of questions. Instead, they focus on a number of specific areas of change as examples of the general themes explored.

Christopher Findlay and Jiang Shu begin by examining how the reforms have changed the balance of economic relationships and power between different groups within society. They argue that the reforms have both precipitated new sets of economic interest groups, loosely defined as groups which share certain types of economic resources or sources of economic power and income, and changed the economic parameters which define the way such groups inter-relate. The consequence is a new set of demands and behaviour patterns which require further changes in social institutions. Should such changes not be forthcoming, they may lead to stress or dislocation within the economy. Changing economic relationships between social groups are thus a source of demand for continued social change.

Clearly this analysis might be broadly applied to many different groups in society. For our purposes, however, the authors focus on those who are key actors in the evolution of the reforms: central cadres who have begun to lose their powers over economic distribution, provincial administrators who now have new sources of wealth at their disposal, urban consumers whose economic expectations have been raised but who fear the risks associated with further institutional changes, and rural producers who are now more sensitive to their opportunity costs and beginning to compete more aggressively with urban residents. These classifications are not rigidly established. They contain overlaps (administrators are also urban consumers, for example) and are based on different criteria (administrative power and sectoral employment). Nevertheless, identifying them as groups or sub-groups with common economic interests and examining how the reforms have impinged on their power and status and changed their behaviour, makes it possible to isolate some of the social and political consequences of the reforms and to consider the mechanisms involved in the resolution of the social tensions created. The failure to anticipate and handle these issues contributed directly to the social protests of May and June 1989, to the associated crisis of leadership and to the subsequent drive to reassert earlier forms of social control and authority.

The following chapters examine how the issues raised in general terms by Findlay and Jiang have affected particular social groups or institutions. Greg O'Leary examines a major focus of party concern, the industrial workforce, focusing on the trade unions and their relationship to both the workers in state enterprises and the new cohort of workers in private, collective and rural enterprises. He shows how the existing structure is no longer appropriate for the situation workers now face. Trade unions established as arms of management and 'transmission belts' between the party and the workers cannot represent worker interests when there is less job security, when welfare provisions are under threat, when there are widening gaps in income levels and when enterprises may no longer adhere to previous norms for job security, age of employment, and other forms of social support. After many years in which the Chinese economic system delivered substantial protections to its urban workers, the economic reforms have begun to introduce new uncertainties and risks. In such a context, pressures to change the nature and function of trade unions have grown. The assumption of identity of interests between management and workforce is becoming harder to sustain, and there is a need for the unions to adopt a more adversarial role in representing workers' interests. It

9

was therefore no surprise to find that these conflicts contributed to the emergence of demands for a more independent trade union system during 1989, and, equally, that the party reaction to such demands, representing as they do an implied parting of the ways between the industrial workers and the party state, has been severe.

In examining the status and role of private entrepreneurs, Susan Young deals with a very different dimension of enterprise operation. The private economy was formerly anathema to the socialist future and the economic plan. The adoption of the market and economic pluralism since 1978 has transformed this view of its social position and role. Furthermore, over ten years the growth of private economic activity has meant that it can no longer be seen as a mere supplement to the state economy, filling in the cracks until the socialist state matures to a level at which it can encompass everything. Instead it has a vitality and momentum of its own, which even the attempts at repression after June 1989 could not hold back. The mathematics appear simple. The cost of each new job in the state sector is far above the capacity of the state to invest at a level to ensure employment for all in urban areas. In the countryside, the possibility of the state taking responsibility for the unemployed or underemployed is not even on the agenda. Economic pluralism with a strong private sector is thus assuming an air of inevitability. Nevertheless, the relationship between the entrepreneur and the state still has many grey areas which have yet to be defined.

Given that situation, what is the status and role of the private entrepreneur? Young shows how the suspicion and low status generated by the centrally-planned system and its socialist morality has hindered the growth of the private sector and led to strategies for self-protection. Private businesses try to disguise themselves as collectives or build links with other types of activity. They support social welfare to prove that they are not exploiters. The effect on their economic behaviour is also significant. Because they are wary of their long-term status and security, they often have short-term horizons and look for a quick return on capital invested. By the same token, party and government authorities often retain their suspicion of private entrepreneurs. They pressure them to conform to party goals and try to manage them through new institutions which reflect old patterns of 'mass organizations'. As they grow, entrepreneurs increasingly find a conflict between the administrative boundaries of party and state and the plasticity of economic linkages shaped by market forces and the profit motive. At the same

10

time, party and government cadres may also exploit private business for their own interests. In effect, entrepreneurs often have little choice but to operate on the edge of legality and subject to pressures from those with administrative power, creating opportunities for many kinds of corruption. Ultimately, the established institutional framework is not properly equipped to handle private activity, and its response is to adapt within existing norms and methods. Private entrepreneurs are forced to protect their future by trying to disguise their true nature, while, at the same time, urgently hoping for an institutional and legal framework which will provide safe parameters for their activities.

Sylvia Chan's contribution also addresses the issue of the relationship between the individual and the state, this time by analysing the nature and role of one of the most crucial social groups, the intellectuals. Historically, intellectuals have always occupied a special position in China. They have been the guardians of ideology and the creators and repositories of cultural values. In modern times they have been in the forefront of the revolution to sweep aside the Confucian past. Nevertheless, there has always been a tension in their relationship to the rulers of China. While many would like to see themselves as the Hai Rui of Chinese society, ready to protect ideals against despotic rulers, few have dared to perform that role. Instead, the demands of the party and their willingness to serve have often made them the mouthpieces of orthodoxy. Given the treatment of intellectuals since 1949, such caution is not surprising. The social liberalization associated with the reforms, however, has begun to break the bonds on intellectuals and to change their attitudes and behaviour. Chan shows how the intellectuals, defined to include the scientifically and technically educated, are coming to see themselves as a special social group which provides the creativity and talent needed for the achievement of the four modernizations. They have played a significant role in the process of change since 1978 and have developed a strong sense of their identity and interests. The old duality of red and expert is being destroyed by the de-mystification of Marxist ideology and the shift to reliance on technocratic expertise.

What, then, is the role intellectuals are seeking to fill? Chan explores the proposition that, with their new sense of identity and crucial function in modernization, intellectuals have become central to the destruction of Marxist ideology and to the development of a new morality of technical decision-making in ways suggesting the

11

emergence of a new class. Their strategy has included working within the party and outside it, and their challenge to authority has been expressed through issues such as the debate over the environment. Chan argues that, in these ways, they are coming to share part of the agenda of intellectuals in other parts of the world. Despite all this, however, only a small number participated openly in the demonstrations of 1989. To some extent, it might be argued that the lack of contact and understanding between the intellectuals and the demonstrating workers and students was a significant aspect of the collapse of the emerging movement. The intellectuals did not provide the theoretical articulation and organizational coherence required. The intellectuals of China have thus not yet emerged to fill the role played by their counterparts in Eastern Europe.

Tamara Jacka examines the impact of economic and social reform on gender relations and the position of women in rural China. Clearly this is an issue in which the weight of cultural tradition is extremely significant. It is also an issue which has been directly addressed since 1949, with a programme for social change and new institutions and laws to achieve it. Jacka argues, however, that many of the underlying patterns in gender relations have not changed in any fundamental way. The rural reforms have offered new types of employment to many rural women and improved their levels of income. They have new roles in domestic sidelines, specialized production and rural enterprises. Nevertheless, women have been restricted by the continuation, modification and reinforcement of a traditional gender division of labour and the values associated with it. In many areas, for example, it is the males who have taken most advantage of access to new jobs or geographical mobility. Women have been left to take over much of the agricultural work, alongside their domestic labour. As such, some of the old dualities of status and expectations have re-emerged in new forms, and the dominance of males has not been affected by the reforms. In effect the programme of reform has itself been developed through a reformulation of existing norms in gender relations.

Zhang Ning explores the reform of the educational system. Given the post-1978 emphasis on economic and technical modernization, the development of human resources and of the intellectual capacity to take the initiative and solve China's problems must be seen as a priority. No wonder, then, that educational development has been one of the major targets of the past ten years. The aim is to

12

improve both the numbers and the quality of the young people being trained. Zhang's analysis, however, demonstrates that there has been a wide gap between aspirations and achievement. The funds have not been provided and have even been directed to other uses. The social status of teachers has not recovered from the battering of the Cultural Revolution and their training has not improved. The low social and economic status of teachers has undermined their morale. Many have left teaching or neglect their work to seek other sources of income, thereby further hindering the development of education. The result? A failure to meet targets for intakes, a huge drop-out rate over the last ten years and a growing sense of disenchantment with the potential for education to improve one's lot. To some extent these outcomes reflect internal tensions within the reforms. Capital is, by definition, scarce. Rapid economic growth absorbs much of it and little is left for other social expenditure. Household farming puts a premium on household labour and keeping children at school, especially girls, entails opportunity costs. Decentralization of economic decision-making powers makes it more difficult to ensure that local cadres obey central directives, especially when those directives are expressed in general terms and have to be adapted to local circumstances where other priorities hold sway. Small wonder then that in 1989 students, uncertain of their prospects and unhappy with the education they were getting, took their disenchantment into the streets with their demands for a better education, for the right to air their grievances and for political change to match their perceptions of the failings of the current system.

My own chapter looks at the changing nature of government and administration in the countryside and considers the relationship between economic development and institutional adaptation. The economic reforms rapidly changed the parameters for the operation of local government and undermined the collective institutional framework. Nevertheless, the new institutional set-up has neither fully escaped from the past nor resolved emerging problems of administration and economic management. The devolution of economic powers has thus created a new sense of local economic identity which is serving to reinforce some of the previous linkages between administrative and economic decision-making, even though the local economy now has a very different relationship with the outside than it used to have. There is thus both institutional inertia and a new context for institutional operation.

13

At the same time, however, the evolution of rural institutions is increasingly subject to pressures from the new social forces at work in the countryside. Among these, a major one in many areas has been the emergence of rural cadres as local entrepreneurs. This is leading to the growth of a network of patronage among them based on their entrepreneurial skills and their powers over distribution. Alongside these cadres are independent households and private enterprises. They want greater economic freedom and operate across administrative boundaries, yet they also need a variety of joint services. They are subject to pressures from cadres, but they are also developing their own independent economic networks.

The evolution of these changes has led to further consideration in the Chinese countryside of the most appropriate systems of ownership and economic organization to promote further development. There is thus a conscious acceptance of the linkage between institutional adaptation and economic growth. Much of the discussion, however, has focused on the relative merits of collective or co-operative organizations and has led to an assertion that dual level management, which retains collectivist features, is most appropriate. To some extent, the events of 1989 resulted in a renewed assertion of collectivist values and an attempt to stop further change. It is my contention, however, that such an attempt cannot work. The underlying tensions remain in place and the need for further reforms is clear. Furthermore, the way institutional change evolves will now be subject to pressures from the diverse economic interest groups that are continuing to evolve in the countryside.

Michael Dutton's chapter addresses the major issues of social control, crime and punishment. He demonstrates how the old systems of management such as household registration, police procedures and education through labour reform no longer correspond to the nature of a society where new types of economic activity and geographical mobility have transformed both the nature of crime and the methods for policing it. The definition of crime has changed, and so has the criminal. Before 1978 political crime predominated. The typical criminal today is a young urban worker who has committed an economic or a violent crime. By contrast, policing and punishment are still fundamentally guided by earlier values and methods, and the process of reform in this area has been shaped by a different agenda. The penal system tries to use old techniques and the result is a high rate of recidivism. Nevertheless, the impact of the reforms has forced some reconsideration and experiments. The use of ID cards to replace the registration system in a highly mobile economy, the introduction of modern urban crowd control equipment such as electric truncheons and rubber bullets (though clearly not yet effectively deployed as shown by the failure of the People's Armed Police to play any role in June 1989), the use of video surveillance and increasing levels of computerization, all offer a new technology of policing, even though the ideology of policing is informed by an earlier set of values. The introduction of these mechanisms since 1978 and the conflict between the effect of the reforms and the 'traditional' methods of social control all demonstrate the changing relationship between the individual and the state in contemporary China.

Finally, Dennis Woodward examines another dimension of social control by analysing the role and nature of the PLA. Tiananmen underlined that it is the ultimate force in the resolution of political and social conflict. Nevertheless, regional tensions and conflicting hierarchies of loyalty remain central to the way the army's role is played out. Although defence has been one of the main concerns of the four modernizations, Woodward shows how, as with education, there has been a gap between aims and achievement. In practice the army has seen its budget allocations and size reduced while its aims of military modernization have been far from realized. Small wonder, then, that there are many signs of low morale and declining quality among its members. At the same time, there has also been conflict between some of the effects of economic reform and military goals. Rural development has provided peasants with many more opportunities for higher incomes and social mobility. Military service is no longer a desirable route out of the countryside. Educated urban youths also look for alternative and higher paid forms of employment. The army no longer offers high social status and an attractive career. Events in Beijing, Tibet and elsewhere are unlikely to revive its old revolutionary image as the people's army. Furthermore, economic change has also affected the performance and goals of military industries. They have to become economic, to produce civilian goods and to compete in the market. Woodward shows how all these events have affected the strategic doctrines of the army, its development and its social role. To a large extent the balance of forces in the political debate within the army remains unknown, as do the changes in hierarchical loyalties created by the generational changes in party leadership taking place. Yet the political stances taken within the army will have a significant impact on China's choices in the next phase of economic development.

Clearly this book does not attempt a comprehensive analysis of all the problems of economic growth and social change discussed at the outset of this introduction. The chapters largely focus on particular aspects of social groups and social institutions. Nevertheless, each of them contributes specific insights into the general problems. The shared conclusions, the contrasts and the implications will be examined in more detail in the concluding remarks.

REFERENCES

1 See Ross Garnaut, *Australia and the Northeast Asian Ascendency*, Canberra, Australian Government Service, 1989, Table 2.1, for Chinese data and a comparison with other northeast Asian economies.
2 Albert Hirschman, *A Bias for Hope*, cited in Bruce F. Johnston and Peter Kilby, *Agriculture and Structural Transformation: Economic Strategies in Late Developing Countries*, New York, Oxford University Press, 1975, p. 155.
3 A useful summary of the evolution of development theories can be found in Yujiro Hayami and Vernon W. Ruttan, *Agricultural Development: An Institutional Perspective*, Baltimore, John Hopkins University Press, 1985, pp. 1–72.
4 Deng Xiaoping, 'On the general principles for the work of the Party and the country', 7 October 1975, in *Zhonggong Nianbao 1977*, section 5, p. 62.

2

INTEREST GROUP CONFLICTS IN A REFORMING ECONOMY

Christopher Findlay and Jiang Shu

Further reform in China depends on the political consequences of the reforms to date. Ten years ago, when economists debated the nature of the relationship between the planned economy and market economy, nobody expected that the planning system might be so deeply affected by the emergence of the market. At the same time, the reforms have promoted new types of economic relationships between people. These have in turn changed the politics of the next stages of reform. Rapid economic growth has generated both new shared interests among social groups and new conflicts of interest. Social groups with common or opposing economic interests clearly existed before 1978, but the kind of interest group interaction now observed is new to contemporary China.

In this chapter we focus on these new interest group interactions and how they influence the process of economic reform which initiated them. We will argue that the emergence of these interest groups[1] reflects the greater autonomy for decision making at the household and enterprise levels and the incentives for pursuit of individual and group interest.

THE ORIGINS OF THE REFORM

Before 1978, China's planned economy was characterized by centralization. General economic decision making and management were monopolized by the central government. The higher the level of governmental organ, the more power it had. Although in the 1950s and 1960s there were some attempts to transform this rigid systems,[2] they did not succeed. The result was a highly centralized management structure.

17

The rhetoric of the regime stressed the national interest and any attempt to pursue individual or group interests were criticized and treated as a departure from orthodoxy. It has been argued that this system achieved a political equilibrium.[3] But a strong case has been made that this equilibrium represented a greater weighting of urban or worker interests against rural or peasant interests.[4]

During the later period of the Cultural Revolution the stability induced by the central party leadership began to break down. There was at that time a tendency to pursue self-interest, which was reflected in the factionalism of the period. This tendency was also illustrated, not by greater effort and thereby productivity, but by the emergence and spread of the 'back door' system, whereby people sought benefit through personal connections. In the Cultural Revolution, the scope for personal gain by the back door was, however, small. It is only since the reform process began that the scope for the pursuit of private interest has been much greater.

The impetus for reform also arose in the Cultural Revolution period. The poor labour productivity associated with the system of fixing incomes under the centrally planned system, combined with the languishing economy, emerged as major problems at that time. Nevertheless the attitudes of the four major pre-reform social strata – the cadres, intellectuals, workers and peasants – varied. Some cadres realized that the slump in the economy would directly threaten the stability of the regime, including the role of the party, and the only solution was to carry out a reform. The intellectuals, when they realized the size of the gap in economic development between advanced countries and China, also advocated reform, expecting a rise in their social position as a result. The endurance of the peasants had almost reached its limits after thirty years of minimal improvement in their standard of living. They welcomed any kind of transformation which could improve their status. The workers, despite the fact that they took a wait-and-see attitude to the reform at first, also had strong expectations.

Underlying the views of all these groups was the implied argument that China's poor economic performance was a result of the suppression of the freedom of people to pursue their own interests. In the early stage of the reform, therefore, one of the topics hotly debated in the economic circles was the principles underlying material benefits and distribution according to work.[5] Both the 'iron rice bowl' and the work point system were attacked at this time for their disincentive effects. The first round of the reforms therefore involved a high degree of decentralization which provided people with the opportunity to pursue their own economic interests. This had dramatic effects on productivity and incomes in rural households and in industry. The new scope for the pursuit of self-interest also had important implications for the structure of interest groups in China.

INTEREST GROUPS AFTER REFORM

We have stressed so far that a key feature of the reform was that it legitimized the pursuit of self-interest, which had the effect of dramatically increasing productivity. At the same time, however, the reforms affected other types of social and political behaviour and it is on those dimensions that we wish to focus.

People recognized after the reforms the scope for and value of collective action to pursue their own interests. As a consequence, new types of social groups emerged and began to contend for shares of national income in ways not experienced previously.

Later in the chapter we give specific examples of the strategies being followed by a selection of the various interest groups which can now be identified in China. We focus on the use of administrative or regulatory powers, either in response to proposals for policy reforms or, at the initiative of the group in question, for the pursuit of individual or group interests.

Options for expressing a reaction to policy changes in China were very much restricted in the period before the reform. We argue that since the reforms, the ways in which those options can be expressed have increased and that there has been a reformation of groups of people around their common interests. Those groups are now critical influences on the progress of the reforms. The behaviour of these interest groups and the outcome of the interaction of groups with conflicting interests will affect the next stages of the reform.

We are using the notion of an interest group as a conceptual device to illuminate the process of reform in China, and it is necessary to define the set of interest groups which is relevant for the period since 1978. There are, of course, a huge number of group classifications which could be adopted. This is because individuals are not restricted to membership of one group. Affiliations are overlapping. An individual's primary allegiance and influence will vary according to the issue so that one person can belong to many interest groups. Because of the range of affiliations, not all members of a group will support the group's position to the same degree of intensity. In addition, the interest group structure of the society will change over time. The groups are defined by the shared attitudes of their members, and events during the reform process will stimulate the emergence of new groups and create new issues on which old groups will focus. It is this transformation of the interest group conflicts in the society which we wish to examine here.

A definition put forward by a Chinese observer in 1987 lists a number of interest groups, all defined in terms of their administrative status, namely central and local governments, specialized departments, families and enterprises.[6] Central government includes central financial and planning organizations. Local governments mainly include provincial governmental organs and those of lower levels. Specialized departments mean central special industrial ministries and their subordinate units. Families mainly include three kinds of people: salaried workers, peasants and private operators. This Chinese scheme of identifying interest groups is not consistent with our review of the origins of the new forms of interest group interaction. The new forms of interaction involve a movement away from interaction between administrative units as such towards interaction between groups with common economic interests. Groups with particular administrative roles, however, can constitute interest groups. For example, we identify the central government as having a different set of economic interests to local government. We also stress the economic interests of the bureaucracy in whose hands the regulation of the market system now lies. In addition to these, we consider the status of the long-standing conflict between the interests of rural compared to urban residents. It is also helpful to divide urban and rural residents into a number of sub-groups and they are discussed in more detail below.

In summary, the discussion in this chapter is organized around three sets of bilateral conflicts in the Chinese economy: central versus local government; urban versus rural populations; and administrative power groups versus the interests of market oriented groups.

RELATIONS BETWEEN THE CENTRAL AND LOCAL LEVELS OF GOVERNMENT

For most of the period since 1949, the economy has been managed by a highly centralized and pyramidical administrative system, in which governmental organs at every level directed economic activity. In this economic model, the relations between governmental organs at different levels played an important role in the operation of the economy.

Centralization and decentralization in the relationship between the central and local governments have been the focus of all the economic system reforms carried out since the late 1950s. One Chinese economist, looking back in 1980, explained this cycle by saying that in China 'centralization leads to rigidity, rigidity leads to complaints, complaints lead to decentralization, decentralization leads to disorder, and disorder leads back to centralization'.[7] Before the recent reforms this cycle took place within the party system, and has been characterized as a long-term 'two line struggle' between branch control or area control.[8] Briefly, branch control meant a top-down system of control and area control meant control by regionally based committees. But in both cases, the role of the party, either from the Political Bureau down in the branch system or through the local committees in the area system, was the common element. A distinguishing feature of the reforms of the late 1970s onwards was that the decentralization pursued at that time involved neither branch nor area control.

Reforms

With the aim of 'decentralizing power and yielding benefit to the lower level', relations between the central government and local governments were reformed, starting with the financial system. In 1980, after several years' deficit in the central budget, a financial contract system was introduced in order to give scope to the initiative of local governments. The centralized system whereby all revenue was handed upwards and all expenditure was allocated from above was replaced by a system whereby each level of government made an agreement with the next level up to meet certain income and expenditure targets. If an administrative level is able to generate additional revenue, this is shared with its next superior level according to an agreed ratio set out in the budget contract.

21

That contract also stipulates any expenditure subsidy provided to the lower level, regardless of changes in its revenue during the contract period. The surplus income retained at the lower level (which may be all such income) can be used to cover new investment or other expenditure at its own discretion.[9]

It has been argued that, for a number of reasons, the reforms of this period were not simply another example of a shift to area control.[10] Conscious efforts were made to separate the party system from management. In addition, the reforms operated at much lower levels than previously, down to county town administration and enterprise levels. An example of the extent of the reforms was the contract system just outlined.

In the first few years, the contract finance system basically achieved its original aims. Local governments' enhanced responsibility and initiative for increasing income and reducing expenditure also contributed to the remarkable improvement in the condition of the state's budget deficit.[11]

The introduction of the financial contract system, however, greatly increased the scope for independent action by local governments, and all levels of government have their own limited interests which differ remarkably from those of the state. Needless to say, local government makes decisions according to the interests of its region. In the past, under the highly concentrated system, although local governments had the incentive to pursue their own interests, they lacked enough financial strength to do so. Now, they have that capacity.

Local government financial behaviour

Since putting the financial contract system into practice, the influence of the central government on national spending has diminished tremendously. In 1984, the central and local governments accounted for about half each of the gross financial expenditure by governments, while the income gained directly through the central government's own financial system was only 20 per cent of the gross financial expenditure. The other part was made up by local finance.[12] This means that the central government has to make up the difference between its share of revenue and its share of expenditure by extracting part of the revenue raised by local governments. Furthermore, following the introduction of the contracting system, the growth rate of expenditure controlled at the local level has exceeded that at the centre.[13] These developments have had some important implications.

First, the central government lacks enough financial power to influence local economic development. The incomplete market mechanism, especially the absence of a national capital market, means the central government does not have a lever for influencing the level of activity in the economy. Instead, it has to depend on its own spending or administrative power, and the new system of financial contracting has weakened its control in that regard. In addition, because of its deficits, the central government cannot afford to finance large infrastructure projects. Local governments are not willing to be involved in these projects either, since their investment criteria focus on regional rather than national interests. As a result, investment in the energy and transportation sectors has worsened rather than improved.

The second major defect of the current financial system is that the boundary between central and local finances is still not definite. Since total expenditure exceeds income, the central government has to force local governments to hand over some of their financial income. The proportion handed over in this way varies. In some cases it is thought to be unreasonable and thus a source of conflict.[14] Although some revenue sources have been assigned to local finance, the central government can also take back revenue in the form of bonds and loans.[15]

A related issue is the period of the contract between the central and local governments. Negotiations between central and local governments on the division of revenue every five years makes the two sides consider how to encroach upon the other's interests in order to get a superior position in the next negotiation. This further undermines the relations between them.

A third defect is the effect of the financial contracting system on the allocation of resources and on the efficiency with which those resources are used. One issue from an efficiency point of view is that local government is likely to pursue objectives related to revenue,[16] which are not necessarily the same as profit. As a result local investment decisions may not be efficient, either in terms of regional comparative advantage or in terms of scale of operation. An example of this is that the financial contracting system has shifted the location of processing of raw materials and thereby affected the pattern of inter-regional specialization and trade. To some extent the passing down of financial power to lower levels has permitted provinces well endowed with raw materials to retain them for further processing. The incentive to do so is created by the distorted prices of processed products relative to raw materials.[17] Access to the capital required to process those raw materials is normally a constraint in the absence of a national capital market. This constraint has been eased by the new financial contract system. The extent of 'economic balkanization' in the 1980s has been compared to earlier periods of decentralization which put local governments in control of their areas.[18]

The coastal and relatively resource-poor provinces are forced, as a consequence of local processing, to compete more strongly for raw materials. This contributed to the 'commodity wars' which have been documented elsewhere. The central government's response was also to promote the policy of placing the 'two ends outside',[19] which meant permitting greater reliance in the coastal provinces on world markets for those raw materials needed for export. By this mechanism, the demand for raw materials spilled over onto the world market.

It is difficult to say whether this re-allocation of processing activity is more or less efficient from the Chinese point of view. It is expected that the degree of local processing is distorted by the structure of relative prices which is biased against raw materials. On the other hand, in the presence of severe constraints on the capacity of the transport infrastructure, for example, it could be argued that local processing does have some economic benefits compared to shipping the material in its raw form. Even so, the combination of distorted prices and local control over investment is not likely to be the most efficient method of resolving that issue. Also, as noted above, the contracting system is itself contributing to the significance of infrastructure constraints.

From the macroeconomic management point of view, since the income of the central government has been reduced, its control over investment has been greatly weakened. Nor does it have an extensive and formal financial system through which it can attempt to influence the rate of investment. The financial resources of local government, especially those at lower levels, come mainly from the funds outside the budget, over which only limited control can be exercised. The macroeconomic problems of 1989 were related to the excessive scale of investment at the local level caused by the pursuit of limited regional interests.[20] In our view, this constitutes the most serious issue in the national economy. The necessity for the

24

centre to respond to macroeconomic problems in a very blunt administrative fashion tends to undermine reforms which aim at decentralization of economic responsibility.

URBAN VERSUS RURAL INTERESTS

As discussed at the outset, the structure of urban society is complex and can be analysed in various ways, as is done in other chapters in this book. For our purposes, however, we shall concentrate on the economic relationship between urban wage earners and the peasants, in order to illuminate one of the key social divisions of interest.

Urban residents

Urban wage earners include four sub-groups of people: production workers, cadres, intellectuals and workers in the tertiary sector. These groups have enormous influence on the reform since they each hold a crucial position in society. Comparative work on other Asian economies at early stages of development suggests reasons why the urban sector will have relatively greater political influence than the rural sector. First, the urban workforce is generally smaller and geographically concentrated and therefore is in a better position to organize so as to lobby the government. Second, group size is important because the industrial and commercial interest groups in a poor agrarian economy suffer much less of a free-rider problem in acting collectively than does the large-number group of farmers. Third, the wages of the urban minority depend both on prices of food, which enter their budgets directly, and on raw materials prices which affect the profitability of enterprises in which they work.[21] The relatively greater political strength of the urban group compared to farmers and workers in the raw material supply sector thus contributes to the distorted pricing structure which favours manufactured products above agricultural products and raw materials. Finally, the process of administration and the establishment of institutions to execute particular policies can lead to the creation of new interest groups which later perpetuate the policy of favouring the urban sector. For example, all state cadres are part of the urban wage-earning group, no matter which level of government they belong to. It is they who work out the economic policy and to a great extent carry it out as well. Therefore, their economic interests will have some influence on their attitudes to policy proposals.

A structure of relative prices biased against primary sectors also reflects publicly held attitudes on policy issues, rather than just the set of limited private interest views. In the Chinese case, one such factor is that, according to theory, the working class is the leading class in the whole society. This theory still plays a role in the weighting of social interests. Second, there was in earlier years a policy of self reliance and the development of capacity to process raw materials. This policy reflected the inability at that time to rely on world markets.

Compared with farmers and the self-employed, the urban wage earners share a number of characteristics. First, their capacity for bearing risk is low, since they are used to a very secure and stable lifetime employment system, in which there is never unemployment. Therefore although their salaries are perceived to be quite low, most are not willing to break away. Second, since most wage earners are not operators of economic enterprises, their hopes of increasing income rely on changing the structure of income distribution. Third, their expectations of short-run gains brought about by the reforms are higher. This is because the successful reform in the countryside set off expectations for reform in the cities. Besides, experience of foreign life styles has a greater influence on urban society and contributes to the anticipation of rapid increases in income as a result of reform. Fourth, the urban residents enjoyed enormous benefits in the old economic system through state subsidies for housing, food and urban infrastructure. Therefore on the one hand they are eager to carry out reform but on the other hand they are fearful of having to give up previous benefits.

Effects of the reforms to date

From 1984 to the present, the attitudes of urban residents has passed through four stages.[22] The first stage – in 1984, when the reform started to unfold in urban areas – was characterized by optimism and enthusiasm for the reform. Encouraged by the initial successful reform in the rural areas, hopes for the economic reform were high. Given the emphasis on reform by the mass media, and some leaders' impatience for success, urban wage earners developed unrealistic expectations about rapid income increases in the short term. They did not anticipate the length and difficulty of the reform period. Besides, urban reform first focused on decentralizing both power and benefits to the lower levels. This stage of reform generated little opposition.[23]

During the second stage, in 1985, complaints from the urban sector began to intensify and concentrated on the rising price of food and some manufactures. These price rises were due to the relaxation of controls over prices of agricultural and non-staple products and the implementation of the two-track price system for industrial raw materials. The complaints arose, even though an ample supply of agricultural products was a result of deregulation of the market. Also at this stage, some income gaps gradually became noticeable, for example between workers employed in more or less successful enterprises. This led to a strong interest among lower-paid workers in matching those higher earnings and created expectations of further increases in income under the reforms. Those urban residents who had already enjoyed benefits brought by the reform had positive attitudes towards the reform, because of its results and not just because of the expectation of its effects.[24]

The third stage was from the end of 1985 to early 1987. Efforts to press ahead with the reforms led to a complex mixture of new and old economic systems, often in conflict with each other. At that time, the shortcomings of reforms which emphasized only decentralization began to appear. The basic defect of the old system – the managerial system of enterprises – had not been changed. Furthermore, having gained more freedom in the economic field, demands for rights in political and social activities began to grow. The limited reform of the political system was a disappointment.

There were three changes in social attitudes during this period. The first was in the range of the complaints, which now extended well beyond concerns about inflation. According to a social survey carried out in twenty cities in February 1986, people were most of all discontented with the abuse of power by rent-seeking private interests. Other dissatisfactions included inflation, nepotism, the imperfect legal system, and policy instability.[25]

The second change of attitudes was in the range of expectations. In pace with the progress of the reforms, expectations began to exceed simply raising incomes. People's expectations also began to vary greatly for different occupations. For example, the workers and staff in the tertiary sector were the most discontented with what they saw as an unfair income distribution, while university students and graduates complained most strongly about the limited opportunities to make money.[26]

The fourth stage began in early 1987. The noticeable feature of this period was the worsened economic situation, including serious inflation. In 1988, the inflation rate was more than 20 per cent,[27] and 79.9 per cent of people in a survey in that year complained about soaring prices, especially the price of food.[28] The expectation of high inflation led to panic purchasing in the last quarter of 1988. This was combined with general problems of corruption and official speculation. The re-distribution of national income caused by inflation and excessive wage payments in some units intensified the contradictions between different urban interest groups, resulting in discontent with the central government and a sense of longing for a return to the pre-reform situation, especially among those whose real standards of living had begun to fall. These pressures culminated in the widespread participation by urban residents in the demonstrations in June 1989.

Complaints about soaring prices were originally interpreted as a demand for reform to create an environment that gave equal opportunities to earn higher incomes.[29] Corruption was also seen as a significant source of inequality. On the other hand, however, even if there were opportunities to increase income in a less regulated environment, people would be hesitant, because the risk brought by new opportunities was often large relative to the benefit. The imperfect market environment, the lack of a social insurance system and a perception that policy is unstable, means that there is tremendous economic, social and political instability in occupations outside the state-guaranteed urban wage sector. The urban wage earners wanted opportunities to increase their income but were unwilling to obtain them by giving up their secure positions.

The views of the urban wage earners are critical to the next steps of reform. They remain a relatively powerful interest group. Their demands, however, are difficult to satisfy. Their interests in both security and high income growth are more costly to meet. They would need to be compensated for the changes that occur, for example, by higher incomes in return for accepting less stability. The dilemma is that achieving higher incomes depends on the successful progress of the reforms, but, in the meantime, resistance by urban interest groups will hold them up.

Rural residents

Rural residents include farmers and others who live in the rural areas, and account for about 80 per cent of the whole population. Although agriculture is thought of as the basis of the national economy, the rural residents are in reality the lowest stratum in society. Since the early 1950s, policy has been to accumulate funds for industrialization through purchasing agricultural products at lower prices and selling industrial products at higher prices. It has been estimated in Chinese sources that during the three decades up to 1979 about 600–800 billion yuan was transferred out of the rural sector by the way of the domestic terms of trade between agricultural and industrial products.[30] This transfer diminished the volume of funds available for investment in the rural sector and, despite the funding of investment from the centre over this period,[31] contributed to a lower growth of rural incomes. Urban wage earners also enjoyed the benefits of subsidies and welfare payments not provided to the peasants. In addition, while not sharing any of the benefits of the planned economy, the peasants' freedoms to change status, to develop private assets or even to decide what crop to plant were all lost.

The long-term exploitation of peasants resulted in a much lower standard of living in the countryside. The ratio of consumption level per capita between urban and rural residents was 2.6:1 in 1957, and by 1978 it had increased to 2.9:1.[32] In addition, during the Cultural Revolution most urban workers did not work so hard as before, while the peasants, without guaranteed wages, had to struggle to survive. The endurance of the peasants had almost reached its breaking point in the period immediately after the Cultural Revolution and in his report to the Central Committee of the party, a provincial party secretary suggested that if the situation of the peasants could not be improved in a few years a peasant uprising on a national scale would be unavoidable.[33]

Economic reform began in the countryside. This was despite the relatively weak power and influence of the rural sector. The policy change was driven by the shortage of agricultural products, and by the relative ease of rural reform in administrative terms compared to urban reform. In 1979, the purchase price of grain, cotton and cooking oil were raised by 30.5 per cent, 17.0 per cent and 23.9 per cent respectively, compared with the previous year.[34] In the following four years, the purchase prices of agricultural products were, to varying extents, raised again. For the first time since the establishment of the People's Republic, the distribution of income shifted in favour of rural residents.

The peasants responded strongly to this new economic environment as is shown by the rapid growth in all aspects of the rural economy. Unlike urban residents, however, the peasants lack effective means for lobbying, so their attitude to the reform is mainly reflected through the market and through their willingness to supply products. In other words, the main reaction of the peasants to the reform reflects their attitude towards how the new policy can contribute to their short-term interests. If the peasants think that a new policy can benefit them they follow it. If not, they will show their dissatisfaction by trying to sidestep it. In the early stages of the reform, the peasants' objective was to attain the rights to manage their own land[35] and as soon as that objective was attained, the rural economy achieved a very high growth rate, at least up to 1984.

Since 1984, however, growth has stagnated for a number of reasons. This switch in performance was due to the neglect of the agricultural production at the policy-making level, a result of the unrealistically optimistic outlook for the agricultural sector based on the high growth rate of agricultural output over the previous seven years. Policy, especially in relation to pricing and land tenure, was inconsistent with the new situation of management responsibility. Also, although the growth rate of rural economy was high, the maintenance of the capital stock in the rural area was not sufficient.[36]

During 1988, therefore, discussion in China began to focus on the division of economic benefits between town and country. Seven years of high-speed growth had improved the living standard of the rural residents. At the same time, it had also deeply affected the structure of interests in the old economic system. The tremendous growth of primary agricultural products moderated long-term shortages. It also triggered off the issue of how to redistribute national income between the state, urban residents and peasants. This was reflected by the fact that, although the relaxation of price controls over agricultural products had led to an unparalleled supply of food to the urban residents, it had also sharpened the contradictions between consumers and producers.

The development of rural industries further intensified interest conflicts between town and countryside. This was reflected in the relative prices of finished products and raw materials and in the conflict over the supply of raw materials. A further feature of the economic relations between the state and the peasants was the growing monetization of the relationship through the higher prices paid for agricultural products. This occurred at the same time as the urban residents remained under the protective umbrella of the state.

The consequence was a tremendous increase in subsidies in the government budget. Owing to their stronger position in bargaining with government, urban residents could transfer the pressures brought by the relaxation of controls over prices of farm and non-staple products onto enterprises and onto state funds. This led to higher prices for industrial products, and larger subsidies from the state. In the face of the dual financial pressures of higher expenditure for crop purchases from rural producers and larger subsidies to urban consumers, the state eventually responded by insisting that peasants supply agricultural products at low prices again.

This shift of policy against the interests of the peasants happened around 1985. This is reflected in the movements of relative income levels. In 1981, the ratio of average annual income between urban and rural residents was 2.24:1; in 1983 and 1984 it was 1.85:1 and 1.86:1 respectively. In 1985, it rose to 2.07:1 and in 1986 to 2.33:1.[37] After 1984 several periods of tightened macroeconomic policy thus had especially severe implications for the agricultural sector.[38]

THE ADMINISTRATIVE SYSTEM AS AN INTEREST GROUP

Before the reforms, the administrative system permitted very little autonomy for individuals. Enterprises were tied to the administrative system. The reforms were stimulated by the shortcomings of this system, but the process also created a dilemma. The government tried to transform social relations by decentralization. One way of doing this was to introduce the market mechanism as a co-ordinating device. But once transplanted into the administrative system, the market mechanism could not work smoothly, because of the residual powers left in the hands of the administrators. The conflicts and uncertainties created by this type of partial reform led to pressure for the administrative system to strengthen its controls again, especially after June 1989. The reinstatement of controls had the effect of creating stability, but at the cost of incentives to productivity growth. Furthermore, from a longer-term point of view, the reinstatement of controls can only be a prelude to the next round of decentralization.

In the process of cycling between centralization and decentralization, the previously powerful administrative system is gradually losing its authority. At the same time, the market mechanism is not sufficiently developed to take its place. The presence of the market mechanism gives individuals at least some degree of autonomy but at the same time, members of the administrative system find they have some residual powers. This coincidence of events provides great incentives to develop networks of contacts and to use those networks to influence the allocation of resources.[39] The development of these networks also serves to constrain the development of the market and thereby to increase the likelihood of 'chaos and instability' in the process of the allocation of resources.

Within the networks, the staff of the administrative system can handle the power they have in the manner of a commodity and so bribery expands rapidly.[40] For example, the members of the network can take advantage of the dual price system and try to transfer commodities from the state distribution system to the market system.[41] When the staff of the administrative system utilize their power to make a profit for others, then it can be argued that a new type of administrative interest group has emerged.[42] An illustration of this is the emergence of waves of establishing trading companies in 1985 and in 1988.[43] As a result, the attitude of the administrative system to further reform depends on the extent of benefit to the administrative interest groups. For example, strong opposition to further price reform came from the administrative system, despite the fact that relaxation of control would relax supply constraints.[44]

CONCLUSION

In the process of reviewing the attitudes of various interest groups in the Chinese economy, we have identified a number of ways in which interest group behaviour has affected the reform process. In this final section, we review those effects and examine the consequences for the future of the reforms.

It was argued that a major theme of the initial reforms was a shift in autonomy to enterprises and lower levels of government, that this shift initially produced spectacular results but that it also involved an exaggeration of the conflicts between interest groups in the economy, especially from 1985 onwards. In other words, having passed down autonomy, there was no new institutional system for the resolution of the conflicting claims by the various interest groups over national income. Previously these conflicts were resolved in a centralized fashion, which had implications for the structure of incentives and which led to a relatively poor economic performance.

The more recent conflicts between interest groups have led to various sorts of inefficiencies noted above, to the macroeconomic problems of 1989 and to demands for reforms of the political institutions, that is, to demands for the development of substitute systems for resolving the conflicting claims between the interest groups. These forces came to a head in June 1989. The events at that time can be interpreted as a mass demonstration of the interests of the urban groups and their reactions to the economic impacts upon them of the reforms to date. Clearly there was a coalition of interests with other groups arguing for political reform; however, the economic motivation amongst even the student groups was strong. The resolution of the conflict at that time led to a forceful reinstatement of the old centralist system and an attempt to suppress individual interest again.

This strategy of forceful suppression in the face of the emergence of relatively more powerful groups based around economic interests sets up many contradictions for the present regime. Nevertheless, the underlying macroeconomic problems still require some immediate action and remain a strong driving force for further institutional changes.

One option is that the centre could continue to operate macroeconomic control through cycles of drastic credit squeeze followed by a boom then another squeeze, a cycle which it has been argued is inevitable in the current Chinese institutional setting.[45] In this situation there is an apparent trade-off between the rate of economic growth and its stability. Recentralization, however, is a crude mechanism to solve macro problems and will undermine the path toward further microeconomic reform. This is another example of a familiar tension in the Chinese economy between unity of control (*tong*) and decentralization (*fang*). The current challenge is to be able to sustain decentralization at a local or enterprise or household level while achieving a sufficient degree of unified macroeconomic control.

Furthermore, as we have argued there will be strong resistance by articulate interest groups to further reforms. The relatively more powerful groups at this time are the urban wage earners, the administrative groups and local government. As we have demonstrated, the first two of these would be opposed to increasing the pace of reform, whatever the macroeconomic circumstance. They gain from the downward pressure on raw materials and food prices and the maintenance of the double track marketing systems, which still involve some degree of state activity. The resolution of macro-economic issues could well become part of the rhetoric of those interest groups opposed to reform in their espousal of conservative policy. Macroeconomic objectives could be used to extend the degree of price control and centralized marketing.

The irony is that the existence of the macroeconomic problems represents the results of the struggle between interest groups. For example, it has been argued[46] that inflation can be understood as a result of a continuing 'tug-of-war' among interest groups as they make claims on the national income. The monetary authorities, and their political masters, can also be seen as actors in this struggle as they attempt to mediate, and a bout of inflation can be a deliberate choice in such circumstances. In the Chinese case, inflation was a much more likely result, once, as we argue in this chapter, the interest groups identified themselves and then pursued their interests in the process of reform, because of the lack of instruments available to the policy makers. This was the result of the problems of the reforms proceeding at different rates in different markets. In general, an inflationary outcome becomes less likely if interest groups learn that their individual pursuit of gain is ultimately frustrated by the reactions of other groups. In the Chinese case, there was little chance of this experience emerging so early in the reforms.

The other relatively powerful interest group identified above was local government. Local government has benefited from the passing down of autonomy. A drastic reinstatement of central control, for the sake of correcting the macro problems, would disadvantage this group. There is evidence that since June 1989, the powers of local government have been constrained. The alternative strategy would have been further to decentralize the remaining economic controls. This is only likely to be successful if the perspective of local governments on development strategies can be more closely aligned with national interests through a new distribution of spending and tax revenue raising powers, otherwise the macroeconomic problems and the issues of the development of infrastructure are likely to be intensified. This implies the development of even more sophisticated contractual relations between the centre and regional governments.[47] Instead of this, the strategy of the Li Peng regime appears to be a recentralization of power rather than a redistribution of power.

NOTES AND REFERENCES

1 The word 'interest group' (*liyi jituan* or *liyi qunti*) has since 1985 become much more frequent in the literature on the reform process. See, for example, Bai Nanfeng *et al.*, 'Zhuzhong dui shehui butong liyi qunti de diaocha yanjiu' ('Paying attention to the study and investigation of different social interest groups'), *Shijie Jingji Daobao* (*World Economic Herald*), 2 March 1987, p. 14.

2 Liao Jili 'Renzhen xiqu wo guo jingji guanli de lishi jingyan zhengque queding tizhi gaige de fangxiang' ('Drawing the historical lessons of China's economic management conscientiously and determining the direction of reform correctly') *Caimao Zhanxian* (*Finance and Trade*), 19 February 1980.

3 Tang Gongzhao and Gu Peidong, 'Jianli shiying gaige yu fazhan de shehui pingheng jizhi' ('Establishment of a social balancing mechanism suited to reform and development'), *JJRB*, 20 December 1988, p. 3.

4 See Andrew Watson, 'New perspectives on China's agricultural development strategy', *Asian Studies Association of Australia Review*, vol. 11, November 1987, pp. 119–39, for a review of debate on the extent of urban bias in China's development strategies.

5 Cf. Wei Xinghua 'Lun shehuizhuyi zhiduxia de wuzhi liyi guanxi' ('On the relations of material benefits under the socialist system'), *JYJ*, no. 1, 1979, pp. 14–20; and Wen Min, 'Yinianlai guanyu an lao fenpei wenti de taolun qingkuang' ('Discussion of the issue of distribution according to work during the past year'), *JYJ*, no. 2, 1979, pp. 76–80.

6 Jiang Hong, 'Liyi zhuti: wo guo jingji yunxing de shenceng jiegou' ('Interest groups: the deep structure of China's economic operation'), *Shijie Jingji Daobao*, 14 September 1987, p. 6. For a review of western literature on the notion of interest groups and their role in the political process, see chapter 1 of Harmon Zeigler, *Interest Groups in American Society*, Engelwood Cliffs, Prentice Hall, 1964.

7 Jiang Yiwei, 'The theory of an enterprise-based economy', *Social Sciences in China*, vol. 1, 1980, p. 55, quoted by Jonathan Unger, 'The struggle to dictate China's administration: the conflict of branches versus areas versus reform', *The Australian Journal of Chinese Affairs*, no. 18, 1987, pp. 15–45. More recently, see Zhou Xiaochuan and Fen Ailing, 'Bimian xunhuan wangfu zhengqu gaige de shizhixing jinzhan' ('Avoiding repeated cycles, strive to make real progress in reform'), *JYJ*, no. 4, 1987, p. 35.

8 Unger, op. cit.

9 *Zhongguo Jingji Nianjian* (*China Economic Yearbook*), Beijing 1981, p. II-130, 1983, p. VIII-56; and Chen Shenshen, 'Zhongguo gaige mianlinzhe xin de xingshi' ('China's reform – facing a new situation') *Shijie Jingji Daobao*, 18 July 1988.

10 See Unger, op. cit.

11 In 1980 and 1981, the state's expenditure fell by 4.8 per cent and 8.6 per cent respectively and the deficit dropped from 17.06 billion yuan in 1979 (5 per cent of national income) to 12.75 billion yuan in 1980 (3.46

per cent of national income) and 2.55 billion yuan in 1981 (0.65 per cent of national income), *RMRB*, 15 December 1981 and 24 August 1982.

12 Tian Yinong, 'Caizheng tizhi de gaige tong jihua jingji de guanxi' ('The relation between the financial system reform and the planned economy'), *JJYJ*, no. 5, 1984, p. 19. Another source, the State Statistical Bureau, *Zhongguo Tongji Nianjian 1990 (China Statistical Yearbook)*, Beijing, 1990, p. 242, reports a higher ratio of central government expenditure.

13 Taking the index value of expenditure by local government in 1980 as 100, the index rose to 115.6 in 1983 and 143.7 in 1984, while the indices of expenditure in central finance over the same base period were 98.8 and 113.5 respectively. Study Group for Macroeconomic Management, Institute of Economics, Chinese Academy of Social Sciences, 'Jianchi shidu fenquan fangxiang chongsu guojia guanli geju' ('Insist on the direction of moderate decentralization and rebuild the state's management pattern'), *JJYJ*, no. 6, 1987, p. 17.

14 For instance, Shanghai had to turn over 76 per cent of its revenues to the central government in 1987 while Guangdong Province handed over only 8.6 per cent. At the same time the central government pays a subsidy slightly less than 10 billion yuan annually to 45 per cent of provinces and regions. Xu Xuehan and Tang Mingfeng, 'Shenhua gaige xuyao jinkuai jianli fenji caizheng tizhi' ('Further reform demands speeding up the establishment of a financial system divided into different levels') *Caimao Jingji (Finance and Trade Economics)*, no. 5, 1988, p. 33.

15 Chen Shenshen, 'Mingque chanquan guanxi shi biyao qianti' ('An essential precondition – defined property relations'), *Shijie Jingji Daobao*, 25 July 1988, p. 15.

16 See C. P. Wong. 'Between plan and market: the role of the local sector in post-Mao China', *Journal of Comparative Economics*, vol. 11, 1987, pp. 385–98.

17 See T. B. Wiens, 'Issues in the structural reform of Chinese agriculture', *Journal of Comparative Economics*, vol. 11, 1987, pp. 372–84.

18 See Unger, op. cit.

19 Wang Jian, 'Xuanze zhengque de changqi fazhan zhanlue' ('Choosing a proper long-term strategy of development'), *JJRB*, 5 January 1988.

20 Zhao Xiaochuan and Zhu Li, 'China's banking system: current status and perspective on reform', *Journal of Comparative Economics*, vol. 11, 1987, pp. 399–409, argue that cycles in macroeconomic performance are inevitable in the current institutional setting.

21 K. Anderson and Y. Hayami, *The Political Economy of Agricultural Protection*, Sydney, Allen & Unwin, 1986, p. 14.

22 *Liaowang (Observation)*, 5 February 1988, p. 46.

23 Social Research Department, The Institute of Economic System Reform of China, 'Gaige de shehui huanjing: bianqian yu xuanze' ('The social environment of reform: change and choice'), *JJYJ*, no. 12, 1987, p. 56.

24 ibid., p. 57.

25 Bai Nanfeng *et al.*, 'Zhuzhong dui shehui butong liyi qunti de diaocha yanjiu' ('Lay emphasis on the investigation and study of different social interest groups'), *Shijie Jingji Daobao*, 2 March 1987, p. 14.

26 Ibid.
27 *Jingjixue Zhoubao* (*Economics Weekly*), 2 October 1988, p. 1.
28 *Liaowang* (*Observation*), 5 Febuary 1988, p. 46.
29 Institute for Economic System Reform of China, 'Ruhe tigao quan shehui dui gaige gongjian de chengshouli' ('How to enhance the capacity of the whole society to bear the effects of reform'), *Shijie Jingji Daobao*, 22 August 1988, p. 12.
30 *RMRB*, 29 June 1988.
31 See Watson, op. cit.
32 State Statistical Bureau, *Zhongguo Tongji Nianjian 1988* (*China Statistical Yearbook*), Beijing, 1989, p. 800.
33 Development Institute, 'Zhongguo de fazhan: caifu, zengzhang yu zhidu shiying' ('China's development: wealth, growth and system adaptation'), *JYJ*, no. 5, 1988, p. 4.
34 Chen Xiwen, 'Zhongguo nongcun jingji: cong chaochanggui zengzhang zhuanxiang changgui zengzhang' ('The rural economy in China is changing from abnormal growth to conventional growth'), *JYJ*, no. 12, 1987, p. 29.
35 Development Institute, op. cit., p. 7.
36 See Chen Xiwen, op. cit., pp. 28–42, and Cai Fang, 'Nongcun jingji fazhan tezheng yu xiayibu gaige' ('The characteristics of rural economic development and the next stage of reform'), *JYJ*, no. 8, 1987, pp. 63–6.
37 Chen Xiwen, op. cit., p. 24.
38 For example, in 1985 the state adopted measures to lower the price of agricultural products and limit the volume of purchase. At the end of 1985, the macroeconomic situation was almost out of control so a tight credit policy was introduced, which seriously jeopardized the development of the rural economy, especially township industry. See the Study Group for Economic Growth in China's Ministry of Agriculture, Animal Husbandry and Fisheries, 'Changgui zengzhang, yihuo fazhan cizhi – dui nongcun jingji fazhan de xianshi panduan' ('Normal growth or sluggish development – a realistic judgement of rural economic development'), *JYJ*, no. 9, 1987, pp. 48–63.
39 Wang Xin, '"Guanxiwang" de jingji fenxi' ('An economic analysis of the "human connection network"'), *Beijing Daxue Xuebao* (*Journal of Beijing University*), no. 6, 1988.
40 Fang Hanting, 'Zhongguo jingji yunxing de "renji-huiluhua" qingxiang cuoshi' ('Wangling and bribery practices in the functioning of China's economy'), *Caimao Jingji* (*Finance and Trade Economics*), no. 3, 1988, pp. 27–32.
41 Ibid.
42 Yi Xianliang and Huang Yan, 'Xingzhengxing liyi quntizhi weihai ji falu duice' ('The harm of administrative interest group and legal countermeasures'), *GMRB*, 27 December 1988, p. 3.
43 In 1985, the number of such companies reached 320,000. After 18 months of intervention to correct this development, the number decreased to 170,000. In the middle of 1988 the number soared again to 400,000 and in addition the proportion of official companies of this type increased rapidly. Wu Yan and Zhang Xuehu, '"Guandao" xianxiang

quanxi' ('Analysis of "official speculation"'), *Gongren Ribao* (*Workers Daily*), 24 August 1988.

44 Zhang Jilin, 'Guandao xianxiang yu xunzu lilun' ('Official speculation and rent-seeking theory'), *GMRB*, 13 October 1988, p. 3.

45 Zhao and Zhu, op. cit.

46 Albert Hirschman, 'Reflections on the Latin American experience' in Leon N. Lindberg and Charles S. Maier, eds, *The Politics of Inflation and Economic Stagnation: Theoretical Approaches and International Case Studies*, Washington, Brookings Institution, 1985.

47 This argument about the importance of establishing new contractual relations between the centre and regional governments is not often stressed in reviews of paths of reform for the Chinese economy. See, for example, J. Fei and B. Reynolds, 'A tentative plan for the rational sequencing of overall reform in China's economic system', *Journal of Comparative Economics*, vol. 11, 1987, pp. 490–502.

3

REDEFINING WORKERS' INTERESTS
Reform and the trade unions
Greg O'Leary

It can be argued that the central contradiction in labour/ management relations in state socialist economies is eliciting adequate worker effort (in terms of the objectives of the regime) whilst not treating labour as a commodity. Within state socialist economies, most regimes have established a significant degree of job security and strict limits on managers' ability to dismiss workers. This awareness of entrenched job security places considerable reliance on the efficacy of political and ideological mobilization behind the objectives of the regime. If such mobilization turns to cynicism (which it often does), then such regimes are faced with serious problems of lack of work effort.[1]

INTRODUCTION

At a time when the legitimacy of the Communist Party in China is at a low ebb and its ideological platform is only loosely related to social practice, the difficulties of mobilizing worker effort and raising productivity – at least in the state sector of the economy – are a major problem.[2] Shifts in labour market and industrial relations policies in recent years have indicated a government awareness that China needs to develop quite new stimuli to maintain and improve productivity.

The economic reforms of the last ten years have attempted to liberalize the economy by the selective replacement of administrative control and planning with market regulation. In the course of these developments many new interests have been aggregated and articulated – some of them, such as the demands for democracy, individual rights and civil liberties in the wake of Hu Yaobang's death in April 1989, have been intense expressions of needs which the political system is not meeting and which are politically destabilizing to an unprecedented extent. The growth of other interests has been more systemic – and in the long run perhaps even more politically challenging. The emergence of small producers and traders as a significant component of both the urban and rural economies with a different set of expectations and, as shown by Susan Young below, requiring significant alterations to existing economic practices, ideology and political sensitivities, has created a notable group of economic interests which has changed the political landscape in significant ways. The generation of large numbers of unemployed has brought profound changes in urban social conduct, although the political mobilization of the unemployed has been sporadic, geographically constrained and ineffective. The increased autonomy of local economic decision makers has led to a strengthening of regional economic interests around orchestrated investment strategies at odds with the centralized political authority of the past. The movement from state to collective and private production has also contributed greatly to a realignment of economic and political interests in ways which directly confront previous patterns of authority.

In general, the hallmarks of the Chinese economic system from the 1950s to the 1970s – collectivity and planning – have been among the central targets of reform in both urban and rural areas. It is not surprising, therefore, that their replacement by market regulation has produced interests which are mobilized around particular markets. In the case of the labour market, these interests are not, as yet, clearly articulated, organized or politically effective, but with the increasing penetration of the Chinese economy by market-regulated wage rates, rewards for productive efficiency, greater managerial discretion and foreign corporate activity with its own managerial methods, there can be little doubt that such interests will find more organized political expression. As was the case in May 1989, when student leaders either endorsed popular demands or were forced to stand aside, the Chinese trade unions may well face the same dilemma – transform party authority and prescriptions into expressions of worker interests or make way for more genuine workers' representatives.

THE NATURE OF SOCIALIST TRADE UNIONS

Chinese trade unions, like their counterparts in other socialist societies, remain something of an enigma. To trade unionists in the west, socialist trade unions appear to adopt the practices of the most compliant western trade unions – acting as management's arm on the shop floor, motivating workers to greater productive effort, monitoring quality, efficiency and productivity and ensuring workplace harmony. A few, such as Solidarnosc, which have attempted to break with this tradition and adopt a genuine oppositional stance both industrially and politically, have done so in ways and with political resonances that cause bemusement and concern for those western trade unions which are most industrially active. Opposition by *Solidarnosc*, particularly, to what was officially 'socialism', has an anti-socialist tenor which makes political dialogue with their western counterparts difficult. The irony is worthy of note. Trade unions which have achieved any political significance and industrial autonomy under 'socialist' regimes have tended to do so with an anti-socialist voice, while within capitalist societies, the most active and progressive unions, with aims of assuming widespread social responsibilities and effecting social change, have usually acted with a strong consciousness of the socialist tradition. If there is a common thread, it is opposition to industrial and political authority – suggesting that there is an irreducible management–worker, if not owner–worker, division which manifests itself within diverse ownership and social forms.

The articulation and representation of workers' interests, both sectional and class, is problematic in capitalist societies. Trade unions and their peak councils attempt and, in part, achieve these ends but since they do not, for the most part, attempt to operate as the representatives of the working class, their goals are largely limited to maximizing workers' conditions and wages within the prevailing capitalist productive and distributive mechanisms. Trade unions in capitalist societies promote the interests of the workers-as-a-class in quite marginal and indirect ways. While they occasionally act to limit the power of capital, it is commonly to thwart capital's excesses rather than undermine its power. Destroying the position of capital seldom forms the focus, conscious or otherwise, of collective trade union activities, despite the adherence of many individual trade union activists to some form of socialist ideology.

There is an awareness among progressive western trade unions that unions in socialist societies necessarily have different political roles from their own. 'Socialism', for their eastern counterparts, has, in theory, already been achieved. The role of their workers as a class is to play their part in the development of socialism and the growth of the economy. Much of what socialist-inclined western trade unions seek, indeed their fundamental goals, has, according to their own perspectives, already been achieved by unions in socialist societies. Production, economic policy, capital accumulation, the distribution of economic output as wages, the organization of work and the conditions of work are, at least in theory, determined in the workers' interests, and, ultimately, by the workers' political representatives. Since workers in a 'socialist' society are, by definition, not exploited – the exploiting class having been abolished – then such issues are not laden with opposing class interests and conflict.[3] Conflict for the worker in the west, generated by the opposing interests of class forces and the workplace environment in which they meet, is, by definition, not present for the worker in a socialist society.[4]

In practice, however, the major preoccupations of western trade unions are wages and conditions, and, to varying extents depending on the country and union concerned, the determination of wider economic, social and public policy issues which affect their livelihood. No matter how socialist oriented, trade unions in the west spend most of their time attending to issues which relate not to overthrowing the capitalist system but to improving the lot of workers within it. Many of these functions arise, arguably, as much from the process of production and the organization of work as they do from the fact that the social formation concerned is capitalist. It is perhaps surprising, then, that for so many years eastern trade unions did not address them with more vigour. The fact that they did not do so almost certainly attests more to the level of social control exercised by the ruling party machines in socialist societies, in the workplace as elsewhere, than it does to the lack of a need for workers' interests to be articulated independently of management, and of political and state leadership. The loosening of party control in socialist societies has invariably been accompanied by claims for greater trade union or worker authority and independence, suggesting that this control is, indeed, the critical factor in the apparent quiescence or absence of employee resistance to management perspectives and decisions. If this is so, then the inactivity of socialist trade unions is at least as much a question of suppression as it is of trade unions having no need of their oppositional functions under socialism as it has been practised.

In the case of Chinese trade unions, the traditional roles they have exercised since 1949 have not differed markedly from their Eastern European counterparts. The attention they have received has often been more concerned with national leadership struggles at peak committee level, the interaction of these with party leadership battles, the way in which national level union hierarchies are composed, the extent of regional as opposed to industry representation, and the like. These foci are consistent with the politically significant aspects of China's trade unions in the past, but are not directed towards an understanding of their shop floor representative functions, their operational arrangements, and their interaction with labour market movements and areas of broad public policy concern. It is the latter areas which are of increasing interest as the political and economic climate in which they operate has, in recent years, given them some encouragement to develop a role as worker advocates.

THE IMPACT OF THE REFORMS

China's reforms have placed significant strains on the model of trade union operation which has existed to date. A more complex set of interests for workers *vis à vis* managers and employers has been generated by many factors including: the emergence of the initial stages of a labour market; the relative decline of the state sector in the economy and the expansion of a collective and private sector with far less control over work organization and remuneration; the growth of wage differentials; reduced job security; heightened enterprise autonomy in employment-related matters; increased initiative and autonomy given to enterprise directors; the development of free trade zones with quite distinctive employment practices; the attempts to promote efficiency by stricter supervisory controls; the emergence of high levels of unemployment; government-initiated redundancy and retrenchment; attempts to implement systems of 'contract responsibility' in the state employment sector; the appointment of managers with contracts linked to reduced output costs and productivity; and, in general, a commitment to a programme of market oriented economic development. It is therefore not surprising that considerable public attention has been given to clarifying a new set of more independent goals and activities for Chinese trade unions in light of these changed circumstances. At the Eleventh National Trade Union Congress in October 1988, the chairman of the All-China Federation of Trade Unions (ACFTU), Ni Zhifu, called for quite dramatic increases in the rights of trade unions to protect the interests of workers from the authority of managers, party and state. He argued in his report to the Congress that previous judgements made about trade union 'syndicalism' and 'economism' were erroneous, that 'the over-centralized political system' made the performance of trade union functions very difficult and that the unions had been 'divorced from the masses'. He concluded that change was imperative to develop the trade union movement into an 'independent and fully democratic mass organization of the working class', though, as always, it was to be led by the party.[5]

There has thus been a belated recognition that while working-class interests may be served by the creation of a socialist state, the interests of workers in any particular employment situation are not automatically met.[6] Government ownership of the economy's commanding heights, as many a workers' control advocate or syndicalist has long since known, does not confer upon any individual work site effective economic or industrial democracy. Workers' ownership of the economy may not be reflected in any obvious way in the treatment received by workers. In fact, the subjective experience of working life in a Chinese factory may well be as alienating, stultifying and powerless as that in any capitalist one. Workers will also be paid much less, though this, of course, is largely a function of China's level of development rather than its particular social formation.

The widespread endorsement by workers in all major cities of student demands in 1989 testifies to an underlying opposition on their part to major aspects of the existing social order. The fact that many workers chose to express their grievances, either through official trade union bodies or through others brought into existence for the occasion, suggests that at least part of their protest was industrially based. Like all other forms of political expression unleashed by the events of 1989, the overt political opposition of organized workers has been suppressed and its leaders have faced detention or execution. In the longer term, attempts to contain worker opposition within boundaries which do not challenge the political and social authority the party has always enjoyed will no doubt be sustained. The expression of interests at a political level, which the logic of the economic developments of the reforms demands, is, at present, simply not possible. There still seems to be no recognition of the need to create forums in which the different interests unleashed by the reforms can publicly debate their claims to resources of various kinds, their appropriate relationship to party and state authorities and their forms of social and political representation. The events of 1989 show that a negotiated solution to the problem is not yet a realistic outcome.

THE HISTORY OF THE CHINESE TRADE UNION MOVEMENT

The Chinese trade union movement has had a thoroughly revolutionary history. Its early energies were generated in the crucible of Guomindang oppression; its founders were revolutionary martyrs; its industrial practice was never separate from intense political struggle and its goals always encompassed a socialist future for China. The movement was not, however, initiated by the Communist Party, though virtually all of the early party leaders worked with trade unions. It grew out of the factories established along the eastern seaboard of China at the beginning of the century, thereby pre-dating the May Fourth Movement of 1919 and the formation of the party in 1920. As in the process of industrialization elsewhere, the Chinese industrial workforce was at first small in relation to the size of the peasantry. It was largely transitory, concentrated in a few major cities and, as a result, vulnerable. There were also ferocious efforts by the combined forces of government and capital to cripple or destroy any attempts at organizing independent industrial or political activity by the incipient trade union movement.

In the literature on the pre-1949 labour movement, most attention has understandably been paid to the 1920s when it was at the centre of the massive political upheavals of the time and the driving force of the Chinese revolution. The bloody suppression of the trade unions in 1927 by the Guomindang, however, decimated them in terms of numbers and political effectiveness. Thus after the massacres of the 1920s had exposed the vulnerability of its industrial wing, the party based its revolutionary strategy on the peasantry.[7] But while the party shifted its strategic emphasis from the urban working class, its commitment to Marxism ensured that class remained central to its ideological considerations. Workers were, in the lexicon of the party, the 'leading force' of the revolution, while peasants became its 'main force'. They were, along with the much larger numerical force of peasants, responsible for the success of the Chinese revolution and its subsequent development, and during the civil war from 1945 to 1949, trade unions in Guomindang controlled areas were responsible for massive industrial and political unrest which played a major role in the Guomindang's eventual demise.

Given their radical past, the apparent passivity of the Chinese trade union movement after 1949 is difficult to understand. A social movement which saw itself as society's industrial and political core and the midwife of socialism was transformed into what, in its worst manifestations, is but a cypher of party policy. A change of this magnitude clearly demands explanation.

Ultimately five main factors contributed to this transformation. First, the importance of the rural strategy described above tended to limit the influence of urban and industrial concerns within the party. Second, the social reorganization after 1949 involved rapid industrialization and expansion of urban employment so that vast numbers of new workers swamped the original workforce. Third, the single-minded pursuit of authority by the party after 1949 meant that all other social organizations necessarily became subordinate to its nation-wide concerns. Stalinist influences combined with traditional absolutism to ensure that party and state were unified into an awesome authority which allowed no rivals and no pluralism. In the arena of industrial relations this meant that, while lip service was paid to the separate concerns of workers and the need for an independent body – the trade unions – to represent them, in practice the relationship between unions and party was one of subordination. The role assigned to unions was to implement party industrial policy and to assist workers in understanding and fulfilling party objectives, be they production quotas, wage limitations, work practices or broader social policies.

The fourth factor stems from the belief that the success of the revolution signalled the arrival of workers on the stage of history as victors. As was the case in the Soviet Union, there emerged a widespread belief that exploitation and oppression in the workplace had been automatically overcome by the demise of the capitalist class. Capital had been displaced by labour, whose voice was the trade unions. Such an explanation ignored the potential for conflict between the political authority of the party and industrial concerns about remuneration and conditions expressed through the trade union movement.

Finally, in the course of post-1949 party history, the trade union movement was the victim of intra-party factionalism and ideological reversals which reduced its independence and authority. During the Hundred Flowers Movement of 1957, trade union cadres pointed out that they were sandwiched between the party and their members. If they bowed to members' wishes and questioned party wisdom, they were accused of syndicalism or tailism or of 'blindly following the masses'. This left union cadres in a position of low status and authority. In the Anti-Rightist Movement that followed, many of those who had openly criticized the role assigned them were relieved of their positions and returned to the factory floor for reform through labour. Li Lisan, the First Vice-Chairman of the ACFTU, was criticized and lost his position, and Lai Ruoyu, the Chairman, was severely criticized and his followers were purged after his death in 1958.[8] Chen Yun was also attacked for his advocacy of increased trade union autonomy along Yugoslavian lines. Lai Ruoyu was eventually replaced by Liu Ningyi who announced that 'all trade union functionaries must always keep in mind the most fundamental truth that trade unions must unreservedly accept the leadership of the Communist party'.[9] The subordination of unions to the party at this time left a legacy of distrust between them which has never been healed.[10]

The trade union movement's historical association with Liu Shaoqi meant that it quickly came under suspicion in the early stages of the Cultural Revolution. By January 1967, the ACFTU had been disbanded and its Chairman, Liu Ningyi, removed. It was not until 1973 that trade unions were restored – their restoration, like their disbanding, being the work of the party. In both instances, the dependence of the trade unions on the party for their very existence was underscored. It was not until its Ninth National Congress in 1978 that the ACFTU was officially rehabilitated.[11]

The outcome of these events is clear: the practice of the post-1949 Chinese trade union movement has, like its Eastern European counterparts, been constrained by party authority into forms of practice which have severely compromised its ability to represent the industrial concerns of workers. While it may have provided useful services to its members, the evidence that independent representation of workers' industrial interests has not been among its major activities is overwhelming. This is not to say, however, that Chinese workers have not benefited from the period of communist rule. They clearly have in substantial ways. There is a quite genuine sense in which Chinese state enterprise workers enjoy conditions which are exceptional for a third world country. Their security of employment, pension rights, maternity leave and child care provisions, attendance requirements and other conditions might even be envied in parts of the developed industrial world. They have also received very high levels of subsidy for their health, education, accommodation and transport costs. These conditions have not, however, been won by the trade union movement as a result of shop floor industrial activity. Nor have they led to significant worker autonomy or widespread effective participation in management and control. Rather, they have been delivered by legislation and regulations which express the commitment of the party to advancing the welfare of workers, as well as to protecting its major source of revenue – urban industry.

THE STRUCTURE OF CHINESE TRADE UNIONS

China's 93 million trade union members,[12] some 89.7 per cent of the country's total workers,[13] are organized in 15 industry unions.[14] As the peak council of these trade unions, the ACFTU has a significant bureaucracy of eight departments dealing with the economy, safety, wages, women, propaganda, international liaison, organization, finance and accounts. The current Chairman, Ni Zhifu, who was appointed in 1983, is also a Vice-Chairman of the Standing Committee of the National People's Congress (NPC) – personifying the interrelationship between union, party and state. Beneath the ACFTU, the federations or councils which duplicate these administrative arrangements at provincial, regional and municipal levels act as local peak councils. Individual industry unions are similarly organized at provincial, regional, local or urban levels and beneath that, at the level of the enterprise. These primary trade union units are mandatory in state enterprises, though membership of them is not.[15] In addition to its membership in urban state-owned enterprises the trade union organization has now reached some 12,000 rural enterprises and 1,000 of the 4,000 foreign-funded enterprises. Altogether, there are said to be 540,000 'grass-roots trade unions'.[16]

Trade unions have also been given the right to organize in private enterprises, where it is recognized that 'with employee–employer relations based on hired labour, the two parties have conflicts as well as common interests'. It is also admitted that 'the contradictions

between employers and workers are increasingly manifesting themselves and many problems have yet to be solved'. As in the state
sector, the role of trade unions is first, 'to help the employer make a
success of running the enterprise and expand the productive forces',
and second, to 'defend the legitimate rights and interests of staff and
workers'.[17]

Since the rehabilitation of the ACFTU in 1978,[18] there have been
continuous efforts to develop and promulgate a 'trade union law'
which would comprehensively modify the existing legislation promulgated in 1950. The move is in accordance with the development
of legislation in other areas aimed at giving greater force to the rule
of law – to some extent as the result of pressure applied by foreign
enterprises, many of which objected to whimsical political decisions
affecting their investments. The efforts to develop the legislation
have all foundered on the central issue of the status of the unions *vis
à vis* the state, the party and enterprise management – the very issue
that has bedevilled the unions since 1949. Over a hundred amend-
ments have been made to the draft legislation. It even reached the
Standing Committee of the NPC, where it excited such controversy
that it was not passed on for consideration at the full NPC.[19] Hopes
were entertained that it would be passed in 1989,[20] but even if
legislation had been enacted, the underlying dilemma would have
remained. There are voluminous local, national and industry-
specific regulations dealing with industrial relations issues, but they
do not have the force which a trade union law could have and are
too easily set aside when they are seen to conflict with more significant political considerations or vested interests. Early in 1989, Ni
Zhifu claimed that trade unions' primary focus should be on
economic construction rather than safeguarding workers' interests[21]
and that trade unions, while giving support to 'workers' reasonable
demands' in labour disputes, should not resort to strikes which 'do
not help resolve problems but can intensify the contradictions'.[22]
Statements such as this suggest that the party remains unwilling to
alter the position which has created the dilemma, despite indications during the 1988 Trade Union Congress of support for greater
independence. Complaints continue to surface, as they have since
the 1950s, of trade union cadres siding with management and party
and of workers being victimized for lodging complaints.

THE LABOUR MARKET

Along with the development of markets in commodities and capital, the economic reforms have also introduced a labour market – despite initial squeamishness about use of the term.[23] Luo Gan, the Minister of Labour, referred to labour exchanges established in a number of major centres as 'socialist job markets'.[24] The hallmarks of Chinese employment arrangements prior to this time were the administrative allocation of life-time jobs by the state, the virtual non-existence of unemployment, redundancy or retrenchment, and a strict separation between urban and rural labour. All of these features have changed with the emergence of a labour market. Pressure to modify the previous arrangements came from reform economists who pointed to serious problems of overstaffing, low productivity, inflexibility, low motivation and the high capital cost of a state employee.[25] While these problems remain,[26] there have been dramatic changes, particularly at the macro level, especially in respect of rural labour and school leavers.

Millions of peasant workers, mostly construction workers, have flocked to urban (and rural) growth areas for employment, pushed by the effects of the production responsibility system in the country-side and pulled by the lure of high wages in the cities. Of the 340 million farm labourers in 1984, 180 million were said to have become redundant. Many more millions are expected to be jobless in the next decade. While some 80 million had been absorbed in township enterprises by the end of 1987,[27] the rural labour surplus has been referred to as 'the biggest problem facing China's economic and social reform'.[28] One estimate suggested that 'surplus labourers' alone will amount to 240 million to 260 million in the year 2000.[29] Guangdong's provincial government revealed early in 1989 that 15,000 labourers per day were flocking into the province.[30] Some 200,000 moved to Hainan – 14,000 arriving at Xingang wharf on 1 March alone.[31] The government's counter-strategy concentrated on blocking the entry of surplus labour into desirable areas and repatriating them to their places of origin.[32] While this strategy might alleviate the difficulties of local urban officials, the structural problem which gave rise to the difficulties remains. The problem was exacerbated by the sharp cutbacks in capital investment and construction in 1988–89 – areas which have absorbed most rural labour.[33]

Students from schools and universities are no longer assured of job assignments on graduation. Many, while not officially un-employed, join the long list of those 'awaiting employment'. A growing percentage of them join collective or private enterprises outside the state's labour allocation system, with much reduced security, welfare and pension provisions. Of the 70 million urban jobs created between 1979 and 1987, 40 per cent were in the collectively owned or private business sector.[34]

The responsibility systems, contract labour systems and labour rationalization programmes introduced into state-owned enter-prises to improve productivity have also begun to smash the 'iron rice bowls' of workers who have been contracted or rationalized.[35] Evidence of the extent of this process tends to be fragmentary but, in Beijing, 44 enterprises undertook 'realignment' of their work-forces by making 12.7 per cent of them redundant in 1988.[36] In Shanghai, 30,000 workers were made redundant and placed on social welfare.[37] In some areas, a system of 'in-factory un-employment' is practised in which workers stay home on a fraction of their pay until work is found for them.[38]

As discussed by Tamara Jacka below, women have been the most severely affected by this rationalization and by the difficulties they face in finding employment in the first place.[39] According to an ACFTU survey, only 5.3 per cent of employers were prepared to accept women workers. Of the young jobless in Guizhou, 70 per cent were women.[40] There have also been warnings against giving women equal treatment in the job market. The aims of gender equality in the workplace, it is claimed, have resulted in high un-employment rates for women, most of whom undertake household chores as well, leading to strains on their health and lowered productivity.[41] While individual enterprises bear the full costs of extended maternity and feeding leave, the financial autonomy they have gained will continue to encourage discriminatory pressures in employment practices.

For those still in the tenured workforce, however, the 'iron rice bowl' seems to remain very much intact. It is primarily new workers who are hired on contractual arrangements.[42] One reporter com-mented:

As there is both the sense of crisis of the contract workers and the sense of superiority of the permanent workers holding the 'iron rice bowl', in many enterprises 'the latter have nothing to do but watch the former working'.[43]

51

Since contract workers are a growing proportion of the workforce –
now over 8 million, or 8.3 per cent of state-enterprise workers[44] – the
contradictions between the rights and privileges of the two groups
will become a more difficult industrial problem.[45] While there is a
stated intention of placing all permanent workers in state-run factories on contract,[46] the political and practical difficulties involved in
this seem to have stalled the process. The theoretical arguments
which preceded the introduction of the contract system – in particular, the argument that such a system involved a return to a
capitalist, wage labour system – has had its reverberations at the
trade union and factory floor level.[47]

Foreign enterprises operating in the special economic zones and
in joint ventures have also made major alterations to the patterns of
appointment, dismissal and management practice in those areas.
The absence of any regulations which have the force of law has
enabled foreign and local managements, often with the compliance
of local officials, to exploit child labour, to extend working hours up
to 17 or 18 hours a day and to provide appalling working and living
conditions. The attitude of a Chinese administrator of a Sino-foreign
joint venture suggests the workers are faced with some formidable
challenges. The administrator claimed:

> It pays to respect and protect the legitimate interests of man-
> agement and accept their temporary exploitation of workers.
> Doing so is conducive to our economic development.[48]

Women, who constitute the majority of workers in the special
economic zones, have borne the brunt of these employment
problems.[49]

WORKERS CONGRESSES

Much trade union work within enterprises currently takes place in
conjunction with the Workers' and Staff Representative Congresses
(workers' congresses), of which the trade unions are the executive
arm and secretariat. These bodies, underpinned by a rationale derived from pre-1949 party industrial practice which is closer to
industrial democracy and worker participation than to collective
bargaining, have had as chequered a career over the last three
decades as the trade unions themselves. They have undergone a
major revival since they were reintroduced at the Ninth Trade Union
Congress in 1978 and are now established in almost all state enter-

prises. The 1986 State Council regulations empower their twice-yearly convocations to design and implement management policies, production plans and technological innovation, to allocate retained earnings and welfare funds, to supervise managerial performance and to recommend or appoint directors. In practice, however, their operations depend greatly on the enterprise concerned and the commitment of its directors to democratic management practices.

The powers of the workers' congresses, while less than those of directors, potentially provide for a democratic management system in which workers have a considerable role in decision making. Workers' domination of the congresses is guaranteed by a maximum staff representation of 20 per cent.[50] Since, however, there are no legal requirements that plant managers carry out congress decisions, it is likely that practice often falls short of the ideal. Nevertheless, the ACFTU claims that, in 1987, the workers' congresses were responsible for removing some 160,000 incompetent enterprise leaders from their offices, suggesting that they have developed considerable authority.[51] Difficulties with the congresses include their inadequate allowance for migrant or casual labour representation, their competition with trade unions in the provision of welfare, and their potential further to reduce the effectiveness of trade unions at industry and national levels.[52]

TRADE UNIONS IN THE WORKPLACE

Most of the traditional workplace functions of Chinese trade unions remain, in addition to those they have acquired as a result of the revival of workers' congresses. Trade unions continue to negotiate with management and party over welfare issues, bonuses and allowances of various kinds, health and safety monitoring, workplace discipline, leave arrangements and the like, as well as taking up the grievances of individuals. They are involved, as in the past, in settling disputes, developing workplace harmony, promoting productive effort and disseminating party industrial policy. They continue also to be largely responsible for social activities, many training and education programmes, and the protection of particular interests such as those of women workers.[53] The roles of trade unions in the state-owned and large collective workplaces, however, particularly those concerned with the representation of workers' interests, have been profoundly affected by various aspects of the economic reforms. The introduction of the directors' responsibility system, rationalization of the labour force, the contract labour system and reform of the standardized wage system have all increased the need for workers' interests to be represented effectively in the workplace.

The *directors' responsibility system* was introduced, after considerable debate, to ensure that responsibility for economic performance lay with directors and managers who had competence in the area, rather than with the party secretary. In the regulations promulgated by the State Council in January 1987, the new directors, bearing some similarities to the 'one man managers' of the early 1950s, became the legal representatives of the enterprise and have ultimate authority over production and operational management issues. The authority given the directors, when aligned with that given the workers' congresses, and that intended to be taken from party officials created ample scope for interpretation, confusion and conflict.[54] A more cynical view claims

> that in the past, the cadres of the labour union acted in accordance with the will of the secretary of the party committee. Now the manager has become the centre of the enterprise, the cadres act in accordance with the manager's will.[55]

The directors' responsibility has been extended by the introduction of the *contract managers system* as a result of which managers are appointed for fixed terms to achieve particular profit or production targets. Potential managers, from within or outside the plant, submit tenders to a selection committee of employee representatives, government authorities and party cadres. Their salaries form part of the bid and can be reduced by up to 50 per cent should they fail to deliver the profit target specified.

A further extension of these arrangements is the *enterprise leasing system* in which plants are leased to individuals or groups who are given greater autonomy over the running of the company. While the regulations require leaseholders to be selected after debate involving the workers' congresses, trade unions report many cases of workers discovering their companies had been leased after the event. Unions have told of those bidding for leases walking through plants advising unsuspecting workers that some of them would be retrenched should their bids be successful.[56] The new autonomy and authority provided for directors and managers, while directed at the worthy cause of productivity enhancement, has clearly made the position of workers more vulnerable and the role of the trade unions more complex and difficult.

Rationalization of the labour force, discussed in its macro aspects above, produces its most intense social result at the enterprise level. Four decades of ideological mobilization which prized workers in socialist China as 'masters of the house' makes retrenchment difficult in practice. So too does the requirement that the trade unions have to endorse dismissals. An alternative method of dealing with surplus labour is *subcontracting* particular stages of a factory's processes to groups of workers who bid to undercut their fellow workers. Even here the difficulty of retrenching the unsuccessful often requires management to keep them on in some reduced capacity. Needless to say, these various attempts at rationalization have produced responses from workers which go far beyond officially sanctioned trade union activity.

As noted above, the *contract labour system* has produced a series of sensitive problems for trade unions. Contract workers do not, as a rule, have their household registration (*hukou*) at their place of work. Consequently, their ability to compete for housing and other provisions with permanent workers is structurally weakened, while their need is often greater. In the Chinese context, it is not surprising that they have been seen as the beginnings of a wage labouring class. The 'mastery of the house' that Chinese workers have seen themselves as enjoying was related to their security of employment, their rights to education, health care, pensions and a range of allowances, and often to hereditary employment, all of which were administered by their unit. None of these rights or privileges is so assured for contract workers. Trade unions, with obligations to protect the interests of both groups, are placed at the centre of this developing polarization of the Chinese workforce. As permanent workers themselves, trade union cadres are identified with the section of the workforce which will continue to diminish if this aspect of industry reform is continued.

Reform economists in China have devoted a great deal of attention to dismantling the 'egalitarianism' or 'eating from the one big pot' of the Cultural Revolution. They regard the traditional wage relativities as insufficient to generate the incentives required for improved productivity, just as they regard the security enjoyed by workers as inimical to sustained worker effort. In response to these views, the government has altered, in a variety of ways, the complex wage structures of Chinese industry. In general terms, the end result has been a considerable expansion of the relativities, as well as a great deal of dissatisfaction with what are perceived as unfair bases of distribution and unfair comparisons of skills and responsibilities. The new arrangements have raised expectations – though often without meeting them. The rapidly emerging disparities between state sector wages and those for some in the private sector, whose wages are often considerably higher, have also generated dissatisfaction, particularly for those state workers unable to supplement their income with part-time work.[57] The stability of the previous system and its comparative wage levels, its control by distant central authorities and the weight it gave to seniority, while not producing the incentives now regarded as appropriate, generated much less conflict and division than the new arrangements. For plant-level trade union organizations, the determination of wages, in whole or in part, at enterprise level has placed greater demands on their abilities to inspire worker confidence and to influence managerial decisions. The need for independent arbitrary mechanisms for dispute settlement and for trade union involvement in them has been recognized.

As with other aspects of industrial reform, changes to the wage system have provided the basis for a weakening of trade union–party relationships. This is especially so at grass-roots levels, where, in the new environment, there is now greater authority to determine many aspects of workers' lives. At a national, policy-making level some progress was made in widening the scope of the ACFTU input into all economic and industrial decisions which affected its members. The ACFTU has been given a role in government and departmental deliberations on labour, wages, benefits, prices and housing.[58] Other developments in their national role have included establishing 'workers' price supervision organizations', of which some 11,000 have been set up to monitor and report on profiteering.[59] There has also been a good deal of public self-criticism as well as criticism by senior party officials of the ACFTU's hierarchical, undemocratic and bureaucratic methods which are said to have stifled grass-roots opinion and membership activism.[60] Experiments with a more democratically elected representational structure began in the summer of 1988 in seven major cities, intended to overcome the problem of unions being 'more or less separated from the masses'.[61]

CONCLUSION

This chapter has discussed the impact of the reforms on workers and trade unions, primarily those in the state enterprise sector. For those working in private industry, small collective industry and the special economic zones, conditions are generally not as favourable and the coverage and influence of the trade unions less.

After the events of 1989 there has been a battening down of ideological hatches, and a resort to political, police and military coercion which reversed, at least temporarily, the general thrust of many of the reforms so far implemented. Both ACFTU and unofficial union bodies were active in support of the demonstrations in Beijing and elsewhere. The Beijing Workers Autonomous Federation campaigned in Tiananmen Square for the development of a voluntary, independent and democratic organization to represent workers' interests. They also sought reduced wage discrepancies between workers and managers, better conditions, workplace representation and improved living standards. They have since been declared a counter-revolutionary organization. The ACFTU, on the other hand, has sided with the official view.[62] The pressure for quiescence in the industrial arena, as in all others, is currently overwhelming. But the expectations already aroused and the changes already made to industry policy, industrial relations, labour market mechanisms and the allocation of workplace responsibilities are not easily or quickly reversed – and one suspects the current leadership has not much time. In short, the direction of change may not be reversed, merely set back.

It has been suggested in this chapter that the reforms, as they affect workers, create a greater need for an independent trade union organization. The economic reforms as they related to workers' conditions were largely inspired by the attempt to elicit greater effort from the workplace. Appeals to ideology, collective benefit and national interest had become less successful, particularly after the Cultural Revolution. The lowered esteem in which the party is now held has made a return to these earlier mechanisms difficult and its outcome uncertain. The alternative path of constructing an environment of economic stimuli to intensify work effort was embarked upon with some vigour, though not always coherence. Since June 1989, however, major efforts have been made to revive artificially the moral and ideological authority of the party in this area as in others.

Trade unions have been both symbol and substance of the break from the monopoly of power held by the party and state in much of Eastern Europe. A number of them ceased to be the compliant transmission belts of party policy when economic reforms required them to assume a more independent and combative role. In China, the events in Eastern Europe have been watched with interest. One banner in the 1989 demonstrations reportedly read 'Where are you, China's Lech Walesa?'[63] Economic considerations have dominated changes to China's industrial relations as they have to other areas of reform. The political reforms necessary to ensure that the interests created by those reforms, in this case the interests of workers, are represented, have not yet, however, been developed. Trade unions are still required to transmit party policy to the workplace, even though the party lacks the moral authority it once had and the policy involved is not necessarily seen by the workers as in their interests.

The imposition of military rule in Beijing and its consequences only intensified the monumental problem facing the Chinese work-force. There are millions of redundant rural labourers leaving the land at a time when major rationalization of employment in urban industry is being undertaken. The likelihood of the trade union movement enhancing its operational independence and authority in the present climate is remote. Its gains in the 1978–88 period were in a time of rapid growth in both rural and urban areas and in real wages. For the moment, when the need for them to be effective has never been greater, they have to make their way in a climate of political threat superimposed upon a highly unfavourable labour market.

NOTES AND REFERENCES

1 Craig R. Littler, *Urban Reforms in China: The Progress of Labour Reforms*, Mimeo, Griffith University, 1988, p. 1.
2 The writers Bai Hua and Wang Ruowang and the dissident astro-physicist Fang Lizhi have claimed that Marxism-Leninism is either dead or dying in China and the thoughts of Mao Zedong are already things of the past, even if they remain the pillars of official ideology. AFP Shanghai, 12 February 1989, quoted in *SWB*, 14 February 1989, FE/0384/B2/5.
3 A typical official Chinese statement claims that, 'In China, the funda-mental interests of trade unions and the government are identical'. Yang Xiaobing, 'Trade Unions: A Major Force for Reform', *BR*, 7–13 November 1988, p. 4.
4 For a discussion of the differences between trade unions in capitalist

and socialist societies, see Craig R. Littler and Gill Palmer, 'Communist and Capitalist Trade Unionism: Comparisons and Contrasts', in Alex Pravda and Blair A. Ruble, eds, *Trade Unions in Communist States*, London and Sydney, Allen & Unwin, 1987.

5 'Proceedings of the 11th National Trade Union Congress', Xinhua, 26 October 1988, *SWB*, FE/0298/B2/6.

6 Zhao Ziyang, at the Eleventh National Congress of the ACFTU, noted that 'trade unions must adhere to the party's lines, principles and policies . . . but, also should remain independent, democratic and non-governmental'. *BR*, 7–13 November 1988, p. 5.

7 Jean Chesneaux, *The Chinese Labour Movement, 1919–1927*, California, Stanford University Press, 1968. Despite Chesneaux' claim that its intention was to satisfy the Communist Party of France's Stalinist ideological predilections of the time, his work still stands as a major contribution to the study of the early Chinese labour movement. See 'My Forty Years of Chinese History', *The Australian Journal of Chinese Affairs*, no. 22, July 1989, p. 134.

8 Lee Lai To, *Structure of the Trade Union System in China, 1949–66*, Hong Kong, Centre of Asian Studies, 1984, p. 53. Lai had proposed workers' congresses with the power to recommend appointments to leading factory posts.

9 Ibid. p. 65.

10 A survey of 20,000 workers in Zhejiang province in 1986, as well as a variety of other national and local surveys, showed a consistent pattern of distrust and dissatisfaction with trade unions as a result of their conformity with the views of the local party secretary, see Chen Lo, 'What is the future of China's labour union?', *Nexus: China in Focus*, Autumn, 1988, pp. 2–3.

11 For a useful summary of Chinese trade union history and operations, see Jeanne L. Wilson, 'The People's Republic of China', in Alex Pravda and Blair A. Ruble, op. cit.

12 The estimated membership at the end of 1987 was 93,365,000, up from 85,866,000 at the end of 1982, see *BR*, 7–13 November 1988, p. 5, and Xue Muqiao, ed., *Almanac of China's Economy*, Hong Kong, Chinese Economic Yearbook Limited, 1983, 1–39.

13 'Workers', in this official sense, are those employed in the state sector. The figures are from Xinhua, 9 October 1988, *SWB*, FE/0280/B2/3.

14 The industry unions concerned are for 'railways, civil aviation, seamen, road transport, post and telecommunications, engineering and metal-lurgy, petrochemicals, coal mining and geology, water and electricity, textiles, light industry, urban development and building materials, agri-culture and forestry, finance and trade, and education', 'China's Trade Unions', *BR*, 13–26 February 1989, p. 28.

15 In 1986 there were 320,000 full-time officials and 100,000 staff members in the national trade unions. Leung Wing-yue, *Smashing the Iron Rice Pot*, Hong Kong, Asia Monitor Resource Centre, 1988, p. 40.

16 Xinhua, 9 October 1988, *SWB*, FE/0280/B2/3.

17 *Gongren Ribao*, 19 July 1988, *SWB*, FE/0222/B2/5.

18 On the revival of the trade union movement after the Cultural

Revolution, see Richard Morris, 'Trade Unions in Contemporary China', *The Australian Journal of Chinese Affairs*, no. 13, January 1985, pp. 51–67.

19 Xinhua, 27 October 1988, *SWB*, FE/0298/B2/8.

20 Xinhua, 25 February 1989, *SWB*, FE/0396/B2/6.

21 Jinan Provincial Radio Service, 8 March 1989, *SWB*, FE/0410/B2/6.

22 Xinhua, 23 February 1989, *SWB*, FE/0396/B2/6. Yu Qinghe, a member of the ACFTU secretariat, in explaining a series of strikes and slow downs, one of which at the North-West Medical Appliance Factory involved 1,100 workers walking out for three months, agreed that 'strikes were not the best way to resolve problems', but claimed 'the major reason for most strikes and slow-downs is bureaucracy and malpractice perpetrated by enterprise leaders, who have seriously infringed on workers' rights and interests'. Xinhua, 25 October 1988, *SWB*, FE/0294/ B2/7.

23 For a discussion of the emergence of contractual employment obligations, the attempts to link wage levels to individual and enterprise performance and other characteristics of a labour market in China, see Gordon White, 'Labour Market Reform in Chinese Industry', in Malcolm Warner, ed., *Management Reforms in China*, London, Frances Pinter, 1987.

24 Xinhua, 23 August 1988, *SWB*, FE/0241/B2/1. Job markets have been formally constituted in a number of places, with a reported one million workers having found jobs in them over the past three years.

25 The origins of such reform plans in socialist societies are well summarized by Charles F. Sabel and David Stark, '[they are] born out of the desire of a loosely defined group of central planners, technically versed party officials and less cautious managers to break the logic of systematic maldistribution and shortages of resources'. 'Planning, Politics and Shop-Floor Power: Hidden Forms of Bargaining in Soviet-Imposed State-Socialist Societies', *Politics and Society*, vol. 11, no. 4, 1982, p. 468.

26 See the survey report documenting widespread sleeping on the job, late arrivals, long lunches and early departures in state firms contrasted with the industry of workers in the private sector, *BR*, no. 40, 3–9 October 1988, p. 29.

27 Xinhua, 23 August 1988, *SWB*, FE/0241/B2/1.

28 Xinhua, 2 March 1989, *SWB*, FE/0402/B2/3.

29 Xinhua, 3 March 1989, *SWB*, ibid. The report stated that the number of China's labourers has increased at a rate of 10 million per year in recent years, 'far outstripping the number of jobs available'.

30 *SWB*, FE/0399/i.

31 Guangdong Provincial Radio Service, 3 March 1989, *SWB*, FE/0402/B2/3.

32 The State Council, early in 1989, issued an urgent circular, drawing attention to the problems created for the railway system, the difficulties of the labourers after they arrive at their destination and the 'confusion in local social order'. Xinhua, 5 March 1989, *SWB*, FE/0402/B2/2.

33 About 110,000 peasants had to leave Beijing in 1989 as a result of cutbacks to spending on hotels and restaurants. Another 200,000 were

temporarily working outside Beijing on the Asian Games site. Xinhua, 14 March 1989, *SWB*, FE/0411/B2/6.

34 Luo Gan, interviewed in *BR*, no 51, 19–25 December 1988, p. 17. In the case of Shandong, for instance, collective enterprises account for 80.9 per cent of all business (national average: 77.7 per cent), for 30.3 per cent of total provincial output (20.7 per cent) and absorbed 42.6 per cent of the newly employed, see Yuko Akiyoshi Nihei, *China Newsletter*, Jetro, no. 38, p. 19. According to estimates by the State Administration Bureau for Industry and Commerce, in 1988 there were 225,000 private enterprises, with some 3.6 million staff and workers, some of them having assets worth 10 million yuan, see *Gongren Ribao*, 19 July 1988, in *SWB*, FE/0222/B2/5.

35 Some 20 million workers in state enterprises are estimated by the Minister of Labour to be redundant and there are approximately 6 million new workers entering the labour force annually, *BR*, no. 51, 19–25 December 1988, p. 18. According to the State Commission for Economic Restructuring, 30 million could be redundant – a number whose pay consumes half of all profits, Xinhua, 22 July 1988, *SWB*, FE/0215/B2/4.

36 Xinhua, 2 November 1988, *SWB*, FE/W0052/A/3.

37 Xinhua, 28 September 1988, *SWB*, FE/W0047/A/4.

38 For an account of the operation of this system, see Zhang Zeyu, 'Enterprises Optimize Labour Organization', *BR*, no. 51, 19–25 December 1988, pp. 21–2.

39 'The Job Hunt – Adventure or Ordeal?' and 'The First Women Employees' Protection Regulations', in *Women of China*, November 1988, pp. 1–3 and 11–12, and Tamara Jacka, 'Back to the Wok', *The Australian Journal of Chinese Affairs*, no. 25, July 1990.

40 Xinhua, 22 October 1988, *SWB*, FE/0298/B2/5.

41 *JJRB*, 24 August 1988, *SWB*, FE/0241/B2/3.

42 See Nigel Campbell, 'Enterprise autonomy in the Beijing Municipality', in Malcolm Warner, ed., op. cit.

43 *RMRB*, 29 July 1988, *SWB*, FE/0226/B2/4.

44 Figures from the Minister of Labour, Luo Gan, Xinhua, 9 December 1988, *SWB*, FE/0333/B2/3.

45 The performance of contract workers generally comes under more scrutiny. One system in use is to test contract workers every six months. If they fail, they are asked to leave. The same applies if they do not fulfil their quota for two successive months. Zhang Zeyu, op. cit., p. 21.

46 *South China Morning Post*, Hong Kong, 11 July 1988, quoted in Leung Wing-yue, op. cit., p. 61.

47 Yun-wing Sung and Thomas M. H. Chan, 'China's Economic Reforms 1: The Debates in China', *Asian–Pacific Economic Literature*, vol. 1, no. 1, May 1987, p. 18.

48 'Child Labour and Exploitation of Workers in Shenzhen', *SWB*, FE/0239/B2/1.

49 Phyllis Andors, 'Women and Work in Shenzhen', *Bulletin of Concerned Asian Scholars*, vol. 20, no. 3, 1988.

50 See Leung Wing-yue, op. cit., p. 108.

51 Xinhua, 21 October 1988, *SWB*, FE/0291/B2/6.
52 For an account of the development and operations of the workers' congresses, see Ng Sek Hong and Russell D. Lansbury, 'The Workers' Congress in Chinese Enterprises' in Malcolm Warner, op. cit.
53 Yang Xiaobing and Feng Jing, 'Unions of Management and Workforce', *BR*, nos. 7–8, pp. 27–31.
54 Yun-wing Sung and Thomas M. H. Chan, op. cit., p. 17.
55 Chen Lo, op. cit., p. 2.
56 Leung Wing-yue, op. cit., pp. 87–92.
57 Dai Nannian, 'Dealing with Unfair Income Gaps', *BR*, no. 33, 15–21 August 1988, pp. 4–5.
58 Xinhua, 2 August 1988, *SWB*, FE/0222/B2/6.
59 Xinhua, 9 March 1988, *SWB*, FE/0411/B2/7.
60 Ni Zhifu's work report to the ACFTU Congress, Xinhua, 26 October 1988, *SWB*, FE/0298/B2/8. Internal reforms undertaken to date are judged to be unsatisfactory. Ni Zhifu claimed that much more effort is needed to transform unions into 'the most important social and political organization in China' as Zhao Ziyang claimed they were at the Thirteenth Party Congress, Zhongguo Xinwen She, 5 October 1988, *SWB*, FE/0280/B2/2.
61 Xinhua, 2 November 1988, *SWB*, FE/0300/B2/7.
62 'Workers in Beijing', *Asian Workers Organizing*, vol. 7, no. 6, July 1988, p. 2.
63 Reported by Louise de Rosario, 'Workers Disunited', *Far Eastern Economic Review*, 1 June 1989, p. 17.

4

WEALTH BUT NOT SECURITY

Attitudes towards private business in the 1980s

Susan Young

The dramatic growth of the private sector from 1978 to 1988 was accommodated by a change in policy from an attitude of toleration and restriction to one of almost no-holds-barred encouragement.[1] The private sector itself also changed, becoming more diversified as it became more established within the Chinese economy. Continued reforms made bureaucrats and state enterprises more willing to co-operate with private entrepreneurs in search of economic gains. After the political turmoil of 1989, to be sure, China's leadership became more determined to keep private business within stricter limits, and this was reflected in the behaviour of administrators at lower levels. But the central government has nevertheless continued to state that the private sector should still be allowed to develop.

This chapter will examine how the changing reform environment has affected attitudes towards, and within, the private sector. It is based on information gained from Chinese media and academic sources and a series of interviews with administrators, researchers and some 50 private businesspeople in Beijing, Chengdu, Zigong and Guangzhou in August–October 1988.

THE DEVELOPMENT OF PRIVATE BUSINESS

Private business was revived in the late 1970s in order to 'fill in the gaps' left by the publicly-owned sector in the production and circulation of consumer goods and services, to stimulate market activity and competition, and to provide employment. Like many reform measures, it was first encouraged in a few localities with no publicity, and public debate on the matter did not emerge until 1979, when results could already be seen. In response to concerns that encouraging private business would lead to exploitation and a revival of capitalism, advocates asserted that these new private ventures would be dominated and controlled by the socialist economy and government and would therefore be unable to develop into more than a very small-scale, marginal sector.[2]

Initially, therefore, the only legally permitted private businesses were the small individual or family concerns known as *getihu* (*geti gongshanghu*: individual industrial and commercial households). Individual proprietors were limited by regulations to employing a maximum of seven people, and five of those were supposed to be apprentices.[3] The earliest regulations also confined private businesses to non-mechanized tools and transport. However, the opportunities generated by economic reforms meant that private operators were often able to ignore these restrictions. The limits on equipment, and several other restraints on supply sources and types of business, were removed from the regulations in 1983. The question of employees was more politically sensitive, and was shelved until 1988, when the Constitution was altered to legalize larger private enterprises or *siying qiye* (privately-run enterprises), defined as privately-owned enterprises with eight or more employees. A set of regulations was then passed which, far from seeking to limit such enterprises, sought to encourage their growth.[4] Thus the situation by 1988 was that there were two types of private business – the *getihu* and the *siying qiye* – which were legal and officially approved; the two being differentiated according to the number of employees.

There are other types of economic endeavour in China which could also be described as private, such as much of agriculture and sideline production or the illegal dealings of cadres who have access to wanted goods, but they are not dealt with here. Although the acknowledged private sector has much in common with these other fields of activity, the fact that it *is* acknowledged gives it a unique position in Chinese politics and society, as its existence must publicly be reconciled with accepted notions of socialism.

Of course, within this private sector there are a wide variety of economic and sociological categories. The more successful among the *siying qiye*, in particular, are very different from the typical *getihu*.[5] However, because of the links in their historical development and their common, important feature of being privately owned, the two types are intrinsically related in public perceptions and in administration and policy. Reports and policy speeches frequently associate them, many of the leaders of the Individual

Labourer's Association (*Geti Laodongzhe Xiehui*) are owners of *siying qiye*, and the administration and licensing of the *siying qiye* was at first simply another of the duties of the Individual Economy Section (*Geti Si*) of the Bureau of Industry and Commerce. There is considerable confusion in the use of the two terms, with the general public using the term *getihu* to describe any private business operator, and some academics and reporters using *siying qiye* to describe, in accordance with its literal meaning, any privately-managed business. The politics of private ownership under socialism override differences in size, trade and location in such a way that factors which affect one type of private business will also affect the others in varying degrees.

This recognized private sector of *getihu* and *siying qiye* has grown into a small but significant part of the economy, and has also become much more complex than its popular image as a small-scale retail and services sector would suggest. In 1978 there were only 150,000 licensed individual businesses (although many more were unlicensed) in the whole country. By 1988 the figure had grown to some 14 million registered individual businesses, employing about 23 million people.[6] In the unfavourable atmosphere of 1989 the trend of rapid growth faltered, and the number of registered *getihu* fell by at least 14 per cent.[7] A 1991 report, giving the figure of 20.24 million private entrepreneurs at the end of 1990 as a 4 per cent increase over 1989, suggests that the decline must have been greater than this.[8]

THE RISE OF THE *SIYING QIYE*

The *siying qiye* began to emerge illicitly in 1981, developing from *getihu* which expanded and took on more employees, from the investment of capital accumulated in rural areas after the introduction of the household responsibility system, or from collectively-owned enterprises which were leased and gradually taken over by individuals.[9] About 80 per cent of these larger enterprises are in rural areas. Since for obvious political and ideological reasons their existence was not officially recognized until 1987–88, they were registered under various guises and included in the statistics on individual or collective enterprises. According to the Bureau of Industry and Commerce, by 1988 there were 225,000 *siying qiye*, consisting of 115,000 registered as *getihu*, 60,000 joint household or share enterprises, and 50,000 registered as collectives.[10] This figure is probably much too small, as it was difficult for the Bureau to determine how many 'collective' enterprises, which may not have come under its direct jurisdiction, were in fact private. Private entrepreneurs have been able to register their enterprises as collectives by paying a fee to a state or collective unit to get its stamp on their registration form, or by claiming that they are indeed run on a collective basis. For example, the director of an enterprise of some five factories in Chengdu which he started in 1982, found it expedient in 1983 to turn over a proportion of the assets as shares to staff members. In 1988 this proportion remained less than 10 per cent and the director retained total control over the enterprise, yet he was thus able to claim that the enterprise was a 'collective share company'.[11] A woman in Chengdu who ran a large fashion retail and manufacturing company distributed a certain portion of the profits to staff as bonuses: hence her company was also 'collective' even though she was a leading member of the Individual Labourers' Association.[12]

After the release of the 1988 regulations on *siying qiye* there was a campaign to make 'fake collectives' register as *siying qiye*, but it is not yet clear how successful this has been. When I asked private entrepreneurs in 1988 if they were planning to change from collective to private status, most said they would try not to, because 'it's easier for a collective to do business', and 'in case policies change'. After June 1989 the drive to clarify ownership status intensified, but the political situation naturally made the 'red umbrella' of collective registration more desirable than ever. While some newspaper items have reported successes in registering *siying qiye* as such, others suggest that some local governments, fearing economic recession in their area, have collaborated with private owners of 'collectives' in obstructing the attempts of the Bureau of Industry and Commerce to ferret them out.[13] In Shenyang it was reported that a 21 per cent drop in the number of registered *siying qiye* in 1989 was accompanied by a 30 per cent rise in the number of registered collectives; apparently many of these were the same *siying qiye*.[14]

While in many cases the difference between a *siying qiye* and a *getihu* consists merely of one or two employees, the *siying qiye* also include the larger enterprises which can have a considerable impact on their local economies. As a type, they differ from *getihu* both in nature and in management personnel. *Siying qiye* tend to be engaged in industry, mining, transport and construction, with very few in pure commerce. According to one survey, 82 per cent of *siying qiye*, 87 per cent of their personnel and 83 per cent of their capital were in industry, transport and construction in 1988.[15] A wider range of trades means that the private sector is becoming more integrated with the rest of the economy: the customers of these enterprises include state enterprises and local government agencies as well as individual consumers. This has been significant for the status and security of private business as a whole. Productive enterprises are more prestigious and more politically acceptable, getting away from the notion, found in both Confucian tradition and Marxism, of the merchant who merely buys and sells, extracting an exploitative income in the process.

Also significant is the nature of the people involved in running *siying qiye*. They tend to be those whose past experience has given them some knowledge of enterprise management and the necessary contacts. According to one report, 60 per cent of private entrepreneurs in rural areas were originally management or supply and marketing staff in state or collective enterprises, or cadres in production teams or brigades.[16] Other sources give much lower percentages but still indicate that owners of *siying qiye* are generally not from a purely agricultural background.[17] Officials and personnel in key units such as state supply bureaux are often involved, less directly, in positions as consultants and directors, or with relatives employed in the enterprise. Some private entrepreneurs have complained that they are forced to give jobs or directorships to cadres or their relatives when they have no wish to do so, but others actively seek out this kind of close involvement with influential people, to make doing business easier and more secure. Whether by choice or not, these close links are a strong incentive for local governments to support private enterprise.

NEGATIVE PERCEPTIONS OF PRIVATE BUSINESS

Individual retail, catering and service businesses, which still dominate the private sector, made up over 80 per cent of outlets in these trades in 1988. Table 4.1 shows the rapid inroads made by the registered private sector (mainly *getihu*) into retail sales of commodities. It should be remembered that these figures are understated, both because they include only registered individual businesses, and because these businesses are likely to understate sales in order to minimize taxation.

Despite official support, these private entrepreneurs have had to contend with considerable opposition and social prejudice. The political campaigns of the past thirty years, especially the Cultural Revolution, had inculcated the general concept of 'state first, collective second, and individual nowhere', and that the bigger and 'more public' an enterprise was, the better and more socialist. A *Renmin Ribao* article described the attitude towards private business as 'if individual business isn't capitalism, it's a tail of capitalism. Anyway it's not socialism.'[18] A much-publicized letter to the *Beijing Daily* in August 1980 expressed horror at the revival of small private businesses, arguing (quite rightly, as it turned out) that

A small-time premise today may well expand into a big one tomorrow. While capitalists of the old days are still living, new ones will before long come on the scene, with so many people intent on money-grubbing and so many small shops and roadside stalls cluttering the streets.[19]

Table 4.1 Value of retail sales by form of ownership, 1978–88

Year	State-run and collective		Individual		Peasants to non-agricultural residents	
	RMB 100m	*% of total*	*RMB 100m*	*% of total*	*RMB 100m*	*% of total*
1978	1,525.4	97.9	2.1	0.1	31.1	1.9
1979	1,748.2	97.1	4.3	0.2	47.5	2.6
1980	2,055.6	96.0	15.0	0.7	69.0	3.2
1981	2,222.1	94.5	37.4	1.6	89.4	3.8
1982	2,383.0	92.7	74.6	2.9	110.8	4.3
1983	2,528.3	88.6	184.5	6.5	133.0	4.7
1984	2,875.1	85.1	323.7	9.6	170.0	5.0
1985	3,340.3	77.6	661.0	15.3	291.0	6.8
1986	3,755.0	75.8	804.8	16.3	375.0	7.6
1987	4,328.6	74.3	1,011.6	17.4	461.0	7.9
1988	5,493.8	73.8	1,324.0	17.8	595.0	8.0

Source: Zhongguo Tongji Nianjian (Statistical Yearbook of China), 1989, p. 601.

The kinds of business most private entrepreneurs conduct, and the way in which some conduct them, reinforce negative perceptions of private business in general. After all, the vast majority of private businesses are *getihu* engaged in small-scale commerce, seen as non-productive and of dubious ethical standing, or in service trades such as catering or repairs – menial tasks for which many people maintain a strong disdain. Most private businesses are involved in these trades because they are easy and cheap to set up, often require no special knowledge or skill, and are in high demand.

Private businesses in these trades are of course highly visible, and interact directly with the public; mostly by taking their money. Not surprisingly their high incomes then engender a certain amount of resentment. This is exacerbated by the common and not entirely unfounded perception that most private operators cheat customers, charge high prices, obtain goods through illegal channels, and in general devote themselves to taking as much as they can from society without contributing to it. *Renmin Ribao* noted in 1987 that 'some people say individual operators earn a lot of money for very little work and rely on loopholes in policy', and that this was a major problem for their image.[20] Private businesses also have a reputation for operating by bribing the officials, though this is partly due to the large number of unlicensed street traders. Supplementing this, many of the licensed private operators, especially larger enterprises in need of producer goods, have been forced to bribe suppliers or key officials in order to stay in business. Tax evasion among both *getihu* and *siying qiye* has also been widely publicized, again reinforcing the impression that the incomes of private entrepreneurs are unfairly high.

A large number of traders, both licensed and unlicensed, specialize in black market and 'back door' goods. Their actions then reflect on all private operators, and popular jingles such as *'jingcha shang ban, geti shou tan'* ('when the police start work, the *getihu* pack up their stalls') do the rounds. During a drive against illegal business in the summer of 1987, legal individual businesses thus also came under attack, blamed for high prices and market disorder; the Bureau of Industry and Commerce was obliged to state that 'currently China's individual economy has not developed too much, but rather too little; we must continue to promote the individual economy'.[21] A series of press reports also pointed out that since individual operators could not speculate in scarce goods all on their own, it was actually corrupt state-employed cadres working behind the scenes who were to blame.[22]

Yet the division between legal and illegal business is a fine one, largely dependent on the politics of the time. The crackdown on illegal business and tax evasion which followed the suppression of the democracy movement in 1989 was felt as even more of an attack on legal private business than its predecessors had been.

The low regard in which the private sector has been held compared to the state and collective sectors is most clearly seen in the marked resistance among urban youth to entering private employment. According to the director of the Bureau of Industry and Commerce, the proportion of young people in private businesses registered as *getihu* increased from less than 10 per cent initially to over 25 per cent after 1985.[23] This was held to be a sign of improvement in the status of private business among urban youth, but it may have been largely the result of the influx of rural youth into cities and towns. Two sisters who did start a hairdressers in 1980 said, 'We were worried because we did not feel that it was proper for young people to be self-employed',[24] and a young man doing business in 1983 told how

> When I applied to do individual business, my friends and classmates were amazed. They said doing individual business had no political future, no security of livelihood, no social position, and even finding a girlfriend would be difficult.[25]

This reluctance to enter private employment has stemmed both from its lack of prestige and from practical considerations: state employment has been seen until very recently as an 'iron rice bowl' offering security for life, while both state and collective employment are seen as far more secure politically. *Renmin Ribao* commented in 1986 that

> For a long time, some people have had fixed in their minds the idea that 'state is first, collective second, and individual is looked down on'; they all want an 'iron rice bowl'. This has led to a contradiction as on one hand there are many people with nothing to do, and on the other many things with no-one doing them.[26]

Not least among the drawbacks of private business is that the private operator must forgo the benefits obtained through a state or collective unit. Depending on the size and wealth of the work unit, these may include anything from housing, access to child care and education, health care and retirement pensions to the occasional load of cheap oranges or a free movie on National Day. And in a society which has been organized on the premise that all individuals

70

would eventually be part of some collective organization, alternative channels for the provision of such benefits can be difficult to find even if one is willing to pay. When possible, people going into business have kept a foot in both camps by maintaining links with a state unit. Many of the private entrepreneurs I interviewed in 1988 obtained housing and some other benefits through spouses or parents with state-unit jobs. Without such arrangements private business looks less attractive, and some young school-leavers have preferred to remain unemployed rather than take up private business, fearing that to do so would influence their chances of a 'proper job' with a state or collective unit. To get around this problem labour bureaux generally continue to count them as *daiye qingnian* (youth awaiting employment) even after they are running a viable, full-time private business: 'Their income is generally enough to keep two or three people, and yet they are still seen as "job-waiting personnel" and also see themselves in this way.'[27]

Probably the major factor in the unwillingness of urban youth to engage in private business is its political insecurity. The rise of the private sector is entirely the result of the current reform programme, and former sudden changes in policy have not been forgotten. By 1988 the passing of time and the continued growth of private business had allayed fears of a change to some extent, but caution remained. When I asked a young woman in Chengdu if she would consider leaving her collective job to make three times as much money with her businesswoman sister, she said she wouldn't, because 'you can't rely on state policy'.[28]

This political insecurity naturally applies not only to the small *getihu* but even to larger, highly profitable *siying qiye* which are able to offer employees far better conditions than they could expect in a state job. As a result it is still very difficult for private enterprises to attract qualified technical and managerial staff. A Shanghai businessman transferred his private enterprise to collective ownership for this reason, saying that suitable people lost interest when they heard that his was a private business.[29] A private chicken-producer on the outskirts of Chengdu offered some of his top staff a lump sum of 50,000 yuan after five years if they would stay for that long.[30] An electrical instrument factory I visited in Chengdu had been able to attract a number of qualified people because of the large amounts of money it was prepared to devote to research and development, including their salaries. Inducements such as these mean that the number of qualified people leaving state jobs for private business

71

appeared to be increasing until recently, albeit still in small numbers.[31] Such transfers were contributing to improving perceptions of private business, both because of the traditional high status of intellectuals and because of the kind of business they undertake.

Generally, though, at the lower end of the market, private enterprise appeals primarily to people who have little to lose by it. Many people starting private businesses in the late seventies and early eighties were the older unemployed, the miscellaneous 'idle personnel' who had been unable to find a permanent niche in the collective system.[32] An estimated 10 per cent of individual businesses are run by ex-convicts who have found it almost impossible to get a job in a state or collective unit.[33] So, too, private business appeals to retired people who are finding their pensions inadequate (it is often they who provide the technical expertise needed by expanding *siying qiye*), and who often find a way to keep on receiving their pensions as well as their new private income. People who actually leave a state job to go into business for themselves or to be employed by a *siying qiye* nearly always seek to keep their options open by paying the unit to maintain their benefits and to keep the job available (*ting xin liu zhi*) in case policies change. In Chengdu in 1988, the going rate seemed to be around 50 per cent of the person's former salary. Finally, of course, there are the rural residents who go into business for themselves or take jobs in private businesses. They have perhaps the least to lose of all, for if private business were to be repressed again they would be in the same position as before in their own village, only richer.

The fact that so many of the ordinary *getihu* are of low-status backgrounds has tended to reinforce negative perceptions of private entrepreneurs: the view is that if they were decent people and had any standards, they'd be doing something else. School teachers have claimed that the children of individual businesspeople are less intelligent and more disobedient than other children, and remarked that this is because their parents are too busy making money to look after them properly.[34] A newspaper article reporting a rise in crimes committed by the offspring of *getihu* attributed this partly to the example set by their parents' 'bad background' and illicit business activities.[35] Such assumptions may be true in some cases; but discussions such as these both illustrate and reinforce negative attitudes towards private businesspeople.[36] The idea that private business is inferior has persisted in spite of the rapid development of the private sector: for example in 1988 a young woman I know in Chengdu would not sell eggs in the thriving market at the college near her home, but went elsewhere because her boyfriend lived at the college. 'I couldn't! Imagine what people would say . . . Xiao Liu's girlfriend selling eggs!' At the time, she was spending some of the proceeds of her egg sales on 'presents' so that she could get a job in a collective factory.

GOVERNMENT PROMOTION OF PRIVATE BUSINESS

Since the early 1980s, the media and certain government agencies have conducted a series of campaigns to improve the image of private business. The aims are threefold: to encourage people to take up private business, to reassure those who have done so that they will not later be attacked, and to secure public acceptance of this aspect of reform policies. The media campaign began by tackling political opposition to private business, stressing the importance of private business to China's economic development, and associating its opponents with the unpopular Cultural Revolution by accusing them of incorrect 'left' ideas.

The benefits of promoting private business were highlighted by articles pointing out how much more convenient life was now that private shops were offering repairs, haircuts, fresh fruit and innumerable small goods and services which were formerly provided inadequately or not at all by state enterprises. Others report on 'model' businesspeople who, having 'got rich first', pay their taxes, go out of their way to serve people well, make donations to charity, and are generally nice to have about. These articles are designed both to improve the image of private businesspeople and to give them models to emulate. The most serious attempt at a 'model' campaign focused on Xing Fuqiang, who was basically Lei Feng reincarnated as a private glazier, complete with an untimely death from cancer and a diary full of thoughts like 'wholeheartedly serving the people is the greatest honour in my life'.[37] In contrast to the common image of the private businessman who has eyes only for profits, Xing seriously wanted to make a contribution to society and would go to great lengths to help people, walking many miles to repair a window for an old lady free of charge. Xing Fuqiang's case was unusual in that he was held up as a model not only for other private operators, but also for youth league and party members to study.[38]

Outstanding private businesspeople have also been honoured at meetings. The most notable of these was in August 1983, when the then Party General Secretary, Hu Yaobang, and other leaders received 609 advanced collective and individual representatives. Their speeches emphasized the role of collective and private business in providing jobs and reiterated that private employment was perfectly respectable.[39] A similar public relations exercise surrounded the establishment of the national-level Individual Labourers' Association in December 1986. National newspapers ran numerous articles on the importance of private business and the propriety of private employment, including a front-page photograph in *Renmin Ribao* of Zhao Ziyang, then Premier, shaking hands with a private businessman.[40]

Before the Tiananmen crackdown of 1989, an obvious sign of improved acceptance by the government had been party membership, but the bulk of party membership in the private sector is the result of party members and cadres moving into private business (often using their connections and expertise to run large and successful *siying qiye*), rather than established private operators becoming party members. In 1989 in the wake of Tiananmen, private employers were finally banned from joining the party; those who were already party members were allowed to remain, but their incomes were to be limited and they were put under renewed pressure to use their profits for employee or public welfare.[41]

Earlier, in the mid-1980s, reformists in the party leadership had fitfully pushed for recruitment of private businesspeople into the party, and occasional articles appeared in the press on private businesspeople joining the party or on increased party activities among them. Among the barriers to such involvement was the attitude of private operators themselves: the party had for so long been the enemy of private businesspeople that many remained suspicious of it, as of all arms of state bureaucratic control. They saw quite correctly that one of the aims behind involving them in the party was to increase control over them: party and youth league activities among private businesspeople were usually concerned with promoting party policies and honest business practices. For example, the model private businessman and party member Bai Shiming busied himself organizing a political study group for young businesspeople, and the youth league co-operates with the Individual Labourers' Association to organize competitions and campaigns to clean up private business practices.[42]

Not surprisingly, such party and youth league activities attracted limited interest from private businesspeople. The party also often lost contact with existing party members who went into private business, because of a failure to adapt its organizational structure to suit new conditions. Private operators, especially those from rural areas, often moved away from their original party branch and no longer attended meetings. More attention was paid to this problem in 1984 as reform policies encouraged peasants to move into towns to do business.[43] Some areas established new party branches, organized into sub-groups according to area or trade, to cater for such people.[44] Some efforts were also made to make party activities more attractive to private businesspeople by organizing trade fairs and the like. In the city of Linfen in Shanxi, a new incentive was added to business ethics campaigns by allowing party members to use their membership for advertising, hanging up signs saying that as party members they guaranteed good service.[45]

In fact, the idea that private businesspeople should be party members (and vice versa) was never really accepted: despite the official line that private operators were 'socialist labourers', there was always grave doubt within the party that they were quite socialist enough. Particular concern was expressed about admitting those who employed others in their businesses, as it was felt that even those who employed only a few assistants, within the limits of the *getihu* regulations, were to some degree exploiting them.

ATTITUDES AMONG PRIVATE BUSINESSPEOPLE

In 1987–88 considerable attention was given in the press to a kind of identity crisis among private businesspeople, amply illustrated by an agony letter published in *Jingji Ribao*:

> Since I started out in private business, I've been very depressed, and wanted to talk about my feelings. But wherever I look, there are only white eyes and red eyes [disdain and envy]. In the last few years, not only have I borne the physical burden of labour, but also a spiritual hardship which is difficult to describe. It's true! I now have money, my material life is very rich. Business has become easier and I now have fixed supply routes and customers. You would think I would be satisfied. But I am actually more and more unhappy and dread my leisure, because as soon as I stop work a voice appears in my mind: 'individual businessman – second-class citizen'.[46]

Chinese reports have noted with concern a tendency among private businesspeople to use their incomes, not for further investment, but for conspicuous material consumption.[47] This may be partly an attempt to gain some of the prestige which private businesspeople are generally denied through other channels.[48] Many intellectuals with whom I discussed private business seemed actually to take some comfort from the supposed spiritual bankruptcy of private operators, as if this made up in some way for the disparity between business incomes and their own. That they resent the disparity is without doubt; several wryly quipped that 'it's better to wield a barber's razor than a surgeon's scalpel' and 'it's better to sell tea-boiled eggs than to make guided missiles'. It may be that one of the aims of the media in reporting on the social and spiritual disadvantages of private businesspeople is to make lower-paid state employees more content with their lot. Ironically, private business-people themselves still envy the prestige of intellectuals and state employees in general: only a very few private operators I interviewed wanted to see their children follow them into private business. In spite of the unfavourable teachers' comments referred to earlier, many hoped that their children would go to university and were pushing them towards this end. It seems that with one generation providing the money, it is up to the next to provide the other trappings of social success.

Some private businesspeople use their money to pay for more education or cultural activities. They may aim towards improving their business skills, like the young man who sold his business to go to university and study management, with a view to starting a better business later.[49] His action is typical of what one private business-man called the 'new-style private operator' (*xinxing getihu*): one who has some education and seeks more, who believes that private business has potential in China and wants to develop it, as opposed to the common concept of the private trader who is content with making a few hundred yuan each month and spending it.[50] Ole Bruun, making tentative conclusions from his interviews in Chengdu in 1987–88, suggests that these entrepreneurs, the type who develop the larger *siying qiye*, differ from traditional *getihu* in their whole approach to social and business relationships. Instead of relying on kinship networks and cultivating connections with local cadres, they prefer market-oriented, businesslike relationships and will quote regulations and policies at cadres instead of relying on *guanxi*.[51] My own interviews did not entirely bear out this hypothesis. Although there were some entrepreneurs of this type, notably in the cities, most were not so sanguine about the reliability of reform policies, and, as mentioned above, did their best to cultivate the 'insurance' of good relations with cadres. For many businesses, good connections and close links with cadres are vital to obtaining premises, energy and raw materials. Some of the more successful private entrepreneurs I interviewed, who had either made or come close to making their first million, had a very positive approach and planned to develop their businesses further, but even they seemed somewhat defensive at times, and were anxious to point out that they were making a contribution to society by providing jobs, helping develop the economy, and building up fixed assets which would be there even if their companies failed or were taken over.

This last, rather wistful thought – that even if their enterprises are taken over, at least the assets will be there for society – expresses the abiding sense of insecurity among private entrepreneurs. Individual Labourers' Association leaders frequently point out that the Constitution guarantees the rights of private business, and it is true that the Constitution was altered in 1983 to confirm the role of individual businesses, and in 1988 to cater for large private enterprises as well. But a Constitution which was altered so easily to include private business, can just as easily be altered to take it out again. In any case, legal guarantees are of only limited relevance to daily life in China; a private entrepreneur whose rights are infringed will normally seek redress through administrative organs rather than the courts. Indeed, it is difficult to imagine a wronged private businessperson mounting a constitutional challenge in China, and even more so to imagine it being successful.

The insecurity of private entrepreneurs arises from their knowledge of past treatment of private business and their awareness that they are now encouraged only as part of a shaky reform programme. The fortunes of private business are tied to those of the reform programme as a whole, so that the political climate is to them what the stock market is to a Wall Street investor. Fear of a policy change was a major issue at the meetings marking the establishment of the national Individual Labourer's Association in December 1986, and Bo Yibo found it necessary to assure private businesspeople that 'on no account will we say you are "capitalist tails" to be cut off'.[52] *Renmin Ribao* noted that the late 1988 drive for 'restoring economic order' was causing alarm among private entrepreneurs, some of whom approached local governments with the idea of handing their enterprises over to collective ownership and then running them under contract.[53] Their fears appeared to be confirmed in June 1989, and while operators of larger enterprises sought collective status, small *getihu* simply handed in their licenses.[54]

Many private businesspeople fully expect the policy of encouraging private business to change, and do business with this in mind:

> If you do individual business for a few years, you will get a fair bit of money, better than several decades in a state unit. Lots of us feel that we should make the best of the opportunity now while there are no big policy changes. In the future they're sure to stop this policy. If I take two years, I can earn enough money for the next 60 years.[55]

As this quotation suggests, the insecurity of private business affects the behaviour of private entrepreneurs, many of whom aim for quick profits rather than long-term development. Some commentators blame much of the cheating, tax evasion and profiteering so rife among private traders on this search for short-term gains.[56] Legal education programmes are also based on this view, and aim to reassure private operators that they are legal and permanent, in the hope that this will make them more law abiding.[57] Another consequence of insecurity is that the development of private business tends to occur in waves of enthusiasm for a particular trade which offers quick returns. In the early years, small retail businesses such as roadside stalls offered high returns for a minimal investment, but in recent years competition has increased and profits are down. The craze for photography followed a similar course, with businesses rushing into first black-and-white, then colour film processing.[58] In 1988 in Chengdu, restaurants were considered the most profitable business; several operators of businesses in quite different trades thought their next project might be a restaurant. While it is to be expected in a market economy that entrepreneurs will follow the highest profits, the sense of impermanence in Chinese private enterprise means that investments with long-term possibilities are likely to be ignored.

More importantly, uncertainty about the future has serious implications for the capacity of private business to diversify and use the capital it generates for productive enterprise. As mentioned above, there has been some progress in this direction, but it remains limited, both by the unwillingness of some operators to commit their funds to long-term projects or costly equipment, and by the difficulty of finding suitable managerial and technical staff. This has important implications for the ability of the private sector to progress beyond the labour-intensive, low-technology enterprises which dominate it at present.[59] Private entrepreneurs who build up the larger enterprises, the *siying qiye*, are obviously willing to commit their funds to long-term goals, although, as noted above, even they often do their best to minimize the political risk by registering their enterprises as collectives. Other private operators do not want to grow too much, as they fear a 'fat pig policy' – that the state will wait until their enterprises have grown, and then take them over.[60] There are of course also the practical constraints of finding space and raw materials for larger enterprises, and the low priority given to easing these contraints on private business also stems partly from the view that it is a marginal, even temporary sector of the economy.

THE MOMENTUM OF CONTINUED REFORM

The above discussion has focused on some negative perceptions of private business and the government's efforts to overcome these. Throughout the 1980s, however, a number of economic factors were at work which have arguably had a far greater influence on the development of private business. The government campaign to promote private business was but a small part of an overall reform programme, many aspects of which have also indirectly benefited the growth of the private sector by altering the political and economic environment. The pressures generated by these changes have in fact made the private sector far more entrenched than common perceptions suggest.

First, the leadership's continued promotion of reforms virtually overcame the overt opposition and blocking of private business which was seen among administrators in the early years of the reform programme. Opponents of private business received little public coverage, but opposition made itself felt in the obstacles private entrepreneurs encountered. Officials who disagreed with the policy of encouraging private business, or who feared that such a policy would not last, often used local discretionary powers to delay or refuse to grant licences. In one extreme case, the local interpretation of the policy of 'appropriate development' of private business was that an appropriate number of private businesses, for a county with over 400,000 residents, was seven.[61] Municipal authorities would close private stalls down, claiming that they were obstructing traffic or ruining the city's appearance. Or they would impose impossible requirements such as that all restaurants must have five rooms, or that private cycle carts could only transport goods in one district.[62]

In some cases state enterprises used their superior political and economic position to ward off private competition. When a Liaoning peasant started a private bus service in June 1984, his state-run competitor used its influence to persuade bus station officials to impound his bus. When this action was overturned by higher authorities, the state company added four buses to the route in question, which not only took most of the customers, but repeatedly attempted to run the private bus off the road. Since the state company could afford to run the route at a loss and repair damaged buses much better than the private operator could, it was a very unequal battle.[63] In another case, a county-run supply and marketing co-operative blamed its falling turnover on private business, and persuaded local authorities to revoke 900 licences at one sweep. (The newspaper article criticizing this action smugly reported that the co-operative's turnover failed to improve.)[64]

Although problems such as these continued to be encountered, their incidence declined markedly from 1984 onwards as further reforms took effect. Initial moves to extend the rural reponsibility system and specific regulations loosening restrictions on private business in 1983 were followed by a strong promotion of the 'commodity economy', including private business, in 1984. The response to Central Committee document no. 1 on the rural economy in January 1984 made it much easier for rural residents to set up businesses in towns, and this encouragement of private business was reinforced by the Decision on the Reform of the Economic Structure in October. In many places the former situation of resistance or simple disinterest changed to one in which Industry and Commerce officials actually went out doorknocking to increase the number of private businesses on their books, clearly in response to pressure from higher levels.[65] Licensing procedures were often simplified and the time required to complete them shortened. Local governments and administrative departments began to take the initiative to set up market areas for private stallholders, in order to encourage private sector growth in their area.

Second, as well as improving administrators' attitudes to the private sector, reforms made it easier to do business. Particularly in the first half of the 1980s, private businesses frequently complained that they were discriminated against in the competition for energy, raw materials and business premises, and it is still the case that state or collective units are given preference in such matters. Even finding customers was more difficult for some businesses because of their private status: some government organs or state enterprises did not recognize receipts issued by private restaurants, hotels and the like, and thus their employees bought state or collective services when travelling on business.[66] However, the growing importance of the profit motive and increased enterprise independence after 1984 helped ease these problems. Production and marketing units became much more willing to sell to individuals. Private operators continued to be at a disadvantage in that they had no legitimate access to subsidized commodities and lacked the influence and prestige of a state unit when seeking supplies, but they were usually able to overcome this disadvantage by paying higher prices and/or assiduously cultivating connections. As a result, wanted goods were even diverted from planned quotas and sold to private buyers in preference to others. Although the problem of finding business premises continued to be acute, it was now more likely to be the result of excess demand than administrative blocking. High demand continued to make finding premises difficult in cities, but the avenues for doing so increased as unprofitable state enterprises rented out premises to private operators and local authorities were also more willing to lease land to private enterprises.

Third, the impact of reforms has begun to diminish the relative advantages of state and collective employment, although the change is slight as yet and depends on the fortunes of the reform programme as a whole. Within the state sector, the 'iron rice bowl' security of employment and income is being challenged by the introduction of contract employment, in which employees are taken on for a set period of time, and by responsibility systems in which incomes are related directly to productivity. Housing remains in short supply and young employees in many state units must wait indefinitely for a flat; meanwhile some units have begun to sell housing, albeit on easy terms, rather than allocating it at negligible rents. The commercialization of housing is still at an experimental stage and is likely to encounter resistance, but it does give hope to private businesspeople outside the collective system, who are also more likely to be able to afford to buy housing than state employees.

Above all, the rising cost of living and increasing consumerism in China make it harder for families to support unemployed members, and also make state and collective jobs less attractive: several private operators whom I interviewed in 1988 said they had taken up private business because they simply could not support their families on their former wages.

In any case, the employment situation in China since the reforms means that many people do not have the option of state employment and competition for collective jobs is also fierce. Many collective jobs offer no greater job security than private business and often a lower income. One effect of the reforms was to cause unprofitable collectives to close down, and others to take the opportunity to divest themselves of unwanted staff. The need to provide an increasing number of jobs, and the inability of the state to do so, is a key factor in the leadership's continued policy support for private as well as collective enterprise.

To China's more conservative leaders, the increasing ease with which private entrepreneurs were able to overcome constraints on supplies, employment and premises signified increasing corruption and an alarming decline in the state's ability to control the economy. Yet the campaign to increase administrative control over private business which began in early 1989, and appeared to escalate into outright attack after June 4, clearly illustrates how the growing importance of the private sector forces those who oppose the private economy to back down. The political and economic crackdown of 1989 had grave implications for private business. Official efforts to popularize private entrepreneurs and justify their high incomes were replaced by a campaign to make them a scapegoat for some of the deep problems China was experiencing. Publicity concerning the annual (but in 1989 exceptionally determined) tax collection drive now implied that most private operators derived their high incomes from tax evasion; the *getihu* were even characterized as an army of corrupt backdoor dealers undermining the integrity of the socialist economy.[67]

Yet the government never actually revoked its support for the private sector as a limited supplement to the public economy, and the effect of the campaign on employment, consumer supplies and investment quickly provoked concern. The government news agency declared in August 1989 that 'the private sector will continue to develop', as this was 'conducive to solving the serious employment problems by invigorating the economy.'[68] In October, Li

Peng himself reiterated that private businesses were 'a necessary supplement', although he characterized them as 'small businessmen and peddlars' and alluded to the need to crack down on tax evasion and illicit wholesale profits.[69] By late 1989 there was clearly concern at the decline in private sector numbers, and officials and press articles again began offering assurances that the policy of promoting both *getihu* and *siying qiye* had not changed. In early 1990, a Bureau of Industry and Commerce report to the State Council noted the need to clarify further that the policies of promoting the private economy, encouraging some people to get rich first, and protecting the legal rights of *getihu* and *siying qiye* had not changed.[70] Although the Bureau's raising of the matter indicates the strength of the attack on the private sector, the fact that it was reported in the *Renmin Ribao* also shows the current leadership's concern that this attack should not be allowed to go too far.

CONCLUSION

The social and political position of private businesspeople has certainly changed since 1978. A decade of sustained promotion by the central government, combined with the economic pressures and opportunities generated by the reform process, has enabled private business to become an integral part of the Chinese economy. In doing so, it has formed complex links with administrators and with other economic sectors, which make it more integrated with the economy as a whole and therefore more difficult to remove. These links will also work against political and economic discrimination, as policies having a detrimental effect on private businesses will also have a like effect on the state enterprises and administrative departments to which they are linked. Even the simple fact of the rapid growth of the private sector has helped improve its position, as it has inevitably become more entrenched and accepted.

The economic incentives for the leadership to continue to support private business – particularly the benefits to employment and the provision of consumer goods – are as important in 1990 as they were in 1980. In spite of the antagonism towards 'privatization' in the more conservative leadership since the fall of Zhao Ziyang, and renewed efforts to control the private sector, the government obviously still considers a private sector necessary. Yet the dependence of the private sector on reform policies, exacerbated by the climate of political uncertainty prevailing in China, remains a severe constraint on both the status of those involved and on its further development.

NOTES AND REFERENCES

1 Part of the research for this chapter was funded by grants from the Australian Federation of University Women–South Australia Inc. and the University of Adelaide. An earlier version of this chapter was published in *The Australian Journal of Chinese Affairs*, no. 25, January 1991, pp. 115–38. I am grateful to Andrew Watson, Jonathan Unger and two anonymous readers for their comments on an earlier draft. Remaining errors are, of course, my own.

2 For example, He Jianzhang, 'Jiji fuchi, shidang fazhan chengzhen geti jingji' ('Actively support and appropriately develop the urban individual economy'), *Hongqi (Red Flag)*, no. 24, 1981, pp. 13–16; and Fang Sheng, 'The revival of individual economy in certain areas', in Lin Wei and Arnold Chao, eds, *China's Economic Reforms*, Philadelphia, University of Pennsylvania Press, 1982, pp. 172–85.

3 'Guowuyuan guanyu chengzhen fei nongye geti jingji ruogan zhengcexing guiding' ('Certain policy stipulations of the State Council on the urban non-agricultural individual economy'), 7 July 1981, in State Bureau of Industry and Commerce, Individual Economy Section, and Beijing Ribao Theoretical Department, eds, *Geti Laodongzhe Shouce (Individual Labourers' Handbook)*, Beijing, Beijing Ribao Chubanshe and Gongshang Chubanshe, 1984, pp. 5–9. This limit on employees remains the distinguishing feature of a *getihu* as far as administration is concerned, and was retained in subsequent regulations in 1983 and 1987.

4 'Zhonghua Renmin Gongheguo siying qiye zanxing tiaolie' ('Provisional regulations of the People's Republic of China on private enterprises'), 3 June 1988, in *RMRB*, 29 June 1988, p. 2.

5 The popular image of a *getihu* is that of the petty roadside peddlar, making perhaps a few hundred yuan per month, but the term may also be used to describe much larger concerns. A 1988 *Renmin Ribao* article, for example, describes an abbattoir run by two '*getihu*' in Guiyang, with 250,000 yuan in capital and handling 40 per cent of the pigs slaughtered in the city. Even a business which is genuinely an 'individual' operation may be quite large in other ways. The individual stallholders in the Hehuachi wholesale market in Chengdu were found to have average cash holdings of over 150,000 yuan at the end of 1988. See *RMRB*, 8 August 1988, p. 2 and *JJCK*, 28 May 1989, p. 2.

6 *SWB*, 15 March 1989, FE/W0068/A/1.

7 *SWB*, 14 March 1990, FE/W0119/A/1.

8 *SWB*, 9 January 1991, FE/W0161/A/2.

9 See Zhong Wenmin and Lu Bingqun, 'Nongcun siying qiye de xingqi ji qi fazhan' ('The rise and development of rural private enterprises'), in *Qiyejia Tiandi (Entrepreneur's World)*, no. 7, 1988; reprinted in Renmin Daxue Shubao Ziliao Zhongxin, eds, *Fuyin baokan ziliao, F 22,*

Nongcun qiye guanli (*Materials from newspapers and periodicals, F 22, Rural Enterprise Management*), no. 9, 1988, pp. 20–2; Liu Xiaojing, 'Siying qiye jiankang fazhan de ruogan wenti – 18 sheng (shi) 130 ge siying qiye shizheng fenxi' ('Some problems in the healthy development of *siying qiye* – a positive analysis of 130 *siying qiye* in 18 provinces and municipalities'), *NYJJWT*, no. 4, 1988, pp. 38–42; and Liu Wenpu, 'Lun nongcun jiti qiye siyinghua wenti' ('On the privatization of management in rural collective enterprises'), *NMRB*, 21 September 1988, p. 3.

10 Zhang Houyi and Qin Shaoxiang, 'Siying jingji zai dangdai Zhongguo de shijian' ('The practice of private enterprise in present-day China'), *JJCK*, 14 November 1988

11 Interview, 14 September 1988.

12 Interview, 9 September 1988. This woman had an excellent relationship with the various officials who could influence her business, and neither she nor they seemed to find her ambiguous ownership status hard to reconcile at that time.

13 See *JJCK*, 15 May 1989, p. 1. Cheng Xiangqing, Li Bojun and Xu Huafei discuss similar behaviour in relation to taxation in 'Siying qiye fazhan xianzhuang yu mianlin de wenti', ('Current conditions and problems in development of private enterprises'), *ZGNCJJ*, no. 2, 1989, pp. 24–31.

14 *JJCK*, 11 April 1990, p. 1.

15 Zhang Houyi and Qin Shaoxiang, op. cit.

16 *RMRB*, 16 March 1988, p. 1.

17 See, for example, Central Committee Rural Policy Research Office and State Council Rural Development Research Centre Rural Survey Office, 'Dui bai jia nongcun siying qiye diaocha de chubu fenxi' ('An initial analysis of a survey of 100 rural private enterprises'), *NYJJWT*, no. 2, 1989, pp. 18–23.

18 *RMRB*, 27 February 1983, p. 5.

19 *Beijing Ribao* (*Beijing Daily*), 18 August 1980, reprinted in *BR*, no. 45, 10 November 1980, p. 20.

20 *RMRB*, 17 May 1987, p. 2.

21 *JJRB*, 20 August 1987, p. 1.

22 *RMRB*, 28 August 1987, p. 2; *RMRB*, 16 August 1987, p. 2; *NMRB*, 1 January 1988, p. 3.

23 Ren Zhonglin, 'Guanyu geti jingji wenti' ('On the question of the individual economy'), speech at the Central Party School, 7 April 1987, in Guojia Jiaowei Gaoji Chubanshe and Guojia Jiaowei Makesizhuyi Lilun Jiaoyu Zhongxin, eds, *Makesi zhuyi lilun jiaoyu cankao ziliao* (*Reference materials for Marxist theoretical education*), no. 5, 1987, pp. 18–23; p. 19.

24 *BR*, no. 44, November 1981, p. 27.

25 *GMRB*, 3 April 1983, p. 3.

26 *RMRB*, 7 January 1986, p. 2.

27 Lin Zili, ed., *Shehuizhuyi Jingji Lun* (*The Socialist Economy*), vol. 1, Beijing, Shehui kexue chubanshe, 1985, p. 161.

28 Interview, Chengdu, 3 September 1988.

29 *JJRB*, 15 March 1988, p. 2; see also *JJCK*, 8 April 1988, p. 4.

30 Interview, 22 September 1988.
31 *SWB*, 30 March 1988, FE/W0019/A2–3.
32 In the mid-1980s 50–60 per cent of registered private businesspeople came under this category, with variations in different localities. See State Council General Office Survey & Research Office, eds, *Geti jingji diaocha yu yanjiu* (*Surveys and research on the individual economy*), Beijing, Jingji Kexue Chubanshe, 1986, for figures on Zhejiang, Guangdong, Shanghai, Nanjing and Wuhan.
33 *RMRB*, 17 May 1987, p. 2.
34 *Zhongguo Funu Bao* (*Chinese Women*), 23 November 1987, p. 1; *JJRB*, 26 November 1987, p. 1.
35 *RMRB*, 13 November 1988, p. 8.
36 For a further discussion of media presentation of *getihu*, *see* Thomas Gold, 'Guerilla Interviewing Among the Getihu', in Perry Link, ed., *Unofficial China – Popular Culture and Thought in the People's Republic*, Boulder, Colorado, Westview Press, 1989, p. 190.
37 *RMRB*, 19 July 1985, p. 4.
38 See also *RMRB*, 4 June 1985, p. 4, and 16 August 1985, p. 2.
39 *GMRB*, 31 August 1983, p. 1.
40 *RMRB*, 5 December 1986, p. 1.
41 *South China Morning Post*, 2 October 1989; *Beijing Ribao*, 25 November 1989.
42 Bai Shiming, *RMRB*, 2 November 1983, p. 4; Youth League, *RMRB*, 27 February 1983, p. 1, and 14 August 1983, p. 1.
43 'Zhonggong zhongyang guanyu yi jiu ba si nian nongcun gongzuo de tongzhi' ('Notice of the Central Committee concerning rural work in 1984'), 1 January 1984, in *Geti Laodongzhe Shouce*, pp. 188–201.
44 *Zhongguo Nongmin Bao* (*Chinese Peasants Daily*), 21 June 1984; *NMRB*, 13 August 1985, p. 1.
45 *RMRB*, 22 April 1987, p. 4.
46 *JJRB*, 18 November 1987, p. 1.
47 Wenzhou Shi Pufa Jiaoyu Bangongshi, 'Women zenyang zuo geti gongshanghu pufa jiaoyu gongzuo de' ('How we conduct common law education among individual businesspeople'), *Nongcun Gongzuo Tongxun* (*Rural Work Newsletter*), no. 9, 1988, p. 42.
48 A. Hegedus and M. Markus note this in relation to similar behaviour on the part of small private entrepreneurs in Eastern Europe. See 'The small entrepreneur and socialism', *Acta Oeconomica*, vol. 22, no. 3–4, 1979, pp. 267–89; esp. pp. 283–4. Anita Chan and Jonathan Unger see the involvement of some *getihu* in the 1989 protest movement as being another kind of attempt to buy prestige: see their article, 'Voices from the Protest Movement, Chongqing, Sichuan', *The Australian Journal of Chinese Affairs*, no. 24, July 1990, esp. pp. 6–7.
49 *JJRB*, 4 March 1988, p. 1.
50 Interview, Chengdu, 9 September 1988.
51 Ole Bruun, 'The reappearance of the family as an economic unit: a sample survey of individual households in workshop production and crafts, Chengdu, Sichuan province, China', University of Copenhagen, Centre for East and Southeast Asian Studies, Copenhagen, Discussion

Paper no. 1, December 1988, p. 111. Bruun's study was really devoted to small, traditional businesses, and only two of his interviews were with larger businesses. He emphasizes that his hypotheses concerning the 'entrepreneurial' type of business are extremely tentative.

52 *RMRB*, 4 December 1986, p. 2.

53 *RMRB*, 21 November 1988, p. 2.

54 *JJCK*, 5 February 1990, p. 2 reported that in Henan after August 1989, 92 of Zhenping county's 202 *siying qiye* sought to become collectives, while 940 *getihu* closed down.

55 Quoted in Hu Guohua, Lin Jinghuai and Chen Min, *Duo sediao de Zhongguo geti jingyingzhe (The many colours of China's individual businesspeople)*, Beijing, Beijing Jingji Xueyuan Chubanshe, 1988, p. 40.

56 *JJRB*, 8 December 1987, p. 1.

57 See, for example, Wenzhou Shi Pufa Jiaoyu Bangongshi, op. cit., p. 42.

58 Bruun, op. cit., describes this sequence as it occurred in Chengdu, with a case study of one of its casualties, pp. 44–5.

59 Michiki Kikuchi points out that this will become even more important as the initial burst of labour-intensive, low-technology production is followed by a need for more advanced industries if they are to remain competitive. See Michiki Kikuchi, 'The "Wenzhou Model" – private enterprise in the regional economy', *JETRO China Newsletter*, no. 77, November–December, 1988, p. 7. For a Chinese discussion of this question, see Ji Jianlin and Zhu Jun, 'Siying qiye lirun liuxiang fenxi', ('An analysis of private enterprise profit uses'), *ZGNCJJ*, no. 9, 1989, pp. 48–52.

60 On a visit to China in January 1991, several researchers and officials told me that one of the effects of political fears since the crackdown of 1989 has been to prevent private operators from using their accumulated capital to expand beyond *getihu* size.

61 *RMRB*, 27 February 1983, p. 5.

62 Liu Long, ed., *Zhongguo xian jieduan geti jingji yanjiu (Research on the individual economy in China's current stage)*, Beijing, Renmin Chubanshe, 1985, p. 114.

63 *RMRB*, 10 July 1984, p. 2.

64 *RMRB*, 27 February 1983, p. 5.

65 *RMRB*, 26 July 1984, p. 2 and 19 October 1984, p. 2.

66 This is one of the reasons why many private enterprises find ways to register as collectives. For an example of the receipt problem, see Office of the County Committee of Tongcheng county, Anhui province, eds, 'Dui siren qiye ruogan wenti de diaocha yu sikao' ('An investigation and consideration of some problems of private enterprises'), *NYJJWT*, no. 10, 1987, pp 51–4.

67 *RMRB*, 2 November 1989, p. 2.

68 *SWB*, 14 August 1989, FE/0534/B2/4.

69 *SWB*, 28 October 1989, FE/0599/B2/1.

70 *RMRB*, 26 March 1990, p. 2.

5

INTELLECTUALS AND REFORM

Sylvia Chan

The Chinese democracy movement in the late 1980s, erupting into mass demonstrations in April and May 1989 and suppressed brutally in June 1989, is without doubt one of the most momentous events in post-Mao China. It has had immediate impact on the power relations among the elite and on the directions of China's domestic policies. It will continue to have effects on China's development in the next few decades.

The majority of demonstrators were university students. In China, university students regard themselves and are regarded by others as intellectuals. Even if we do not accept such a loose definition of intellectuals, we cannot doubt that· university students are being trained by intellectuals to join their ranks. There is thus a close affinity between the two. In the aftermath of the Beijing massacre, the Chinese authorities have accused some leading intellectuals of instigating 'turmoil' (*dongluan*).[1] The regime is, of course, using this as an excuse for further suppression of the democracy movement, but there is some truth in this accusation. Intellectuals did play a crucial role in the student unrest. Through their publications and lectures, radical and reformist intellectuals exerted a profound influence on the thinking of the younger generation in the years leading up to June 1989. Many demands for democracy and freedom voiced by student demonstrators were exactly those intellectuals had been fighting for for many years. Even if most of them refrained from direct participation in demonstrations at the beginning, their sympathy was clearly with their students. In the end, many were so provoked by the government's increasing intransigence that they threw caution to the four winds and joined in the marches and hunger strikes, signed petitions, and gave public lectures in support of the demonstrators. The most committed among them are said to have acted as advisers to student leaders. At critical moments in the movement, it was their support that greatly boosted students' morale, sustained the momentum and helped win for it widespread popular support.

There have been similar opposition movements before in the history of communist China. The first was in the spring of 1957, when large numbers of intellectuals and university students took advantage of the party's 'hundred flowers' policy to voice their disenchantment with communist rule.[2] This movement was quickly squashed and the severity of the suppression effectively cowed intellectuals into total submission for the next twenty years. From 1957 to 1977, there was not even a single case of significant organized intellectual opposition, though timid dissent voiced by individuals was heard from time to time.

Towards the end of 1978, however, there was a spontaneous outburst of intellectual dissent. Big- and small-character posters mushroomed in the main streets in China's major cities to denounce various aspects of Maoism. The most radical among them went so far as to reject the socialist system.[3] Though most activists in this movement were ordinary young people who had no formal higher educational qualifications, they were self-educated intellectual thinkers, some of whom have since become prominent literary figures.[4] The movement was crushed when a number of the most outspoken dissidents were arrested.

Mass protests broke out once again in September 1985, on the anniversary of Japanese invasion of Manchuria in 1931. Angered by the Nakasone government's defence of Japanese imperialism, Chinese students publicly criticized what they considered to be the Chinese government's current capitulationist policy towards Japan. The situation was defused only after top-level party leaders went around to university campuses to talk with students. Then, in the winter of 1986–87, dissatisfaction with erosion of their living standards by high inflation, and disappointment with the lack of progress in political reform, again sent disgruntled university students in several cities onto the streets. This movement, too, was quickly put down by the authorities. Some activists were arrested while others were blacklisted, to be punished upon graduation by being assigned to unsatisfactory jobs in undesirable locations.[5] The party's General Secretary, Hu Yaobang, was blamed for being 'too soft' with the demonstrators and dismissed. The suppression was less bloody and therefore less visible to the outside world than the

Beijing massacre, but it must still have been fresh in the memory of university students in 1989. When students marched again – and some of them may have taken part in demonstrations in 1986–87 – it was clearly a conscious decision to revive the failed cause of 1986. Appropriately, Hu Yaobang became their rallying symbol.

The frequency of mass protests involving large numbers of students and intellectuals within such a short time was unprecedented in communist China. Even more significant is that each outbreak drew more participants and stronger popular support, showed more sophisticated organization and co-ordination, and was characterized by more uncompromising antagonism towards the regime than the previous one. This fact testifies eloquently to the political maturity and growing political influence of intellectuals. They have changed from a submissive into a self-assertive social group.

Intellectuals throughout the world have risen to social prominence and political independence in modern times, owing to their possession of the knowledge and skills essential to the development of a modern economy and to the management of a modern society. In countries where the ruling class can successfully organize society to undertake modernization, intellectuals are usually co-opted by and eventually incorporated into the ruling class. Such intense antagonism between intellectuals and the authorities as occurred in China in May–June 1989 is rarely seen elsewhere.[6]

In China, however, the ruling communist party elite under Mao Zedong's leadership had led the nation to the brink of social chaos and economic bankruptcy, and had antagonized intellectuals, suppressing them politically, preventing many of them from using their knowledge and expertise constructively, and restricting the recruitment and training of new intellectuals. After Mao's death, the party faced a serious legitimation crisis. Its last chance to regain the mandate to rule rested with its ability to provide leadership in modernizing the country. The party thus had no choice but to make peace with a demoralized and hostile intelligentsia. Its success in co-opting intellectuals, however, also depends on the attitude of the latter. Until the Beijing massacre, intellectuals were not simply passive recipients of the party's policy, but actively tried to influence the way policies were made. In this chapter, I propose to examine the party–intellectual relationship from the perspectives of intellectuals, that is, to look at how intellectuals have responded to policy towards them since 1979, how the modernization programme has changed their perception of their own strength *vis-à-vis* that of the party, and what initiatives they have taken to try to re-define their relations with the party and to improve their overall economic, social and political position.

DEFINING CHINESE INTELLECTUALS

There has been a great deal of unresolved controversy as to who exactly in China constitute intellectuals. Are they simply people with a higher education or should they be defined by the social function they perform, the nature of their work or by the cast of their minds? Do they share common attitudes and interests, which can distinguish them as a social stratum or even as a class?[7] These are clearly important theoretical and practical questions, but it is not my intention to discuss them here. I shall use the word 'intellectuals' as a convenient translation for the Chinese term *zhishi fenzi*, literally 'elements with knowledge'. Knowledge in this context means theories and information about the physical world, human beings and human society which require a relatively advanced level of education (formal or informal) to gather, formulate and learn. Intellectuals are those who earn their incomes by producing, interpreting, transmitting, evaluating and applying knowledge. In concrete terms, they include thinkers, creators and researchers in all areas of knowledge; artists; university teachers and senior teachers in high schools; administrative bureaucrats in government and party agencies and economic institutions, and professionals such as engineers, lawyers, doctors and journalists. In its more restrictive usage, the large number of university students, technicians, low-ranking white-collar office workers, and the majority of primary and secondary school teachers are not regarded as intellectuals. However, in so far as government policies towards intellectuals also impinge on their lives, or affect their future, they share a great deal of common interests with intellectuals. I shall therefore regard them as constituting the mass base of China's intellectuals. It can thus be seen that the term intellectuals used in this chapter applies to a larger group of people in China than is usually the case in western countries. Nevertheless, their leaders who articulate and initiate actions to advance their group interests, and who exert great influence on the group and on society, are by and large intellectuals *par excellence*, i.e. they are creative producers of knowledge and culture. Because they are articulate, high-profile representatives of the group, this study tends to focus on their attitude and behaviour.

Intellectuals' income is derived mainly or solely from their possession of knowledge. Knowledge is thus their capital. Their economic interests dictate that they favour the principle of free competition in the acquisition and sale of knowledge, and that they oppose intellectual work being restricted or judged by criteria other than professional ones, i.e. those derived from the accepted beliefs, agreed conceptual frameworks, and common sets of symbols used in the pursuit of their particular area of knowledge. They also want intellectual work rewarded more generously, both in normative and material terms, than non-intellectual work. Their claims to higher rewards are justified by the argument that they, with their special knowledge and skills, contribute more towards raising social productivity and enriching culture than other people, and that they are better qualified than other social groups to provide normative standards and high ideals for the ordering of society. This last perception gives rise to intellectuals' self-image as guardians of the social conscience, and makes them more keenly aware of imperfections in the existing order than other groups; they are thus social critics by profession.

Intellectual elitism and intellectual social conscience are not peculiar to Chinese intellectuals, though such attitudes may have deeper roots in China's traditional culture than in other cultures. That culture also posits a much wider gap between the well-educated and the under- or un-educated than that between people educated in different specialities. For a long time, there was only a uniform generalist–humanistic education for the entire Chinese intelligentsia. It was not until the latter half of the nineteenth century that the education system allowed for specialization in languages, natural science and technology. This was done with the specific nationalistic goal of self-strengthening in mind, and the first generation of Chinese technical personnels and professionals were motivated to 'learn the superior techniques of the barbarians in order to control them'.[8] This linkage between science and technology on the one hand and socio-political goals on the other has given rise to a stronger group identity between Chinese humanistic intellectuals and technical intellectuals than would be the case in other cultures. Chinese engineers or medical doctors, for example, regard themselves and are regarded by others as intellectuals simply because of their higher level of education, which is thought to give them better insight into social problems and imposes on them greater responsibility for social well-being. Not surprisingly, among the most active in the recent democracy movement were students from some of China's best science and technological universities, including Qinghua University in Beijing and the Chinese University of Science and Technology in Hefei, and the best-known Chinese dissident intellectual is the astrophysicist Professor Fang Lizhi.

'EXPERT' VERSUS 'RED': AN OVERVIEW

The stated policy of the party is for intellectuals to become both 'red' and expert. Under Mao, overwhelming emphasis was placed on becoming 'red', and even non-party intellectuals were expected to embrace Marxism. The official line was that Marxism is the highest truth that holds the key to understanding 'the iron laws' governing both human society and nature, and that the initiated are therefore all-powerful. Other special branches of knowledge were seen to be at best of a second order, pertaining only to compartmentalized truth, and at worst, if they ran counter to Marxism, packs of lies concocted by the bourgeoisie. Falsehoods should, of course, be eliminated and compartmentalized knowledge should be guided by the universal holistic truth of Marxism. The 'red' must therefore lead the expert.

The conflict between professional experts and officialdom is a world-wide phenomenon. Intellectuals everywhere resent interference in their professional work by political appointees. In today's China, however, tensions between intellectuals and those responsible for controlling them, i.e., the political–ideological cadres (*zhengzhi sixiang gongzuo ganbu*), are particularly acute, because not only the former's professional work but also their thinking and even their private life are subjected to close scrutiny. This applies to party and non-party intellectuals alike. The situation is aggravated by the great disparity in the intellectual and cultural levels between the supervisors and the supervised. Intellectuals constitute an extremely small proportion of party membership; according to an official source in 1985, only 4 per cent of party members had received a tertiary education.[9] Political cadres, selected on criteria of political loyalty rather than specialized expertise, are thus usually less educated than the professionals they supervise. To subject intellectuals to the control of anybody at all is bound to create conflicts, but to subject them to the control of their intellectual and cultural inferiors is adding insult to injury. How much importance Chinese intellectuals attach to the intellectual ability of their political leaders can be seen in the following two examples. During the Cultural Revolution, the leadership of the *Renmin Ribao* was re-shuffled several times, but none of the top appointees was more hated by staff members than Lu Ying. This was not simply because of Lu Ying's loyalty to the Gang of Four, but because of his abysmal ignorance, according to one of his former colleagues.[10] On the other hand, a person scorned for his politics can still retain the respect of intellectuals if he is seen to be erudite and cultured. The dissident intellectual Wu Zuguang confessed to having a tender spot in his heart for the cultured ideologue Hu Qiaomu, who is his political enemy.[11]

It is not that the party has never been sensitive to this problem. After the urgent demand for large numbers of political cadres in the first years of the Republic was eased, the party did try to improve the quality of cadres. Wherever possible, qualified people were assigned to political posts in institutions with a high concentration of intellectuals, such as universities and research institutes. But in the 1960s, as Mao became increasingly obsessed with the fear of a 'capitalist restoration', anti-intellectualism resurfaced with a vengeance. The policy of appointing intellectuals to do political and ideological work was denounced as revisionist. During the Cultural Revolution, ordinary workers and soldiers with very low levels of literacy were moved into universities and research institutes to assume direct control.[12] This not only intensified tensions between intellectuals and the party, but also sowed dissension between workers and intellectuals.

The distrust of intellectuals stems from fear. China's capitalists were dispossessed in the mid-1950s, and so were the peasants, through several stages of collectivization and communization. Workers had had nothing to be dispossessed of from the start. The intellectuals' capital of knowledge cannot be dispossessed, but it can be devalued and its use and acquisition can be controlled. This is exactly what the party has tried to do. Under Mao, 'white' experts were prohibited from or restricted in practising their expertise, and people judged to have little prospect of becoming 'red' were often denied educational opportunities to acquire expertise. This, however, could only be done to a certain extent. As long as the party had to rely on specialized knowledge in its socialist construction, it could neither completely destroy intellectuals as a social group, nor devalue their knowledge to a point where there were no material and normative incentives for them to work. Mao's policy was to make use of the expertise of the majority while stepping up vigilance against perceived ideological deviations among them. A series of unprovoked attacks on many intellectuals finally culminated in a decade of indiscriminate suppression of all of them in the last years of Mao's rule. Who can blame them for harbouring strong resentment and mistrust for a regime that has so outrageously mistreated them?

THE POSITION OF PARTY INTELLECTUALS

Ironically, even as the party is attempting to regain its mandate to rule after Mao's death by launching the modernization programme, it is also laying its political power wide open to challenge. Its failure to provide leadership in modernization in the past inspires little public confidence in its ability to do the same in future. Intellectuals as the social group with the knowledge and skills most essential to modernization are thus placed in a strong position to challenge the party's leadership. Many intellectuals, believing that modernization is the only road to national salvation, also feel that it is their patriotic duty and social responsibility to provide, or help to provide, leadership in modernization. It is this sense of mission that has given them the moral strength they need to pit themselves against an entrenched system many times stronger than they.[13]

In the post-Mao era, party intellectuals have played a leading role in challenging the party's absolute authority.[14] Party intellectuals have dual identities. As party members, they are often required to supervise the ideology and politics of other intellectuals on behalf of the party, but as intellectuals, they are also controlled by political–ideological cadres, the full-time professional revolutionaries. This has led Gouldner to see them as a 'second-class elite'.[15] But Gouldner has underestimated the precariousness of their elite position, that their position is predicated upon their subjugating their intellectual identity to their political identity. Party discipline does not allow for what Gouldner calls the culture of critical discourse[16] but demands unconditional acceptance of party dogma. Those perceived to have allowed their critical faculty to get the better of their sense of loyalty to the party have been hit hard in successive purges since the Yan'an rectification campaign in the early 1940s. Stripped of their political privileges, disgraced party intellectuals often felt a strong affinity with those critical non-party intellectuals who shared the same fate as they.

During the Cultural Revolution, the across-the-board attack on all intellectuals, regardless of whether they were conformist or non-conformist, party or non-party, made many party intellectuals realize that their personal well-being depends more on the general well-being of intellectuals than on their party membership. This cannot but affect the balance of their allegiance towards their social group and towards the party. This is why, in the aftermath of the Cultural Revolution, a number of party intellectuals have shown sincere contrition about their former role in the persecution of other intellectuals; Zhou Yang was only the most visible of them. The more moderate post-Mao policy towards intellectuals has further blurred the distinction between party and non-party intellectuals and strengthened solidarity between them, because party intellectuals have benefited from it as intellectuals, not as party members. True, their political status still gives them certain advantages over their non-party colleagues, notably in competing for promotion to leading positions and for opportunities to go overseas, but this is not serious enough to create sharp division between party and non-party intellectuals, as leaders and those going overseas constitute only a very small number. Party intellectuals, too, are still more involved in the political process than non-party intellectuals. Ironically, this has tended to give them more confidence in challenging party authorities, and to make them feel even more resentful, because even though their party membership should, in theory, give them equal political status to that of political cadres, in practice, they can only play second fiddle in the political process to those who are intellectually inferior to them.

A 'BLOC WITHIN' THE PARTY AND AN 'OPPOSITION' WITHIN THE GOVERNMENT?

One of the most effective ways for intellectuals to have greater influence over decision making is for them to infiltrate the party and take control from within. This was a strategy openly advocated by the leading dissident Fang Lizhi.[17] On the other hand, the party is also eager to recruit intellectuals into its ranks, so that it can bind them to its ideological and organizational principles, while making use of their specialized expertise. In the early 1980s, there was a national drive to recruit intellectuals. Reports in the Chinese press suggest that there was no lack of enthusiasm on the part of intellectuals to join the party, but that there was considerable resistance from entrenched party bureaucrats at all levels, who feared that their positions might be threatened by more capable new recruits.[18] Opposition was so strong that Deng Xiaoping had to take firm actions to overcome it. From 1982 to 1985, there were major reshuffles of party and government leadership at the central and provincial levels. Party and government leaders obstructing this policy or deemed unequal to the task of modernization were demoted or retired, and educational qualifications became important criteria in the selection of new leaders to replace them. As a result, provincial leaders with tertiary education increased from about 10 per cent to nearly 40 per cent in 1983,[19] and to 60 per cent in 1985.[20] Of the new appointees in 1985, 80 per cent had tertiary education.[21] All eight new ministers appointed in that year had higher education and professional experience relevant to the speciality of their respective ministry.[22] At the same time, in September 1985, a total of 131 members of the old guard in the Central Committee, the Central Advisory Committee and the Central Discipline Inspection Committee were retired to make room for younger and more qualified new members. Of the 91 new members and alternate members of the new Central Committee, 76.6 per cent had a tertiary education.[23]

With the policy-making process of the party shrouded in secrecy, it is difficult to determine exactly how a more educated leadership influences outcomes. The decision to suppress the democracy movement in 1986–87 and 1989 and the swiftness with which party and government leadership at all levels fell into line (in spite of Hu Yaobang in 1986 and Zhao Ziyang in 1989) seems to suggest that a more educated leadership does not necessarily work in favour of intellectuals. After all, it is reasonable to assume that people are promoted to high leadership positions primarily for their loyalty to the party, and their academic qualifications are merely additional assets. But the leadership reshuffle in the first half of the 1980s did establish the precedent of making the level of education a criterion for promotion, and helped to facilitate the recruitment of intellectuals into the party and their promotion to leading posts. There is also evidence to suggest that at the lower levels, a higher proportion of intellectuals in party membership and in leading bodies often influences the implementation of policies, if not their formulation. For example, the literary critic Liu Zaifu and the journalist Qin Benli could, with the support of their respective constituency, use their power as leaders in the Institute of Literary Research and in the newspaper *Shijie Jingji Daobao* (*World Economics Herald*) to over-rule the anti-intellectual decisions of their immediate superiors. Liu Zaifu refused to publish critiques of the expelled party writer Liu Binyan in the journal he edited,[24] and Qin Benli refused to suppress from publication the speeches of several leading intellectuals demanding Hu Yaobang's posthumous rehabilitation.[25]

Another way of influencing policy making is for intellectuals to serve as advisers. Pro-reform leaders are usually more aware of their own intellectual limitations and more receptive to advice by experts. Some leaders, such as Zhao Ziyang, even institutionalized their consultation with intellectuals through the establishment of research bodies within government or party agencies under their direct con-trol. In the absence of reliable information, however, it is impossible to determine the exact role these 'think-tanks' have played in policy formulation.

Another strategy for intellectuals to gain greater political influence was to agitate for greater representation of the so-called democratic parties in government. Many democratic parties have a large intel-lectual membership, and present themselves as representing intel-lectuals' interests. In the early 1980s, they also made considerable effort to expand their intellectual membership. Democratic parties have never been a meaningful opposition, but at times they could criticize the party's policies and make suggestions at the Political Consultative Conference. Even though the latter wields no real political power, it provides them with a legitimate and prestigious forum to influence public opinion. Reports of meetings of this body in recent years show that the overriding concern of most of its members has been improvement of the political and social status of intellectuals and of their working and living conditions. True, their opinions have seldom been heeded, which has generated much disillusionment and cynicism, but their grievances could at least be heard, and this has exerted some pressure on the government.

'PRACTICE IS THE SOLE CRITERION OF TRUTH': OPENING THE FLOODGATE

Political power starts with the power to define social realities, and intellectuals are a social group whose function is to define social realities. The party has maintained its monopoly of power by making its official definitions of social realities, codified as Marxism-Leninism and Mao Zedong Thought, legally binding on Chinese citizens.[26] In this way, it uses legal sanction to try to reduce the role of intellectuals to that of the party's mouthpieces. For intellectuals to play a more independent political role, they must have freedom to propose alternative definitions of social realities and alternative ways to change them. In the last four decades, the intellectuals' fight for more political power has primarily been a fight for freedom of expression. Under Mao, the party's domination over intellectuals was secure. In the twenty-seven years of Mao's rule, only twice did the party decide to concede more freedom of expression to intellectuals, in 1956–57 and in 1960–61, and both times the decision was quickly reversed. This contrasts sharply with the frequent concessions in the scope of that freedom in the post-Mao era. More significantly, in Mao's time, the freedom conceded to intellectuals became increasingly limited; the so-called 'second hundred flowers movement' in the early 1960s was but a shadow of its former self in 1956–57.[27] In the post-Mao period, however, with each round of change in the party's policy towards intellectuals, they managed to win more freedom and grew bolder. The first major concession they won was when the proposition that practice is the sole criterion of truth was endorsed by the reform faction of the party leadership. This proposition essentially stripped the official ideology of its privileged exemption from critical examination.[28] After this, all sorts of daring arguments could be advanced to loosen up official doctrinal rigidity and to dispute formerly sacrosanct dogmas. One only has to compare the writings of some intellectuals in the late 1970s and those written in the last few years to realize how far they have gone in testing the party's limits. If readers consider vanguard intellectuals such as Su Shaozhi and Wang Ruoshui to be atypical, I invite them to compare two pieces of writing by the conformist writer, Cong Weixi. The first is his 1979 novelette *The Red Magnolia by the Prison Wall*, hailed as China's first piece of Gulag literature,[29] and the second, *Heading Towards Primordial Darkness*,[30] his recent reminiscences of his life as a rightist in the 1950s and 1960s. The stark realism with which the author unflinchingly depicts the hellish realities of labour camps and prisons in the latter piece is a far cry from the timid half-truths of the former.

The struggle for intellectual freedom has made intellectuals more conscious of their common interests and enhanced their group solidarity. Those who have been in the forefront of the struggle and have thereby incurred the wrath of the authorities have invariably won the respect and support of their peers. For example, in 1981, the writer Bai Hua was criticized by the military authorities for his anti-Mao filmscript *Unrequited Love*. In the same year, one of his poems was awarded a 'best poetry' prize, much to the chagrin of his critics. In the anti-spiritual-pollution campaign of 1983, enormous political pressure was brought to bear on alleged offenders. Prominent intellectuals were mobilized to denounce them. Under pressure, the principal offender, Zhou Yang, was forced to make a self-criticism, and subsequently suffered from a nervous break-down. In December 1984, at the Fourth Congress of the Writers' Union, over 800 delegates responded with a two-minute standing ovation as a brief message of greeting from the sick Zhou Yang was read to them, while a similar message from his detractor Hu Qiaomu was received in complete silence.[31] The delegates also defiantly voted Bai Hua, Liu Binyan and Wang Ruowang into the Presidium and the Council of the Writers' Union,[32] at a time when all three fell foul of the authorities. In 1987, in the campaign to combat 'bourgeois liberalization', the writer Liu Binyan was expelled from the party for his heretical views. Several national newspapers, obliged to print criticism of him, could not get anybody of any standing to write the criticism. On the contrary, Liu was defended by such prominent party intellectuals as the poet Shao Yanxiang and the novelist Zhang Jie,[33] and received massive support from the general public.[34] Another two prominent intellectuals purged in the same campaign, the Marxist scholar Wang Ruoshui and playwright Wu Zuguang, had similar experiences.[35] Probably the most significant indication of the growing collective consciousness among intellectuals was the fact that a large number of leading intellectuals of very diverse backgrounds bravely rallied behind the cause of political prisoners in early 1989. Among the signatories of open letters demanding their release were Chen Jun, a young Chinese émigré in the US involved in the Chinese Democratic League (a US-based organization of overseas Chinese dissidents), Yan Wenjing, a veteran party literary bureaucrat of the Yan'an era, Wang Ganchang, an old German-trained nuclear physicist, and Xie Bingxin, a liberal intellectual of the May Fourth generation, educated in the US in the 1920s. [36]

Repeated crack-downs in the last decade on real and imaginary dissent have shown how nervous the party still is about intellectual opposition. Even Hu Yaobang, who is now remembered posthumously as champion of the intellectuals' cause, at no time favoured unrestricted freedom of expression.[37] His successor Zhao Ziyang seems to have adopted a more *laissez-faire* attitude in ideological matters.[38] During his term of office, not a single intellectual was subjected to officially–organized criticism. His downfall, however, has shown how powerless he was against strong inner-party opposition to his policy. As long as there are no legal safeguards for basic human rights, intellectual freedom is precarious, dependent on the good will of top party leaders. Thus, in a bid to protect their freedom, some intellectuals agitated for the removal from the constitution of provisions protecting the supremacy of the official ideology.[39]

BORROWING FROM THE WEST

To overturn or even to modify an entrenched dominant ideology, it is often necessary to borrow alternative ones from other cultures. This has happened time and again in China and elsewhere. In modern times, those committed to transforming China from a traditional society into a modern nation-state were naturally attracted by the successful experience of western modern nation-states, and even the more conservative among them (such as Zhang Zhidong) admitted that traditional ideas were inadequate and needed to be supplemented by western learning. When repeated attempts to westernize the political system failed, radical intellectuals in the May Fourth period were led to conclude that partial westernization would never succeed unless the entire traditional culture was fundamentally revolutionized through extensive western borrowing.

From the point of view of the party, the most important result of the May Fourth borrowing of western culture was the introduction and the final victory of Marxism in China. The party has thus always seen itself as the true inheritor of the May Fourth mantle and argued that the anti-imperialist and anti-traditional ('anti-feudal') revolution set in motion by the May Fourth Movement was carried to its victorious conclusion by the party-led 'new democratic' revolution in 1949.[40] The official line is that the success was due to the astuteness with which Mao and the party adapted the western theory of Marxism to Chinese conditions. The post-Mao leadership continues to adhere to the principle of selective borrowing from the west and adapting foreign things to Chinese needs. The problems are: what are China's most urgent needs, and what are the most effective ways of meeting those needs? Clearly, answers to these questions will determine what is best to borrow from the west.

On the first issue, most Chinese people agree that China's most urgent problem is to build up a strong modern economy, but they cannot agree on the second. Opinions are divided, and the division is most apparent between politicians and pro-reform intellectuals. The post-Mao leadership, including the pro-reform faction, believes that science and technology are what China needs most to learn from the west. It believes that science and technology have no value or institutional implications. It concedes that there is room for improvement in certain socialist institutions, but insists that perfection of socialist institutions is through a self-regulatory and self-rejuvenating process within the system, and that socialism has sufficient dynamism to initiate and sustain this process. This has led to an ambivalent open-door policy; while the regime has thrown its door wide open to western science and technology, and its managerial skills and investment, it is wary of the influence of western culture and decidedly hostile to western social and political ideas.

Leading intellectual exponents of reform, on the other hand, see things very differently. While there are differences among them, they are united in their common belief that ideal factors – cultural and institutional – play no less important, if not more important, a part in modernization than material factors. They do not believe that science and technology are value-free, and argue that over a century of importing western science and technology has failed to modernize China's economy because there has not been a concomitant importation of western institutions and western values to make the science and technology work. There is thus much continuity between the May Fourth movement and the last decade of intellectual ferment in China, in that the anti-traditionalism of both springs from cultural determinism. In fact, pro-reform intellectuals all look upon themselves as keepers of the May Fourth flame. They all heartily endorse the goal of the May Fourth movement to remould China's traditional culture in the modern spirit of science and democracy, but they think that the May Fourth enlightenment was aborted by the party-led 'new democratic' revolution. When Marxism established its unchallengeable dominance over China, they argue, this was the end of the cultural openness of the May Fourth period and the end of democracy and the modern rationalistic critical spirit (science).[41] The problem, according to pro-reform Marxists, does not lie in Marxism itself but in the distortion of Marxism. China borrowed Marxism not from the west, but through Soviet Russia. It is Leninism–Stalinism rather than Marxism that has guided the party. The party has inherited Lenin's emphasis on centralism in political life,[42] his anti-humanist determinism that denies the relative autonomy of will and consciousness (*zhutixing*),[43] and the Stalinist distrust of market forces and use of violence and coercion to suppress dissent.[44] In their opinion, these are all distortions of Marxism, some of which have been made worse in the course of transplantation, because Chinese traditional culture is congenial ground for such distortions.[45] The most iconoclastic thinkers even argue that what is being passed off as socialism is nothing more than the traditional order in a socialist guise, 'feudal socialism' or 'petty peasant socialism' as they label it, and call for its total rejection and 'wholesale westernization'.[46] Even moderates believe that much in China's tradition is inimical to modernization, and propose '*xi ti zhong yong*',[47] a verbal antithesis of Zhang Zhidong's '*zhong ti xi yong*' ('Chinese learning as the basis, and western learning for practical use').

There is thus a strong anti-Leninist–Stalinist proclivity in the post-Mao agitation for westernization. It is western ideas such as freedom, democracy, humanitarianism, individualism and subjectivism, thought to be most wanting in the official brand of Marxism–Leninism, that have been most appealing to intellectuals. Western thinkers and literary figures such as Sartre, Freud, Husserl, Kafka, Herbert Marcuse and Nietzsche, virtually unknown a decade ago, have become familiar names among intellectual circles. Chinese Marxists, too, have sought inspiration in Marx's *1844 Manuscripts* and his *Grundrisse* and in the writings of other humanistic western Marxists such as Lukàcs and the Frankfurt school. On the other hand, there is little enthusiasm for such a 'Stalinist' Marxist as Althusser. Even Su Shaozhi, who approves of Lenin while rejecting Stalin, emphasizes Lenin's later ideas of democratization of the party and the state.[48]

In the wake of the suppression of the movement, the regime has accused intellectual activists of spreading pernicious bourgeois ideas to instigate students to overthrow socialism and establish a bourgeois democracy. Some western observers, on the other hand, see the whole movement as basically a 'loyal opposition', posing no threat to the socialist system.[49] It is difficult to be conclusive about the ultimate goal of the 1989 student unrest, because there was no carefully thought-out general programme to guide their action and, according to eye-witnesses, student leaders were unable to see eye to eye on many issues. But it is not true that anti-socialist slogans were 'conspicuous by their absence' in the student unrest.[50] Official sources might have exaggerated the number of such slogans, but eye-witnesses confirmed their presence. Radical intellectuals such as Fang Lizhi and Liu Xiaobo have never bothered to hide their opposition to socialism,[51] and the fact that both these people were influential among student demonstrators shows that their anti-socialist stance had a following. More important, there are all kinds of socialism. What the party leadership says is that the free thinkers are trying to subvert *their* model of socialism, the 'socialism with Chinese characteristics', as Deng Xiaoping calls it. The fundamental features of this model are best summed up by the four basic principles proposed by Deng, the essence of which is monopoly of power by the party. Not only are radical ideas such as the introduction of a multi-party system favoured by Fang Lizhi and others anathema to such a model; even moderate proposals such as expansion of freedom of the press (*Hu Jiwei*), recognition of the relative independence of the judiciary (*Yu Haocheng*), and less state intervention in the citizen's private life (*Zhang Jie*) are all unacceptable. Take the question of freedom of the press as an example. In the week or so before the massacre, the regime had bowed to public pressure and relaxed control of the media. When the media started to report events with more openness and honesty than it had ever done before, China was, of course, still a socialist country, but it was a socialist country with a difference. That difference, moreover, could lead to other differences, and it is this 'domino effect' that the regime fears most.

ECONOMIC GRIEVANCES

An immediate goal of intellectuals has been to fight for better living and working conditions. Ironically, even though intellectuals were politically oppressed under Mao, they enjoyed a living standard higher than workers and much higher than peasants. In the post-Mao era, however, although their living standard, like that of most other people, has improved in absolute terms, in relative terms, it has fallen behind. The people that have benefited most from Deng's economic reform have been peasants and those running small private businesses, people who have relatively little education. Moreover, since the mid-1980s, inflation has been high, and this has hurt most badly people on fixed salaries, who include most intellectuals, particularly humanistic intellectuals, researchers, teachers and government employees. This problem has caused widespread disenchantment with the regime. Even better-paid 'big' intellectuals were complaining loudly about this 'inverted scale of remuneration for manual and mental labour' (*nao ti shouru daogua*),[52] for the devaluation of knowledge not only affects their living standard, but ultimately weakens their political muscle.

One way of increasing intellectuals' incomes is to open up a free market for their services and work. The growth of a market economy has created a limited free labour market, but the state has tried to impose many restrictions, such as setting a ceiling on intellectuals' income outside their regular salary, introducing an income tax, and restricting job mobility for state employees. As might be expected, these restrictions are strong disincentives to intellectual work. For example, in 1985, the Shanghai municipal government allowed academics to retain 30 per cent of the fees they earned in their spare-time consultancy jobs, instead of the previous 20 per cent. That year saw consultancy work by higher institutions jump by 100 per cent, bringing in a total income of 89 million yuan as against 38 million yuan in the previous year. In the following year, the 30 per cent was revised back to 20 per cent, which immediately brought about a sharp decline in the amount of consultancy work done.[53]

In spite of restrictions, in the three or four years before the Beijing massacre, intellectuals were more able than ever before to make a living outside the centrally controlled labour market. There were some cases of state employees leaving their posts to take up administrative and technical responsibilities in private operations, particularly in foreign-owned enterprises or joint ventures. Private show business was thriving, rivalling state-run cultural operations, absorbing a large number of staff retrenched from the latter, and threatening to lure away their top performers. A private fine arts market was also growing, its clientele being mainly tourists and foreign residents. State film-studios were for hire to private individuals to make films. Even writers, who had formerly been tied most tightly to the state-owned presses, were given slightly more freedom of operation. The most adventurous among them used pseudonyms to publish popular fiction, which is often a euphemism for pornography. Others were encouraged to negotiate contracts directly with publishing houses.

A free labour market not only generates extra incomes for intellectuals, but also gives them some degree of economic independence, which is a precondition for political autonomy. An interesting example is the writer Can Xue. Her avant-garde fiction won much critical acclaim in 1986, but was considered anti-social and decadent by the authorities. One suspects that her fiction would not sell very well, but she was financially secure because she ran a private tailor shop and employed several people to work for her. She thus enjoyed a degree of freedom denied to writers on the government pay-roll.

MORAL CRITIQUES OF THE PARTY

Intellectuals' aspirations to play a bigger and even a leading role in modernizing the country arise partly from their conviction that they are morally superior to the ruling party elite. With a long tradition of intellectuals acting as moral mentors to rulers behind them, Chinese intellectuals today are only too eager to assume that role. In the last decade, literature in particular has played a vital role in exposing the moral bankruptcy of the ruling elite.

In the Confucian tradition of benevolent government, it is immoral for rulers to fail to provide a reasonable livelihood for the people. In the past, the party's strongest defence of its record in government was its achievement in eliminating hunger in the most populous country in the world, but such a defence has become increasingly weak. With the introduction of a degree of openness in government, shocking stories of starvation and poverty have come to light through reportage writings such as *Migration in the West*[54] and *Apocalypse in the Beginning of the World.*[55] Such writings are shattering, because they are based on post-Mao reality, and Mao's leftism cannot be held responsible for it.

The Confucian theory of benevolent government also condemns those who rely on coercion and violence to rule, and no social group has suffered more from repression than intellectuals. When they write about ruthless purges of innocent people like themselves, their moral outrage is often overpowering. This is why 'scar literature', for all its artistic crudity, drew such overwhelming public response.[56] This is also the reason why Deng Xiaoping eventually found 'scar literature' too damaging to his government, even though it had helped create public opinion for his faction to repudiate Mao's ultra-leftism and to discredit his political rival Hua Guofeng. Through his spokesman Hu Qiaomu, intellectuals were requested to refrain from harking back to the negative experiences of the past.[57] By the time this restriction was applied, however, there was no need for critics of the party to draw their ammunition from past mistakes; public grievances against current corruption and abuse of power had overshadowed people's concern with the past. The best-sellers were now writings such as *Between Monsters and Men*[58] and *If I were Real*[59] exposing corrupt practices of party people in authority in Deng Xiaoping's regime. It is of course true that corruption is rampant within the party and the government, but so is it among other strata, including the intellectuals themselves. It is an open secret that writers, for instance, have often bribed adjudicators of various literary prizes, and that patients have to grease the palms of doctors and nurses in order to get reasonable medical treatment. But there seems to have been a conspiracy of silence among intellectuals about corruption elsewhere, so that all public anger could be directed against the party elite.

A more recent issue which has provided intellectuals with ammunition to criticize the ruling elite is protection of the environment. The rallying point of the environmentalists is opposition to the construction of the world's biggest dam over the gorges of the Yangzi River. Though still inchoate, the green movement, involving both humanistic intellectuals and natural scientists and technical experts, could turn out to be an important integrative factor among intellectuals. This is not to say that there is already a schism between the two groups, but the government's pragmatic policy of favouring applied science and technology has widened the income gap between them,[60] which is a potentially divisive issue. Some of the humanist intellectuals involved in the green movement, such as the writers Zhang Jie and Dai Qing, have been known for their pro-reform politics. Since it has been rumoured that it was the conservative Premier Li Peng who promoted the Yangzi dam project, this particular environmental issue may have been politicized. It is interesting that a strong argument against the project is the damage it would do to China's cultural heritage, because the natural beauty of the three gorges has inspired many traditional Chinese poets and painters.[61] Environmentalists have also lamented the spoiling of historical sites through over-development.[62] But as a matter of fact, leading pro-reform intellectuals have never been noted for their great love for the national cultural heritage. On the contrary, in their iconoclastic anti-traditional mood, they have seen historical relics such as the Great Wall and ancient temples and palaces as symbols of the nation's 'feudal' backwardness. Most representative of such anti-traditional sentiments is the much-acclaimed – now much-maligned – commentary accompanying the six-part TV documentary series *Elegy to the Yellow River.*[63] Interestingly, Su Xiaokang, who headed the team writing the commentary, was also a most vocal critic of the government's senseless destruction of many historical sites in the ancient city of Beijing.[64] While one cannot hastily draw the conclusion that people such as Su have no sincere commitment to the environment, one can say that the environmental issue has clearly been used as a strategy to expose the moral bankruptcy of the party leadership.

Moral critique of the ruling class is particularly effective in winning public support in China, which has a long tradition of cherishing moral government. This was the major reason behind the spectacular boom in the market for literature from 1978 to the early 1980s. People read literature avidly because they felt that literature was speaking up for them, through its sympathetic portrayal of their miserable lives, and through its explicit or implicit condemnation of the party. Unfortunately, not enough effort has been made to sustain the rapport that grew up at that time between writers and their readers. In recent years, the social prestige and income of writers seem to have risen in inverse proportion to public enthusiasm for literature. The reason for this is complex, but writers themselves are at least partially responsible for the decline in their popularity. In their frustration with the lack of genuine political reform, writers have become increasingly alienated, and many have begun to withdraw into the ivory tower of pure art. However much one may applaud their effort to free literature from its subservience to politics, one can hardly blame the people in the street for losing interest in a literature far removed from their intimate concerns. Such elitist and escapist tendencies in literature have drawn sharp criticism from concerned intellectuals such as Liu Binyan.[65] As a matter of fact, there are signs that intellectuals as a whole are seen by other social groups as increasingly selfish and insensitive to popular sentiments. For example, in the 1989 democracy movement, a worker wrote an open letter warning students that they would lose public support if they focused exclusively on issues of democracy, better pay for intellectuals, and increased spending on education, and ignored problems of general concern such as in-flation and shortage of housing.[66] Regardless of whether such public perception of intellectuals is fair, it does point to a communication barrier between intellectuals and the rest of the population. Intellectuals have failed to convince the ordinary people that their cause *is* the common cause. This has been a fundamental weakness of the intellectuals' opposition movement in the post-Mao era.[67]

AFTER THE BEIJING MASSACRE

Conflict between intellectuals and the ruling party elite has been at the centre of the Chinese political arena in the last decade. The crushing of the democracy movement by brutal force in June 1989 has done little to change social and power relations, and has therefore not removed the sources of conflict. If anything, it has only intensified the antagonism between intellectuals and the party. Since the Beijing massacre, the party's intellectual and cultural policy has appeared to be directionless. On the one hand, hard-line rhetoric has been kept up, promising to carry out an unrelenting anti-bourgeois-liberalization campaign.[68] Work teams have been dispatched to take control of institutions deemed to have been heavily involved in the democracy movement; books by perceived dissidents have been banned; compulsory political study sessions for state employees have sharply increased; free debates on socio-political problems have stopped, and students of some key universities are required to undergo military training.

On the other hand, the authorities have repeatedly reaffirmed the 'hundred flowers policy'.[69] They seem to be particularly eager to court scientists and technical personnel. Soon after the massacre, *Guangming Ribao* front-paged a glowing account of the achieve-ments of the nuclear scientist Wang Ganchang.[70] Considering that Wang was a signatory of a much-publicized pro-democracy open letter and a vocal critic of Premier Li Peng's pet Yangzi dam project, one cannot but see this as an extraordinary gesture calculated to reassure scientists of similar political views. Since then, Jiang Zemin and other party leaders have received scientists and technical experts many times, paying tributes to their contributions.[71]

The regime's handling of intellectual dissidents has also been rather low-key. While a lot of publicity has been given to the arrest and execution of democracy movement activists of non-intellectual background, punishment of intellectual dissidents has as a rule been carried out secretly. When it has become impossible to conceal such punishment, the regime has tried its best to play down its political implications. The best-known case is the dismissal of the former Cultural Minister Wang Meng. Wang Meng was the only minister who refused to endorse the imposition of marshal law on Beijing and failed to turn up at hospitals to comfort soldiers wounded in the military operations to suppress students. Yet according to official sources, he was relieved of his ministerial duties at his own request, so that he could concentrate on creative writing.[72] Recently, the regime has even released a number of prominent political prisoners.[73] It has also been rumoured that the expulsion from the party of several pro-democracy veteran party members is opposed by Chen Yun and that their party membership is currently under review.

These conflicting signals indicate deep divisions among the top leaders, which came to a head in the so-called '*Zhongguo Wenhua Bao* [*Chinese Cultural Gazette*] incident'. A mouthpiece of the hard-line faction, the *Zhongguo Wenhua Bao* published an editorial on 24 June 1990 to attack by innuendo Li Ruihuan, the political bureau member responsible for cultural and intellectual matters, for his alleged soft line towards 'bourgeois liberalization'.[74] Even though Deng Xiaoping is said to have subsequently arbitrated in favour of Li Ruihuan, Li was denied the satisfaction of having his detractors punished.[75] Since this setback, Li Ruihuan has been assuming a rather low profile, confining himself to uncontroversial matters such as promoting patriotism and denouncing pornography. But the fact that he has retained his position in the political bureau shows that the hard-liners have not yet carried the day, and that further instability can be expected.

Eighteen months after the suppression of the democracy movement, the regime is still beset by a host of problems. It has done little to win back public confidence which it lost completely in the massacre. It has maintained its unpopular hard-line position with regard to the Tiananmen incident. Corruption in officialdom has remained widespread. The economy has been stagnant, and government officials have admitted that the financial situation is deteriorating.[76] The resultant adverse effect on the people's living standard is thus bound to fuel further public discontent. People in China today are eagerly waiting for some catalyst for change to come. If the party does not have sufficient internal dynamism to rejuvenate itself by a complete change of course, it will be made to do so by external forces. Either way, such changes are most likely to be spearheaded by intellectuals, who of all social groups possess the most advanced science and technology and organizational skills. If the current ruling elite were once the grave-diggers of the old ruling classes (be they 'feudal' or 'capitalist' or both), their own grave-diggers could well be the intellectuals.

NOTES AND REFERENCES

1 Official accounts of intellectuals' involvement in the student unrest include Chen Xitong's report to the Standing Committee of the National People's Congress, *RMRB*, 7 July 1989, pp. 2–3, 'Dongluan "jingying" Yan Jiaqi' ('Yan Jiaqi, a member of the "turmoil elite"'), *RMRB*, 3 August 1989, pp. 1 and 4, and Kuang Yan, 'Dongluan "jizhe" Dai Qing' ('Dai Qing, the "journalist" specialising in turmoil'), *GMRB*, 13 September 1989, pp. 1–2.

2 For informed analysis of the movement, see Roderick MacFarquhar, *The Origins of the Cultural Revolution, 1. Contradictions among the People, 1956–1957*, London, Oxford University Press, 1974, T. H. E. Chen, *Thought Reform of the Chinese Intellectuals*, Hong Kong, Hong Kong University Press, 1960, pp. 117–201 and Merle Goldman, *Literary Dissent in Communist China*, Cambridge, Mass., Harvard University Press, 1967, pp. 158–242. English translations of some source materials are collected in Hualing Nieh, ed., *Literature of the Hundred Flowers*, vols 1 and 2, New York, Columbia University Press, 1981.

3 The two volumes of *Documents on the Chinese Democratic Movement 1978–80: Unofficial Magazines and Posters*, edited by Claude Widor, Paris, École des Hautes Études en Sciences Sociales, and Hong Kong, The Observer Publishers, vol. 1, 1981, vol. 2, 1984, have collected a large amount of invaluable Chinese source materials. For English translations of some source materials with critical analysis, see James D. Seymour, *China's Human Rights Movement 1978–1979*, Stanfordville, New York, Human Rights Publishing Group, 1980 and David Goodman, *Beijing Street Voices, the Poetry and Politics of China's Democracy Movement*, London, Marion Boyars, 1981. For an eye-witness account, see John Fraser, *The Chinese*, Glasgow, William Collins, 1982, particularly Pt III and Pt IV 13, 14, and 15.

4 The poets Bei Dao, Gu Cheng and Mang Ke are some of the best-known examples.

5 Arrests were reported by Yang Yunwen, 'Neng zai zhou ye neng fu zhou de Zhongguo xueyun' ('The Chinese student movement that could make or break a government'), *Ming Bao Yuekan (Bright Monthly)*, no. 2, 1987, pp. 14–15.

6 Scholars have taken different views concerning the relations between intellectuals and the ruling class in capitalist and developing countries. Zbigniew Brezinski posits a harmonious relationship between the two, with intellectual politicians providing moral and intellectual leadership

to the moneyed class (Zbigniew Brezinski, 'America in the technetronic age', *Encounter*, vol. 30, January 1968, pp. 16–26.). Chomsky, on the other hand, stresses the subservient role of intellectuals to the capitalist class (Noam Chomsky, 'Objectivity and Liberal Scholarship', *American Power and the New Mandarins*, London, Chatto and Windus, 1969, pp. 23–129). Edward Shils and Joseph Schumpeter see intellectuals primarily as critics of the ruling class, but do not suggest that this will lead to a hostile confrontation between the two (Edward A. Shils, *The Intellectuals and the Powers and Other Essay*, Chicago and London, The University of Chicago Press, 1972, particularly 'The intellectuals and the powers' and 'Ideology and civility', pp. 15–21, 42–59, and Joseph A. Schumpeter, 'The sociology of the intellectuals' in George B. de Huszar, ed., *The Intellectuals, A Controversial Portrait*, Illinois, The Free Press of Glencoe, 1960, pp. 55–79).

7 Gramsci is of the opinion that intellectuals are distinguished by their special social function, Antonio Gramsci, 'The intellectuals' in Quintin Hoare and Geoffrey Nowell Smith, eds and trans, *Selections from the Prison Notebooks of Antonia Gramsci*, London, Lawrence and Wishart, 1971, pp. 5–23. Alvin Gouldner, on the other hand, thinks that intellectuals should be distinguished by their rational critical spirit, Alvin W. Gouldner, *The Future of Intellectuals and the Rise of the New Class*, New York, The Seabury Press, 1979, pp. 28–30.

8 These were words used by the Qing scholar Wei Yuan in his *Hai Guo Tuzhi (Maritime Countries)*, translated in Ssu-yu Teng and John K. Fairbank, *China's Response to the West, a Documentary Survey 1839–1923*, New York, Atheneum, 1975, p. 34.

9 *SWB*, FE/8065/C/6, 25 September 1985.

10 Wang Ruoshui, 'Cong pi "zuo" daoxiang fan you' ('An about-face from criticising "leftism" to criticising rightism'), *Ming Bao Yuekan*, no. 3, 1989, pp. 3–12.

11 Zeng Huiyan, '"Dang de zhengce chang bian, wo shizhong mei bian" – Wu Zuguang "zai Jiazhou de yixi hua' ('"The party's policy changes constantly, but I have never changed" – so says Wu Zuguang in California'), *Jiushi Niandai (The Nineties)*, no. 12, 1987, p. 19.

12 Yao Wenyuan's article 'Gongren jieji bixu lingdao yiqie' ('The working class must exercise leadership in all areas'), *RMRB*, 26 August 1968, p. 1, was written to counter intellectuals' resistance to this move.

13 Old and middle-aged intellectuals often talk with pride of their sense of mission (*shiming gan*) and their anxiety for the fate of the nation (*youhuan yishi*), which they feel is lacking among the younger generation. See, for example, Jin Guantao, 'Lun zhongguo zhishi fenzi de shiming gan' ('The sense of mission among Chinese intellectuals'), *Zhongguo Qingnian Bao* (Chinese Youth Daily), 29 January 1988, p. 3. But the recent student movement shows that students were no less idealistic than their elders.

14 Most intellectual leaders in the recent democracy movement now on the regime's hit list are party members. See Song Ping's speech at a meeting of the party's organizational department, *RMRB*, 23 August 1989, p. 1.

15 Alvin Gouldner, op. cit., p. 79.

16 ibid., p. 28–30.

17 See the decision to expel Fang from the party, *RMRB*, 20 January 1987, p. 1. Fang Lizhi confirmed that he had indeed advocated party intellectuals changing the party from within. See Fang's interview with Ao Hua, *Zhengming*, no. 9, 1988, p. 15.

18 'Ping "women da tianxia, zhishi fenzi zuo tianxia"' ('Comment on (the saying) "We have fought to win political power, only to hand it over to intellectuals"'), *RMRB*, 6 February 1983, p. 1.

19 William deB. Mills, 'Leadership change in China's provinces', *Problems of Communism*, May–June 1985, p. 29.

20 *SWB*, FE/8052/BII/1, 10 September 1985.

21 Ibid.

22 *SWB*, FE/7982/BII/1–2, 20 June 1985.

23 *SWB*, FE/8065/C/6, 25 September 1985.

24 Liu Binyan's interview with Li Yi, *Jiushi Niandai*, no. 5, 1988, p. 25.

25 A post-Beijing-massacre official account of this incident was given by Xin Huashi, '"Shijie jingji daobao" shijian zhenxiang' ('The truth of the "World Economics Herald" incident'), *RMRB*, 19 August 1989, p. 4.

26 The 1982 Constitution of the People's Republic of China, Preface, *RMRB*, 5 December 1982, p. 1.

27 Comparing the two 'hundred flowers' movements, both Dennis Doolin and Merle Goldman arrive at the same conclusion that the second was much more restricted. Dennis Doolin,'The revival of the "hundred flowers" campaign: 1961', *China Quarterly*, no. 8, 1961, pp. 34–41, and Merle Goldman, 'The unique "blooming and contending" of 1961–62', *China Quarterly*, no. 37, 1969, pp. 54–83.

28 It is true, as Stuart Schram argues, that from a purely theoretical point of view, the proposition can be given an interpretation consistent with the Maoist orthodoxy, but *in effect*, it was interpreted otherwise by its proponents and supporters, a fact which Schram does not deny. See Stuart R. Schram, '"Economics in command?" ideology and policy since the Third Plenum, 1978–84', *The China Quarterly*, no. 99, 1984, pp. 417–20.

29 'Daqiang xia de hong yulan', *Shouhuo (Harvest)*, no. 2, 1979, pp. 5–38. From this story is derived the Chinese term for Gulag literature, *daqiang wenxue* ([prison] wall literature).

30 *Zou Xiang Hundun*, Beijing, Zuojia Chubanshe, 1989.

31 Liu Binyan, 'Wo de riji' ('My diary'), *Wenhui Yuekan (Wenhui Monthly)*, no. 2, 1985, pp. 6–7.

32 *Wenyi Bao (Literary Gazette)*, no. 2, 1985, pp. 7 and 10.

33 Liu Binyan's interview with Li Yi, *Jiushi Niandai*, no. 5, 1988, p. 24.

34 ibid., p. 27.

35 Ren Jianbai, 'Zhonggong zheng wu junzi neimu' ('Inside story about the purge of five scholars by the CCP'), *Zhengming (Free Debate)*, no. 9, 1987, p. 14, and Zeng Huiyan, op. cit.

36 *SWB*, FE/0391 B2/1–2, 22 February 1989; *SWB*, FE/0404 B2/4–6, 9 March 1989.

37 On the contrary, in 1985, he reaffirmed the necessity of party

censorship of the press. See Sylvia Chan, 'Two steps forward, one step back: towards a "free" literature', *Australian Journal of Chinese Affairs*, nos. 19 and 20, 1988, p. 105.

38 He allegedly said that in literature and art, the best policy was non-interference, i.e. neither praising nor censuring anything. *RMRB*, 16 August 1989, p. 4.

39 In a conference sponsored by the Stone Company on the revision of the constitution, some participants proposed that the revised constitution should be above any ideology. *Shijie Jingji Daobao*, 24 April 1989, p. 5.

40 The classic statement in this respect is Mao's exposition of the politics of new democracy in 'On new democracy', *Selected Works of Mao Tse-tung*, vol. II, Peking, Foreign Languages Press, 1967, pp. 347–52.

41 Most articulate of this view is Liu Zaifu's article '"Wusi" wenxue qimeng jingshen de shiluo yu huigui' ('The loss and recovery of the spirit of enlightenment in May Fourth literature'), *Wenyi Bao* (*Wenyi Daily*), no. 16, 1989, pp. 3–4, and no. 17, 1989, p. 3.

42 Li Honglin, 'Women jianchi shenmeyang de Makesi zhuyi' ('What kind of Marxism should we adhere to'), *Makesi Zhuyi Yanjiu* (*Study of Marxism*), no. 1, 1989, reprinted in *Xinhua Wenzhai* (*New China Digest*), no. 5, 1989, pp. 1–3.

43 Wang Ruoshui, 'Xianshi zhuyi he fanyinglun wenti' ('The problem of realism and the theory of reflection'), *Wenhui Bao* (*Wenhui Daily*), Shanghai, 12 July 1989, p. 3, and 9 August 1988, p. 4.

44 Su Shaozhi, 'Dui Buhalin de zai pingjia' ('A re-assessment of Bukharin'), *Makesi Zhuyi Yanjiu*, no. 2, 1988, reprinted in *Xinhua Wenzhai*, no. 9, 1988, pp. 63–9.

45 One of the most succinct expositions of this theme is Jiang Jianqiang, 'Makesi zhuyi zhongguohua de wu da "shizhen"' ('Five major distortions of Marxism in the process of sinicisation'), *Shehui Kexue Bao* (*Social Science Bulletin*), 14 July 1988, reprinted in *Xinhua Wenzhai*, no. 8, 1988, pp. 9–10.

46 Liu Xiaobo is probably the most extreme iconoclast. This can be seen in all his writings. See, for example, his book *Xuanze de Pipan* (*Critique of choices*), Shanghai, Renmin Chubanshe, 1988.

47 This is Li Zehou's formula, which means 'Westernisation of social being (*ti*) in China'. His concept of *ti* is different from Zhang Zhidong's, in that it does not refer to ideology and culture alone but includes the economic base and everyday life. See Li Zehou, 'Manshuo "xi ti zhong yong"' ('Random thoughts on "Westernisation of Chinese social being"'), *Zhongguo Xiandai Sixiang Shi Lun* (*Theories of the Intellectual History of Contemporary China*), Beijing, Dongfang Chubanshe, 1987, pp. 331–41.

48 A symposium on Marxism in China today: an interview with Su Shaozhi, with comments by American scholars and a response by Su Shaozhi, *Journal of Concerned Asian Scholars*, vol. xx, no. 1, 1988, pp. 17–18.

49 E.g. Colin Mackerras, 'The political situation in China in 1989', in Colin Mackerras, Kevin Bucknell and Russell Trood, *The Beijing Tragedy: Implications for China and Australia,* Research Paper no. 51, Centre for the Study of Australia–Asia Relations, Griffith University, 1989, pp. 34–5.

50 ibid., p. 35.
51 E.g. interview with Fang Lizhi by the Austrian radio correspondent Helmut Opletal, *SWB*, FE/0483 B2/12–13, 15 June 1989; and Liu Xiaobo, 'Zhongguo dangdai zhishi fenzi yu zhengzhi' ('Contemporary Chinese intellectuals and politics'), *Zhengming*, no. 3, 1989, pp. 68–71, no. 4, pp. 78–81, no. 7, pp. 74–7, no. 8, pp. 90–1, no. 9, pp. 88–90, no. 10, pp. 68–70, no. 11, pp. 72–4, and no. 12, pp. 53–5.
52 Xie Bingxin, who is within the top circles of the intellectual elite, complains about this in her recent short story 'Luo jia' ('A slump in price'), *Shouhuo*, no. 5, 1988, pp. 48–9. A veteran writer in semi-retirement, Xie seldom writes now except when she feels very strongly about something.
53 'Gei xuexiao chuang shou kai lü deng' ('Turn on the green light for schools to create income'), *RMRB*, 22 January 1988, p. 3.
54 Mai Tianshu, 'Xibu zai yimin', *Renmin Wenxue* (*People's Literature*), no. 5, 1988, pp. 49–77. Unlike fiction, reportage is basically factual.
55 Su Xiaokang, 'Honghuang qishilu', *Zhongguo Zuojia* (*Chinese Writers*), no. 2, 1986, pp. 144–59.
56 Typical of this kind of 'scar literature' are the celebrated reminiscences of purges of intellectuals since 1949 by Ba Jin, collected in several volumes of *Suixiang Lu* (*Random Thoughts*), published by Joint Publishing Co., Hong Kong, from 1981 to 1986. Whatever artistic merits these pieces may or may not have, their political significance is indisputable.
57 Hu Qiaomu, 'Dangqian sixiang zhanxian de ruogan wenti' ('Some current problems on the ideological front'), *Wenyi Bao*, no. 5, 1982, pp. 21–2.
58 'Ren yao zhijian', a reportage by Liu Binyan, *Renmin Wenxue*, no. 9, 1979, pp. 83–102, translated as 'People or Monsters?' in Perry Link, ed., *Liu Binyan: People or Monsters? and other Stories and Reportage from China After Mao*, Bloomington, Indiana University Press, 1983, pp. 11–68.
59 Sha Yexin, Li Shoucheng and Yao Mingde, *Jiaru Wo shi Zhende*, special issue of *Xiju Yishu* (*Art of Drama*) and *Shanghai Xiju* (*Shanghai Drama*), Shanghai, 1979, translated as 'What if I really were?' in Perry Link, ed., *Stubborn Weeds, Popular and Controversial Chinese Literature after the Cultural Revolution*, Bloomington, Indiana University Press, 1983, pp. 198–250. I have discussed the socio-political impact of this play and *Between Monsters and Men* in 'Two steps forward . . . ', op. cit.
60 A survey carried out in Beijing and Guangzhou shows that the salaries of intellectuals working in factories, telecommunications, public transport and other public utilities were higher than those working in state agencies, cultural and educational institutions, and scientific research. Li Cheng, 'Nao ti shouru daogua mianmian guan' ('An examination of the problem of inverted scale of payment for mental and manual work from different angles'), *GMRB*, 6 October 1988, p. 1.
61 Jasper Becker, 'China Greens try to halt Yangtze Dam', *The Guardian Weekly*, vol. 140, no. 11 (week beginning 12 March 1989), p. 10.

62 In October 1988, two separate conferences were held in Xi'an and Hangzhou at which experts called for the introduction of environmental laws to halt over-development at scenic and historical sites. *GMRB*, 24 October 1988, p. 1, and 17 November 1988, p. 2.

63 'He Shang', originally published in *RMRB*, *GMRB* and *Wenhui Bao* (Shanghai), reprinted in *Xinhua Wenzhai*, no. 9, 1988, pp. 106–19.

64 Su Xiaokang and Cai Yuanjiang, 'Zuihou de gu du' ('The last ancient capital'), *Hua Cheng (City of Flowers)*, no. 6, 1987, pp. 12–39.

65 See, for example, his interview with Chen Zhaohua, 'Yensu wenxue de bu jingqi wenti' ('The problem of a depressed market for serious literature'), *Dagong Bao (Ta Kung Pao)*, 9 September 1986, p. 2, and his interview with Li Yi, op. cit., p. 30. Another leading intellectual, Jin Guantao, expresses similar concern. 'Jin Guantao tan yishujia de shiming gan' ('Jin Guantao on the artist's sense of mission'), *Xinhua Wenzhai*, no. 6, 1989, pp. 157–8.

66 *Zhongguo Minyun Yuan Ziliao Jingxuan (Selected Source Materials of the Chinese Democracy Movement)*, vol. 1, Hong Kong, Shiyue Pinglun Chubanshe, 25 June 1989, p. 33.

67 The problem was acknowledged by Fang Lizhi. See his interview with Helmut Opletal, op. cit., p. 13.

68 *RMRB*, 21 July 1989, pp. 1–2.

69 Jiang Zemin's speech at the mass rally to commemorate the May Fourth Movement, *RMRB*, 4 May 1990, p. 3, and Li Ruihuan's speech at a cultural work conference, *RMRB*, 15 May 1990, p. 3.

70 *GMRB*, 3 October 1989, p. 1.

71 *RMRB*, 29 August 1989, p. 1; *SWB*, FE/0583 B2/2, 10 October 1989.

72 *SWB*, FE/0562 B2/2–3, 15 September 1989. Several newspaper editors supporting the democracy movement were removed on grounds of their advanced age. See *SWB*, FE/0517 B2/8–9, 25 July 1989.

73 *RMRB*, 11 May 1990, p. 1; *SWB*, FE/0983 B2/2, 30 January 1991.

74 The same issue of the newspaper printed two pages of 'instructions on ideological problems' by Deng Xiaoping and other members of the political bureau, with the conspicuous omission of Li Ruihuan. *Zhongguo Wenhua Bao*, 24 June 1990, pp. 1–2.

75 According to the *New York Times* reporter Kristof. *New York Time*, 17 July 1990, p. A2.

76 *SWB*, FE/1031 C1/9–13, 27 March, 1991; *SWB*, FE/1033 C1/5, 29 March, 1991.

6

THE PUBLIC/PRIVATE DICHOTOMY AND THE GENDER DIVISION OF RURAL LABOUR

Tamara Jacka

Reforms introduced in rural China since 1978 have created new areas of work and have profoundly changed the nature of others.[1] In doing so they have resulted in changes in the work patterns of women and men and have altered the existing gender division of labour and the values associated with it. In this chapter I will look at these changes in relation to a dichotomy between public and private spheres.

In the 1970s some western feminist anthropologists explained what they saw as the universal subordination of women in terms of an identification of women with a private or domestic sphere and men with a public sphere. Michelle Rosaldo argued, for example, that women's subordination is due to the fact that given their child bearing role, women in all societies are inevitably tied to a restricted domestic sphere, while men are free to operate in a wider public domain.[2]

Other anthropologists have claimed that this is a very eurocentric model – that in other societies the private sphere is not necessarily seen as inferior to the public, or that public and private are defined in quite different ways, or else that a division between private and public and an association between the private and women and the public and men simply is not made.[3]

I argue that in rural China there *is* evidence of a public/private dichotomy, but my argument for it is significantly different from Rosaldo's. In China, as in the west, the actual work of women and men does not fall strictly into separate categories according to a public/private dichotomy. Rather, the public/private dichotomy can be thought of as a set of norms governing the work opportunities and choices of women and men and the ways in which work is to be recognized. These norms are reproduced at all levels of society, from children's education through to employers' recruitment policies. Accordingly, the very identity of individual men and women and the position of each in terms of relations with other people and institutions and access to and control of material resources, are shaped both by the norms themselves, regardless of whether they are accepted or not, and by the degree to which they are accepted or contested.

In contrast to Rosaldo, I would argue that, like any norms, the public/private dichotomy is neither universal nor inevitable. Thus, the public/private dichotomy in rural China has a range of meanings and associations different from in the west. And within rural China, the meanings associated with this dichotomy and the relations between it and the actual work women and men do, have been changing over time. Since the introduction of reforms in 1978 the changes have been particularly marked. Nevertheless I will argue that since 1978 women have been constrained by the fact that such a public/private dichotomy still exists. It has meant that despite major changes in work patterns, the rural reforms are as yet resulting in neither a breakdown of the gender division of labour, nor a re-evaluation of women's and men's sides of the division. Instead, what is happening is that what is included in the ideal of women's work and men's work is changing, but the division remains, as does the lesser regard for women's side of that division.

Before dealing directly with the question of changes that have emerged since the introduction of recent rural reforms, I will put this issue in context by giving a brief outline of the public/private gender division of labour that existed before 1949 and communist interventions into that division between the 1950s and the late 1970s.

THE PUBLIC/PRIVATE DICHOTOMY IN PRE-1949 CHINA

In the first half of the twentieth century, as indeed today, the basic unit of all economic and social relations in China was the household; a group of usually, but not always, related people bound by a common budget. The bulk of the time and labour of most rural households was spent on the cultivation of food grains for their own consumption and on domestic work, by which I mean work involving the processing of goods for household consumption, the physical maintenance of the household and its members, the care of the elderly and the rearing of children. In addition, activities such as the production of handicrafts, small-scale animal husbandry and farm labour for other households were undertaken to supplement the household's diet and/or cash income. John Buck, undertaking a survey of Chinese farms in the 1930s, found that, not including domestic work (for which he had no information), agriculture occupied the full time of a little over two-thirds of the farm population, subsidiary work one-eighth and agriculture and subsidiary work combined one-fifth.[4]

The type of work undertaken by women (and men) was heavily influenced by Confucianism, according to which women were not to take part in public affairs and were to be confined to the physical boundaries of the home. In fact, one of the words for wife, *neiren*, literally meant 'inside person'. This ideal was enforced to a great extent in reality through very strict control of a woman by her family (or husband's family once she married) and through the practice of footbinding. It meant that across the whole of China women performed only 13 per cent of all agricultural work and 16 per cent of subsidiary work, though these figures varied considerably according to class, local customs and the economic necessities of the time and place.[5] Although we have no statistical information on domestic work, contemporary accounts of the period suggest that women performed most of the domestic work of a household. They worked long hours doing tasks such as grinding grain, collecting firewood, fetching water and making shoes and clothes, as well as cooking, washing and childcare. They also did a large proportion of the work involved in home industries, especially spinning and weaving[6] and in the rearing of domestic livestock. Their work was often arduous and was as vital to the household economy as the men's work in the fields.[7]

COMMUNIST INTERVENTIONS INTO THE PUBLIC/PRIVATE DICHOTOMY FROM THE 1950s TO THE LATE 1970s

The programme of communization of agriculture and rural industry undertaken by the CCP in the 1950s was an attempt to eliminate the individual household economy; in a sense it was an attempt to eliminate the distinction between 'private' and 'public' spheres of work and to make all work public. This ultimate goal was not achieved. Instead, what resulted was a much clearer distinction between 'public' work and 'private' work and an altered meaning for each. 'Public' work now meant work for the commune whilst 'private' work encompassed everything else.

TAMARA JACKA

By 1959 all rural households were grouped together into communes. The communes owned all land and almost all the means of production, and employed peasants to work in production teams in return for a share of the total output of the team. The role of the household as a unit of production was, in this way, greatly reduced. It was not eliminated, however. Peasant households were assigned small private plots of land (*ziliudi*) and retained ownership of scattered fruit trees, domestic livestock and small farm tools. They were allowed to use time outside commune work hours and the labour of household members not engaged in commune work to gather wild plants, to cultivate vegetables and fruit trees on their private plot or in their courtyard, to rear small numbers of domestic livestock and to make handicrafts on a small scale. Much of the work involved in these 'domestic sidelines' (*jiating fuye*), as they were called, was done by women.[8] CCP policies towards domestic sidelines fluctuated from the 1950s to the late 1970s between cautious encouragement and repression. On the one hand, they were regarded by the CCP as competition with and a threat to the commune economy and as an area where class inequalities could re-emerge. On the other hand, they were a concession to the peasant population which, on the whole, was opposed to communization and, in addition, they could provide an important supplement to commune production. In most periods the latter considerations won the upper hand. Peasants generally obtained grain from communal distribution, but a large proportion of other food items and cash they obtained from domestic sidelines.[9]

In addition to the household maintaining this role of unit of production, it continued to be the basic unit of consumption. Thus, although in theory peasants were to be remunerated for their commune work as individuals, in practice pay-packets for all members of a household were distributed to the (usually male) head of the household who then had ultimate authority over how that income was to be spent. Members of the household who did not participate in productive work were dependent on those who did, and the woman or women of the household generally undertook domestic work for the whole household.

Communization was accompanied by attempts on the part of the CCP to increase women's participation in agriculture and by somewhat less vigorous attempts to remove the responsibility for domestic work away from the individual woman into the public sphere. This was partly to overcome a shortage of labour in the

120

fields. It was also because the CCP believed in the Marxist notion, expressed most clearly in Engels' *The Origin of the Family, Private Property and the State*, that women's confinement to the private sphere and their exclusion from the public was the cause of their oppression and that

> the emancipation of women becomes possible only when women are enabled to take part in production on a large social scale, and domestic duties require their attention only to a minor degree.[10]

During the Great Leap Forward (1958–60, henceforth GLF) large numbers of women were drawn into commune work, and their domestic work was reduced to some extent through the provision of some social services such as communal dining halls, sewing groups, laundries and childcare centres. In addition, during this period, especially in 1958, domestic sidelines were discouraged and rural markets were closed,[11] thus reducing further women's work in the private sphere.

However, other problems notwithstanding, the GLF revealed a number of limitations and problems with the Chinese adoption of the Marxist approach to women's emancipation. Many of these problems were due to the fact that the Marxist solution of bringing women into public production and reducing their private work to a minimum was achieved only very imperfectly and was not backed up with more direct attempts to change traditional ideology relating to the gender division of work. Thus, although the number of women participating in commune work was enormously increased, and although the establishment of some communal services lessened individual women's burden of domestic work, where communal services were minimal women continued to bear the entire responsibility for their households' domestic work and where domestic sidelines were undertaken women did a large proportion of that work also. The result was a double burden for many women, and, for the commune, constant difficulties in increasing the number of hours women devoted to commune work.

Other problems with the Chinese adoption of the Marxist approach to women's emancipation were less a result of an incomplete implementation of the approach, as due to the fact that the original approach itself was based on assumptions that were at odds with the Chinese situation. In *The Origin of the Family, Private Property and the State* Engels argued that the reason why men came

121

to dominate women was that 'gaining a livelihood had always been the business of the man; he produced and owned the means therefor'.[12] When, in the middle stage of barbarism men took to domesticating animals and were able to produce more than was needed for consumption,

> all the surplus now resulting from production fell to the man; the woman shared in consuming it, but she had no share in owning it . . . The woman's housework lost its significance compared with the man's work in obtaining a livelihood. The latter was everything, the former an insignificant contribution.[13]

Recent research has thrown doubt on Engels' version of world history. For example, there is much anthropological data which suggests that it was women, rather than men, who first developed horticulture and thereby generated productive surplus.[14] This problem aside, Engels' account clashes with what we know about women's work in the twentieth century. Engels' claim that the emancipation of women can come only when they take part in production on a large social scale was based on the assumption that their work in the private sphere did not produce surplus and, therefore, in his mind was insignificant. In rural China, however, although domestic work did not produce surplus, it was vital to the workings of the household economy. To regard it as insignificant was to reinforce a sexist outlook in which regardless of what women do, because they are women their work is undervalued. Furthermore, other aspects of women's work in the private sphere, such as feeding the pig or making handicrafts or other domestic sideline occupations, certainly did produce surplus and that surplus was exchanged in the market.

While women were undoubtedly better off after the Chinese adoption of the Marxist approach to women's emancipation than they were before it, the incomplete implementation of the approach and the failure to tackle directly a number of aspects of traditional peasant ideology, combined with the unsuitability of the original approach, resulted in some new problems. As I have mentioned, it created for women a heavy 'double burden' of work in both the public and private spheres. In addition, I would argue, it not only failed to eliminate the public/private gender division of work, it devalued even further women's side of the division, i.e. the private. It did this in two ways. First, while the state's attempt to free women from domestic work which was considered unproductive and akin to slavery to the man failed, the rhetoric did reinforce peasants' low opinion of such work, and the women who did it. Second, women's work in domestic sidelines was, again, not eliminated, but was devalued, ironically both because of its close association with unproductive domestic work and also because it was, in fact, productive and was part of a private market economy, which was considered a threat to the commune economy.

After 1960 when the GLF ended in economic disaster, the number of women participating in commune work continued to increase, but women also undertook domestic sidelines and remained responsible for domestic work. Much less attention was paid to the socialization of domestic work than during the GLF, in part because it proved so expensive, and although it was claimed that in agriculture and industry 'what men can do, women can do too' the reverse claim was never made. The view that women are responsible for the private sphere remained unchallenged, except to a small extent during the 'Criticize Lin Biao and Confucius' campaign (1973–74) when some attempt was made to urge men to share domestic work with their wives.

THE IMPACT OF RURAL REFORMS

The rural reforms begun in 1978 combined changes to the agricultural pricing system, attempts to diversify the rural economy, decentralization of agricultural management, and a strict family planning policy. They introduced radical changes both to the way in which work was organized and to the type of work available to peasants.

Various forms of a 'rural responsibility system' were introduced as a means of improving incentives for peasant production by linking the remuneration of work more closely with performance. Initially, this was done within the commune framework. Under the earliest forms of the responsibility system specific production tasks were contracted by the production team to a group of peasants or to a peasant household in return for a quota of workpoints and a bonus for surplus production. By 1983, however, the commune system had broken down. Most areas had adopted a type of responsibility system in which households managed their own economies entirely, and simply paid taxes to their production team.

Concurrently, the CCP abandoned its earlier policy of aiming for

self-sufficiency in grain in each region in favour of an encouragement of diversification and specialization in the rural economy.
Peasants were encouraged to engage in more cash-cropping,
forestry, animal husbandry, fishing and handicraft production and
even to abandon agriculture altogether to work in processing,
manufacturing and services. The trend toward diversification and
specialization both led to and itself was further intensified by the
growth of markets, an improvement of transport and service facilities and a relaxation of restrictions on the movement of labour both
within rural areas and between rural and urban areas.

The combination of the responsibility systems and measures
aimed at encouraging a diversification of the economy enabled
peasant households to make their own decisions about what areas
of production to engage in, according to their particular abilities and
the interplay of local prices, supply and demand. This in turn
resulted in significant changes to the structure of rural production.
For example, between 1978 and 1984 grain acreage decreased by 8
per cent and the acreage sown to economic crops increased by 47
per cent. At the same time, the proportion of the total rural labour
force used in crop farming declined from 75.2 per cent to 62.7 per
cent. The proportion of the rural labour force involved in secondary
industry increased from 6.7 per cent to 13.3 per cent and the proportion involved in tertiary industry increased from 6.2 per cent to
11.3 per cent.[15] It is important to note, however, that although in
terms of their basic thrust the economic reforms have been implemented right across rural China, the details of their implementation
and the changes they have effected have differed from place to
place. The most obvious difference has been between areas on the
eastern coast and around large cities and areas further inland and far
removed from large cities. In the former areas industries are now
well developed, as are trade networks with other parts of China and
with overseas markets. A relatively large proportion of peasants
work at non-agricultural occupations and households are fairly
well-off. In the latter areas the market economy and industries are
as yet relatively underdeveloped, and most peasants rely on agriculture for their livelihood and are relatively poor.

Another reform which needs to be considered in an examination
of work and the division of work in the countryside since 1978 is the
CCP's new one-child family policy. Under this policy, which was
introduced in 1979, various forms of economic incentives have been
given to couples who, after the birth of their first child, pledge to

have no more, and penalties, often in the form of fines, have been imposed on couples who bear a second or third child.[16] In urban areas, a relatively long history of family planning education, combined with socio-economic pressures for having fewer children, such as housing shortages, has made the implementation of the one-child family policy relatively easy. In rural areas, however, the policy has met with less success. According to 1988 statistics, Chinese couples of child bearing age on average had 2.6 children. The figure for urban college-educated couples was 1. By contrast couples in rural areas had 4.2.[17]

One reason for this discrepancy between urban and rural areas has been that there are few welfare services in the countryside. Most elderly peasants do not receive a pension, and children (or more particularly sons, because under the patrilocal marriage system daughters leave their native village upon marriage) are considered vital for the care they will provide their aging parents. This situation became more critical with the introduction of the rural responsibility system because of the decline in collective welfare systems due to the breakdown of commune management and the reluctance of individual households to contribute to its upkeep.[18]

A second reason for the failure of the one-child family policy in rural areas has been that, to a great extent, the economic prosperity of a rural household depends on the amount of labour power it can muster. Once again, this has become more critical following the introduction of the recent economic reforms, since the closer link between remuneration and work performance, and the diversification of the rural economy mean that labour power can now be used more effectively to generate income. In addition, the increased autonomy of the household relative to the commune and the state has meant that CCP cadres have lost much of their authority over peasants' lives and their exhortations for family planning have often been ignored.

Some people have claimed that having fewer children lessens women's domestic work, thus enabling them to be more involved in the public sphere. One woman wrote, for example,

> the amount of domestic work [a woman has] is dependent, to a great extent, on the number of children [she has] . . . For China's women to be liberated they must practise birth control, otherwise their participation in social production and social affairs will be restricted, and the existing inequalities between men and women will not be overcome.[19]

It might be supposed that such a claim would be used by the CCP to back up its family planning campaign. In fact, however, it has received very little publicity. Ironically, family planning since 1979 has been accompanied by a strong affirmation of the importance of the family and, in particular, of women's work as mothers and domestic workers. Thus, whilst during the Cultural Revolution and the 'Criticize Lin Biao and Confucius' campaign women who devoted too much time to their families were criticized as bourgeois and selfish,[20] in the 1980s the All-China Women's Federation mounted many propaganda campaigns to encourage women to develop a good family life.[21] Whereas during the 1970s it was claimed that 'what men can do (in industry) women can do too', in the media of the 1980s this notion has been rejected as exaggerated[22] and women's work in industry and agriculture has assumed a low profile, while their domestic work, and as an extension their responsibility for social morality, has been seen to be their primary contribution to society. As Hu Yaobang, the then party chairman, put it in his report to the Twelfth National Congress of the CCP in 1982,

> women are not only an important force in national economic construction, they also have a particularly significant role to play in the building of socialist spiritual civilization.[23]

On its own, party ideology admittedly has only a limited influence on rural people's behaviour, but in the case of attitudes toward women and the family it is much strengthened by the fact that it is a reassertion of traditional values, rather than a challenge to them.

CHANGES TO THE PUBLIC/PRIVATE DICHOTOMY

Domestic work

In rural China of the 1980s domestic work continued to be women's work. In my investigation of sixty-five rural households in Beijing, Shandong and Sichuan in 1989, I found that, almost without exception, the bulk of domestic work was done by women. Furthermore, both party ideology and pressures resulting from the economic reforms outlined above combined to create a widespread increase in the number of women whose *only* or *primary* occupation was domestic work. A recent article about the structure of women's work in rural Sichuan claimed, for example, that before

126

the introduction of the rural responsibility system, except for the elderly and the weak, women's primary occupation was work for the commune, and domestic work was always secondary to this. Today, however, domestic work is the primary occupation (in that they devote more time to this work than to any other) of 23.38 per cent of all women, 63.14 per cent of women over the age of 55, 15.98 per cent of middle-age women and 20.88 per cent of young women.[24]

One of the economic factors behind this trend is the appearance of a large amount of 'surplus labour' in agriculture in many areas, due to improved productivity stimulated by the rural responsibility system and, to a lesser extent, mechanization. Many Chinese analysts see this generation of surplus labour in a positive light, for it is the starting point for the development of industries and other non-agricultural ventures.[25] However, in the early stages of reform, and even today in the least developed areas, not all the surplus workers from agriculture can be absorbed in other forms of (paid) employment. One report claimed, for example, that in Huairen county, Shandong, shortly after the introduction of the responsibility system (but before 1983 when new lines of production were developed) one-third of all labourers were no longer needed in agriculture and the majority of women had no paid work.[26] Similarly, a survey carried out in 1986 in Heze prefecture, a very poor region also in Shandong, found that local enterprises were developing very slowly and there were no outlets for surplus female labour. Women were keen to earn money, but lack of funds, skills, avenues for work and sales outlets thwarted their enthusiasm.[27] In areas inland and far from large cities, in particular, markets, services and transport are all relatively underdeveloped. Many such areas still have few local industries and those that exist often employ workers on only a part-time, temporary basis. In addition, peasants in these areas lack the capital and the skills necessary for non-agricultural work. All this makes it difficult for peasants in less-developed areas to find non-agricultural employment, either in their home county or elsewhere, or to start up their own non-agricultural ventures. Nevertheless, many peasant households have found it advantageous to withdraw surplus workers from agriculture (rather than that person be underemployed in the fields as would have happened under the commune system), so that they can do the household's domestic work and perhaps rear some pigs and chickens or other domestic livestock, grow some vegetables or do some craftwork as a subsidiary occupation.

127

Most have found it natural that if someone is to be withdrawn (or kept out of) agriculture to concentrate on domestic work that person should be a woman, preferably an older woman if there is more than one woman in the house. An article written in 1979 claimed, for example, that where mechanization resulted in a reduced need for labour in agriculture women were the first to lose their jobs.[28] This is because, on the one hand, since childcare is perceived to be women's responsibility it is more efficient for women, if they have children, to take charge of affairs around the home that can be fitted in with childcare, than for men to leave the fields to undertake such work. On the other hand, it is often perceived that women are less capable of agricultural work than men because they are physically weaker and because they are generally less well trained than men. The above-mentioned article claimed, for example, that women were rarely given agricultural jobs involving new machinery. This was partly because young women were not given technical training, since it was considered that their skills would be 'lost' when they married into another village.[29] Wolf, in her survey conducted in 1980, confirmed this and found also that women were barred from a number of agricultural tasks because they were deemed too heavy for them (though in many cases the work women *did* do was even heavier).[30]

Domestic sidelines and the courtyard economy

As mentioned, many women whose primary occupation is domestic work also spend time in activities previously termed 'domestic sidelines'. One step further on, is the situation in slightly more developed areas in which markets and services have improved and large numbers of women have developed their domestic sideline activities into significant income-earning ventures. Many households in these areas have found it profitable to have young women undertake domestic sidelines as their primary occupation, while domestic work is done either by the same young women or by older women and children, and agriculture is undertaken by the man or men of the household. One article written in 1984 claimed, in fact, that this was the most common sexual division of work in peasant households at that time (though no mention was made of domestic work).[31] In order to understand the implications of this division of labour in terms of changes in the public/private dichotomy, it is necessary to examine the recent history of domestic sidelines and associated ideological trends.

Whereas for much of the period between the 1950s and the late 1970s domestic sidelines were barely tolerated by the CCP and during the Cultural Revolution and the Gang of Four era they were repressed as 'capitalist tails',[32] at the Third Plenum, December 1978, the CCP reaffirmed commune members' rights to undertake domestic sidelines, stating that

> small plots of land for private use by commune members, their domestic side occupations and village fairs are legitimate adjuncts of the socialist economy.[33]

Following the breakdown of the commune system the distinction between 'domestic sidelines' and commune work became an anachronism. In the media, the term 'domestic sidelines' continued to be used occasionally throughout the 1980s. However, from about 1983 another term, which once more stressed the physical location of such work in the private sphere rather than its form of management, began to appear more frequently. This was the 'courtyard economy' (*xiao yuan jingji* or *tingyuan jingji*), which referred to vegetable and fruit growing, animal husbandry, handicraft production and services (including commerce and small-scale tourism) undertaken in the home or courtyard.[34] Significantly, activities which had been included in a 1978 definition of 'domestic sidelines'[35] but which involved travelling and work at a distance from the home, such as fishing and hunting, are generally not seen as part of the 'courtyard economy'.

Since 1978 the CCP has made a strong push, both in terms of ideology and practice, to link domestic sidelines and the courtyard economy with women. One article published in 1988 claimed, for example, that in Pingyuan county, Shandong province, 100,000 women participated in the courtyard economy. It said that

> in rural commodity production the county government found that because of their physiological, psychological and biological characteristics women were not being made full use of. In order that this group of people might also contribute to commodity production, the county government called on women to develop the courtyard economy, this being particularly suited to women's special characteristics.[36]

One of the most important aspects of the Women's Federation's work in rural areas in recent years has been to implement concrete measures to encourage women in the courtyard economy. It has made links with other bodies to help women obtain bank loans and to assist them with the supply of raw materials and feed for livestock, etc., and with the marketing of their produce.[37] In addition, it has run numerous short-term courses to teach women basic skills in sewing, handicraft production and animal husbandry. In 1987, for example, the Women's Federation in one county in Hebei ran 552 classes to teach women skills to be used in the courtyard economy. Some 58,000 women participated in the classes.[38]

In the media numerous articles have appeared in which women who had earnt large incomes by working in the courtyard economy have been raised for emulation. For example, in 1979 the official journal of the Women's Federation *Zhongguo Funü* ran an article entitled 'Mrs Xie Fu and her long haired rabbits' about a sixty-one year old woman whose income from selling fur from rabbits that she looked after amounted to 530 yuan in 1978, which was enough to buy four months worth of grain for her eleven family members when the harvest failed, to buy the family's condiments and to pay for the children's education expenses that year.[39] An editorial accompanying the article praised ventures such as this for helping the state's export trade, providing manure, increasing collective and individual income and helping to advance the diversification of the economy. It called on its readers to 'wholeheartedly support and encourage it'.[40]

In many examples such as this, it is assumed not only that domestic sidelines benefit society, but also that the income a woman earns by working in domestic sidelines or the courtyard economy improves her status and welfare. For example, in one article published in 1985 it was claimed that in one township in Lichuan county, Jiangxi province, women now have an important role in the commodity economy, particularly in domestic sidelines and this 'has changed the structure of the family economy and has improved the women's own political status'.[41]

I would argue, however, that the encouragement of domestic sidelines and the courtyard economy as being particularly suited and beneficial to women has masked, and in fact further contributed to, a number of problems for women. One problem has been that although some women have earnt substantial incomes through their work in the courtyard economy, in many cases such work is the most poorly remunerated of all that is available (not including domestic work) and is tedious, undercapitalized and done in poor working conditions.[42] Encouragement of women's work in the courtyard economy has masked the fact that, as I have shown, such work has been developed by women in a context in which they are losing their jobs in agriculture and have no alternative sources of remunerated work. The Women's Federation's emphasis on training women for the courtyard economy and claims that women are particularly suited to such work may have helped women to make the best of this situation, but they have left unchallenged the public/private division whereby such a situation was originally justified, and have helped instead to perpetuate it.

A further problem with the recent encouragement of women's work in the courtyard economy has been the over-simplistic link made between income and status and the lack of consideration of power relations within the household. Yet, there are numerous instances in which, even though a woman's work in the courtyard economy generates a large proportion of the household income, she has no control over that income and little say in the household's use of resources. Those decisions are made by the male head of the household.[43] While the commune system did not eliminate the male household head's authority, it did reduce it by taking from him the major decisions over labour allocation and income distribution. The rural responsibility system, however, restored that decision-making power to the male head of the household. That power has been underpinned by women's relative insecurity in the household due to the patrilocal marriage system.

In addition, in some cases women's work in the courtyard economy has itself further reinforced men's authority. As Davin has pointed out, under the commune system the majority of women worked in the fields with women and men from other households, but under the new system many women working in the courtyard economy have had fewer opportunities to communicate with people outside their household.[44] This is particularly true of women whose work in the courtyard economy is solely for household consumption. An important part of the reform programme has been to encourage, once more, the commoditization of produce from the courtyard economy and its integration into a market economy. However, in many cases where a woman's produce is exchanged in the market her contact with those outside her household is still limited, because it is not she who purchases raw materials, arranges loans or business deals and sells the produce, but rather her husband or father.

When I discussed this with peasants and grass-roots cadres, most said that this is because of the continued dominance of the idea that while private affairs are managed by women, public affairs are a man's realm. There were some interesting variations in the elaborations given, however. One person in Xindu county, Sichuan, told me that in local rural markets women sell fruit, vegetables, chickens and handicrafts, but they do not sell pigs or pork because the pigs are too heavy for them to cart to market and too difficult to chop. Many people said that while women might séll small amounts of produce at the local market or from their home, it is generally the men who investigate markets, and make business deals and large sales because all this involves travelling long distances from home and women do not travel. One local cadre in Jinniu, a suburban county of Chengdu, said, however, that the fact that it is men who do business deals has nothing to do with travelling, since in that county there is little travelling involved. The main reason is that women do not smoke or drink, so it is difficult for them to discuss business.[45]

Specialized households

A small proportion of women have been able to develop their courtyard economies into 'specialized households' (*zhuanyehu*). Specialized households are rural households which derive most of their income from just one form of production. Many of them started out as households engaging in both agriculture and domestic sidelines. Then, finding the 'sidelines' to be most profitable, they concentrated on turning them into their major line of production.[46] Perhaps because of this origin, a fairly large proportion of specialized households are run by women. According to an investigation carried out by the Women's Federation, in fourteen regions specialized households run by women (*funü wei zhu de zhuanyehu*) comprise 35 per cent to 40 per cent of all specialized households and in some developed regions the figure is as high as 55 per cent.[47] The total number of specialized households is relatively small, however. One report claimed that at the end of 1987 there were 3.98 million rural specialized households in China.[48]

Particular instances cited in the media suggest that a woman running a specialized household is in control of most aspects of the production process, including contracting with other bodies, taking out loans and being responsible for investments and the sale of produce.[49] In addition, some women running specialized households achieve positions of considerable status in their village by employing other people, by teaching others their skills or helping them to set up their own businesses[50] and by joining the party or receiving 'labour model' status.[51]

It might be supposed then, that women running specialized households are breaking down the public/private division of labour, both in terms of the work they do and in terms of their social status. There are a number of caveats to be made to this proposition, however. In the first place, there are considerable variations in meaning attached to the term 'running a specialized household' and in the powers and responsibilities a woman in this position has. In Beijing and Shandong the women running specialized households that I interviewed were middle-aged married women whose husbands were cadres, township enterprise workers or contract workers working away from home. They did seem to be in control of their line of production, and in Huairou county, Beijing, one of the counties I visited, I was told that in an investigation in 1988 of 403 specialized households run by women it was found that 65 per cent of the women earnt incomes higher than their husbands and in 80 per cent of the households the women managed all financial matters.[52] In Sichuan, however, the situation was somewhat different. Women running specialized households did most of the work, and it was they who had the technical skills required, for example, to raise chickens. However, in some cases their husband was also involved and, in keeping with the traditional public/private gender division of labour, it was he who arranged loans, signed contracts, sought business, and in general was the household representative to the outside world.[53] Researchers in Chengdu told me that in other cases where the husband works in another line of business the fact that a woman runs a specialized household tells one very little about her status, for the man might still be the household's business representative and major decision maker. It does not even necessarily mean that her income is higher than her husband's. Often, specialized households are defined locally in terms of a standard of output. For example, 5,000 chickens might be the standard set for a chicken-raising specialized household, but in any one household the income from this number of chickens might in fact be less than the man's income in another line of production.[54]

It must also be recognized that the people who run specialized households are a privileged minority among peasants. Many have been able to get loans and arrange contracts, either because they have relatives who are cadres, or because they are known to be exceptionally hardworking.[55] They also tend to have above average levels of education (some were young people educated in urban areas and then 'sent down' to the countryside during the Cultural Revolution). An investigation of 212 specialized households run by women in Huaide county, Jilin province, found, for example, that 38 per cent of the women had junior or senior secondary school education and 95 per cent had upper primary school education. Among all women in the county aged 18 to 45, however, 57 per cent were illiterate or had junior primary school education.[56]

Lack of education is likely to limit any increase in the number of women running specialized households, either in terms of absolute numbers or as a proportion of the total. According to the 1982 census 49 per cent of rural women aged twelve and above were illiterate, compared to 21 per cent of rural men, and at each level of education there were fewer women than men.[57] Since then there have been numerous reports in the Chinese media of both a decline in overall school attendance rates and an increase in the inequality between male and female attendance rates. The main reason given is that since the introduction of the rural responsibility system many families have been withdrawing their children from school so that they can contribute to the household economy, either by doing domestic work or by working in agriculture, domestic sidelines or industry. Among children withdrawn for this reason, girls far outnumber boys. A further reason given for the decline in school attendance rates is that there has been a decline in collective funding for education and, as a result, school fees have increased and for some households have become prohibitively expensive.[58]

In fact, the emergence of specialized households run by women is being overshadowed by other changes associated with increasing industrialization. The same aspects of development that have made possible the emergence of specialized households in some areas, i.e. the accumulation of capital, the development of a market network and transport and service facilities, and the removal of restrictions on labour movement, have also resulted in an increase in the number of jobs available in individually owned businesses (*geti qiye*) and township industries (*xiangzhen qiye*) and in a migration of rural workers to industries in cities and in the special economic zones on the east coast.

Industry

As the economy has developed, more rural men than women have been employed in industry and there have been significant differences between their occupations – differences once more related to a public/private division of labour.[59] Thus, in the late 1980s men formed the majority of rural workers in urban industry or in other non-agricultural work such as transport or construction work which was likely to take them away from home for extended periods of time. Women were more likely to work in industries run by their village or a nearby township Nationally, women now form about one-third of the labour force in such industries, though about 80 per cent of those involved are in services or light industry.[60] In most cases such work is part-time or temporary and done in conjunction with domestic work, domestic sidelines and agriculture. Often it is done as outwork in the woman's home. In an article published in 1984, it was claimed that since the introduction of the rural responsibility system in Xinjin county in Sichuan, many men have gone to work outside the area. Women now perform 60 per cent of work in agriculture and more than 80 per cent of work in domestic sidelines.[61] Another article published in 1987 claimed that in well-off areas in Shandong, after the introduction of the rural responsibility system the majority of men went away to work in commerce or become workers in city factories. The women stayed in the villages and undertook agriculture, domestic sidelines and domestic work and worked in village-run factories.[62]

There are also peasant women working away from their home village. There are, for example, approximately 3 million peasant women working as nannies in cities around China.[63] However, almost all these women are young and unmarried and return to their home village after a few years at most. In Shenzhen and other special economic zones the majority of workers are young women from outlying rural areas. Again, however, they are almost all hired as temporary workers and return to their villages after a few years.[64]

One major reason for the emergence of such a division of work has been the strong identification of women with childcare and other domestic work and, as a result, a tie, both in ideology and in practice, of women to the home. This tie has functioned in two different ways. On the one hand, peasant households (and individual women themselves) have found it preferable that women undertake work that can be accommodated with their domestic

135

responsibilities. On the other hand, industries have taken advantage of this preference. In the case of outwork it has meant that enterprises have not had to pay for the provision of machines, buildings and services, such as childcare services, because it is all provided by the women themselves in their own homes. Both township enterprises and industries in the special economic zones are characterized by low skill and low wage levels and a vulnerability to market fluctuations. Young women are regarded as an ideal workforce for such industries because they themselves see their work as only temporary. This makes it less likely that they will fight against exploitation and means that it is easier to sack them in times of business contraction. In the special economic zones women hired as temporary workers fall outside all the labour insurance and social benefit schemes designed for contract and permanent workers. Their employers do not have to provide housing, medical benefits, retrenchment benefits, family benefits, retirement benefits or maternity leave.[65] A report on industries in Shenzhen published in 1988 claimed that 'in Shenzhen today exploitation not only exists – it is protected and respected'. It cited an example of a factory which employs women to make artificial flowers:

> In this factory the workers' living and working conditions are unbelievably bad. They work 14 to 15 hours a day. . . . Child workers receive far less wages than adult workers. Although their average monthly pay is from 80 to 100 yuan, they have to pay for room and board, utilities and training, leaving them with only a meagre amount. A little girl from Guangxi who injured her hand receives only 10 yuan a month. She sadly told me: I cannot even afford to pay my way back home.[66]

The situation may not be as extreme as this in most township enterprises. However, there has been concern on the part of the Women's Federation in recent years over poor working conditions and a neglect of women's welfare and health in township industries in which women form the majority of the workforce.[67]

There are other factors involved in the difference between women's and men's employment in industry which have more to do with a new tie being made between women and agriculture. Thus, whereas in its early stages, reform resulted in a movement of women out of agriculture, in later stages and in the more developed areas there has been a complete turn around, so that women now form the backbone of the agricultural workforce (and also do domestic work, domestic sidelines and part-time work in township industries) while men move out of agriculture to take up newly available opportunities in urban industry, transport, commerce and construction work in other counties.

In a survey report published in 1987, the author described this situation in rural Sichuan in terms of a new form of the traditional gender division of labour exemplified in the phrases 'men plough, women weave' (*nan geng, nu zhi*) and 'men work outside, women work inside' (*nan zhu wai, nu zhu nei*). Nowadays women's 'inside' work includes not just domestic work and domestic sidelines but also work in agriculture. Men's 'outside' work involves leaving family and land and going to work in industry or in other non-agricultural activities such as forestry, fishing, transport or construction.[68]

This conceptual shift of agriculture from the public or 'outside' sphere to the private or 'inside' sphere, or to put it another way, the expansion of the concept of the private sphere, coincided with first, a change in perception of what work is suitable for women and second, a downgrading of the status of agricultural work. Before the availability to many peasants of work in industry, a restriction of women's participation in agriculture was justified by claims that such work was both too heavy and too skilled for women. Now that possibilities for non-agricultural work are opening up, however, agricultural work is considered the least desirable, being 'bitter' (*ku*) and 'tiring' (*lei*) work, and all those who can are leaving.[69] This situation is being accompanied by new claims about the gender division of labour. The author of one article published in 1986 said, for example, that when industries were developed,

> in determining who did what work within the household, not only levels of skills but also biological characteristics had to be taken into account, so it was natural that women, the young and the old should stay on the land and young, fit men should go into industry.[70]

At the same time, the whole thrust of economic reforms since 1978 has been based on the assumption that 'development' means the development of industry and a shift of the majority of the workforce out of agriculture. Thus, the concentration of women in agriculture means that they are being left behind in the backwaters, as it were, excluded from what is perceived to be the most important part of the economy.

Even as the identification of women with agriculture is being made, however, it is also being challenged. Concern is sometimes voiced by economists, for example, that the 'feminization' of agriculture is causing a decline in agricultural productivity.[71] An interesting article written by Shi Chenglin claimed that in 1987 rural China had entered a second period of movement of labour out of agriculture into other forms of production (the first period was 1979–86) and proposed that in this second period women should be the driving force. Shi claimed that

> agriculture in China still requires heavy physical labour. If the majority of male labour leaves agriculture this will be hard on women and detrimental to agriculture. Whereas if the majority of women were to move out of agriculture, old members of the household could take over domestic work or else the women could move into industry nearby and still do some domestic work after their eight hours in industry.[72]

If, as Shi suggests, a division of labour emerges such that men work in agriculture and women in industry, it will be interesting to see what happens with regard to the public/private dichotomy.

CONCLUSION

Rural reforms introduced in 1978 resulted in a number of changes to women's and men's work and to the gender division of labour. In some cases women have been able to take advantage of these changes to enhance their position in society in terms of relations with others and access to and control of resources. On the whole, however, the reforms have not led to an improvement in rural women's status, either within the household or in the wider community. Rather, certain aspects of women's subordination have intensified and others have been altered or broken down, only to form new patterns of subordination. In this chapter I have argued that central to this process has been, on the one hand, a public/private dichotomy and, on the other, a continual redefining of the concepts of 'public' and 'private' work.

An ideology in which women are associated most strongly with work in the 'private' sphere and men with work in the 'public' sphere has gained strength in the last decade, being bolstered by claims in the media that this is a 'natural' division of labour. The responsibility for 'private' domestic work has lain entirely in the hands of women, and this in turn has ensured that their involvement in the 'public' sphere of work has been restricted where the availability of such work has been limited. Thus, at the time when the introduction of the rural responsibility system resulted in a reduced need for labour in agriculture, but alternative forms of employment were as yet scarce, women were the first to lose their jobs in the fields.

Later, when the reforms generated new avenues for employment and women moved into the 'public' sphere of work in large numbers, the continuing tie between women and 'private' domestic work was used by employers to maximize their profits and minimize the benefits to women. Many women have been employed, for example, to do outwork in their own home. This has meant that they have also been able to attend to their domestic work responsibilities and the employer has not had to provide machinery, work space or welfare services. Other women, especially young unmarried women, have formed a large proportion of temporary workers in township industries and especially in industries in the special economic zones where employers have sought docile workers who can be paid low wages and few welfare benefits and who can be retrenched in times of business contraction.

While the association of women with 'private' work and men with 'public' work has been strengthened, the boundaries between 'public' and 'private' spheres are also changing, and it is through this change also that women's subordination is being transformed and re-formed. Thus, while in the early stages of reform agriculture was considered 'public' work and was dominated by men, the expansion of opportunities for industrial employment has led to a shift of men out of agriculture into more prestigious industrial jobs, while women are being left behind in agriculture. The devaluation of agricultural work and the corresponding concentration of women in such work has been achieved through, and legitimized by, the re-characterization of agriculture as 'private' work and, ironically, following this re-characterization, the same references to women's biological characteristics that were used as a justification for the restriction of women's employment in agricultural work are now being used to justify a concentration of women in such work.

NOTES AND REFERENCES

1 This chapter draws on findings from five months' fieldwork in China in 1989 funded by an Adelaide University Overseas Travel Grant and a D. R. Stranks Fellowship.

2 Michelle Zimbalist Rosaldo, 'Woman, culture and society: a theoretical overview' in Michelle Zimbalist Rosaldo and Louise Lamphere, eds, *Woman, Culture and Society*, Stanford, Stanford University Press, 1974, pp. 17–42.

3 E.g. Carol MacCormack and Marilyn Strathern, eds, *Nature, Culture and Gender*, Cambridge, Cambridge University Press, 1980, and Caroline Ralston, 'Deceptive dichotomies: Private/public, and nature/culture. Gender relations in Tonga in the early contact period', *Australian Feminist Studies*, no. 12, Summer 1990, pp. 65–82.

4 J John. L. Buck, *Land Utilization in China*, New York, Council on Economic and Cultural Affairs Inc., 1956, p. 289.

5 Ibid., p. 293 and p. 298

6 In a study of rural households in Ding county, Hebei province conducted between 1926 and 1933, Sidney Gamble found that 88 per cent of home industry workers were engaged in spinning or weaving or both; 95 per cent of spinners were women and 82 per cent of weavers were women. Sidney Gamble, *Ting Hsien. A North China Rural Community*, Stanford, Stanford University Press, 1954, pp. 288–301.

7 Jan Myrdal, *Report from a Chinese Village*, New York, Random House Inc., 1965, pp. 229–39, and Delia Davin, *Woman-Work. Women and the Party in Revolutionary China*, Oxford, Clarendon Press, 1976, p. 123.

8 *ZGFN*, no. 3, 1962, editorial.

9 This was reflected in the peasant saying 'We depend on the collective for grain, but on ourselves for cash', *RMRB*, 20 November 1964, p. 2.

10 Frederick Engels, *The Origin of the Family, Private Property and the State*, Moscow, Progress Publishers, 1977, p. 158.

11 Erika Platte, 'The Private Sector in China's Agriculture: An Appraisal of Recent Changes', *The Australian Journal of Chinese Affairs*, no. 10, 1983, p. 82.

12 Op. cit., p. 158.

13 Ibid.

14 See Alison Jaggar, *Feminist Politics and Human Nature*, Sussex, Rowman and Allenheld, 1983, p. 72.

15 Nongcun Jiaocha Lingdao Xiaozu Bangongshi, *Nongcun Zai Biange Zhong Qianjin – lai zi jiceng de diaocha baogao* (The Rural Areas Advance in the Course of Change – Reports on Grass-Roots Investigations), Beijing, Nongye Chubanshe, 1987.

16 For details see Elisabeth Croll, Delia Davin and Penny Kane, eds, *China's One-Child Family Policy*, London, Macmillan, 1985, Introduction, pp. 1–36.

17 *SWB*, 7 April 1989, FE/0428/B2/3.

18 In a few places the problem has been mitigated recently by the establishment of pension schemes for elderly peasants by local government and private insurance companies, *NMRB*, 29 December 1988, p. 3.

Concern over the failure of the one-child family policy combined with greater wealth may make such schemes more common in the future, but they are unlikely to become widespread among peasants for a long time.

19 *RMRB*, 20 January 1981, p. 5.
20 Elisabeth Croll, *Feminism and Socialism*, London, Routledge and Kegan Paul, 1978, pp. 311–6 and pp. 323–9.
21 Marlyn Dalsimer and Laurie Nisonoff, 'The new economic readjustment policies: implications for Chinese urban working women', *Review of Radical Political Economics*, vol. 16, no. 1, 1984, p. 35.
22 See, for example, *Funü Shenghuo (Women's Life)*, no. 1, 1986.
23 Quoted in Jean C. Robinson, 'Of women and washing machines: employment, housework and the reproduction of motherhood in socialist China', *The China Quarterly*, no. 101, March 1985, p. 51.
24 Wang Shuhui 'Sichuan nongcun funü de zhiye jiegou' ('The structure of women's work in rural Sichuan') *Hunyin yu jiating (Marriage and the Family)*, no. 11, 1987, pp. 20–9.
25 *ZGFN*, no. 10, 1984, p. 5.
26 *FNGZ*, no. 9, 1984, p. 24.
27 *FNGZ*, no. 7, 1986, p. 12.
28 *ZGFN*, no. 5, 1979, pp. 38–40.
29 Ibid.
30 Margery Wolf, *Revolution Postponed: Women in Contemporary China*, Stanford, Stanford University Press, 1985, pp. 84–5.
31 *Zhongguo Nongmin Bao* (Chinese Peasant Daily), 30 September 1984, p. 3.
32 Elisabeth Croll 'The promotion of domestic sideline production in rural China 1978–79', in Jack Gray and Gordon White, eds, *China's New Development Strategy*, London, Academic Press, 1982, p. 237.
33 Erika Platte, op. cit., p. 83.
34 *NMRB*, 17 July 1986.
35 In 1978 a reporter form the New China News Agency claimed that 'According to the provisions of the Party's current policies commune members are allowed to keep a small number of pigs, sheep, rabbits, chickens, ducks, geese and other domestic animals; they may also keep sows; they may engage in small-scale sideline production such as weaving and knitting, embroidery, collecting wild crops, fishing, hunting, bee-keeping and so on which are not suitable for collective or unified undertaking; and they may plant and own bamboos, trees and fruit trees in front of and behind their houses. As to what crops to plant on private plots, the commune members have the right to make their own arrangements according to their own needs', *SWB*, 27 April 1978, FE/5799/B2/8.
36 *NMRB*, 17 May 1988, p. 2.
37 See, for example, *ZGFN*, no. 10, 1984, p. 41, and *NMRB*, 18 December 1985, p. 2.
38 *RMRB*, 10 October 1987, p. 4.
39 *ZGFN*, no. 3, 1979, pp. 8–9.
40 *ZGFN*, no. 3, 1979, p. 4.

41 *NMRB*, 3 March 1985.
42 Delia Davin 'The implications of contract agriculture for the employment and status of Chinese peasant women', in Stephen Feuchtwang, and Athar Hussain, eds, *Transforming China's Economy in the Eighties Vol.1: The Rural Sector, Welfare and Employment*, Colorado, Westview Press, 1988, p. 140.
43 Personal interviews, Sichuan, 1989.
44 Ibid.
45 Ibid.
46 Wang Guichen *et al.*, *Smashing the Communal Pot. Formulation and Development of China's Rural Responsibility System*, Beijing, New World Press, 1985, pp. 86–7.
47 *RMRB*, 31 October 1986, p. 4.
48 *SWB*, 5 October 1988, FE/WOO46/A/1. The figures given here can be used as only a very rough guide, as definitions of 'specialized households' vary widely.
49 For example, *NMRB*, 12 June 1985, and *Zhongguo Nongmin Bao*, 26 June 1984.
50 For example, *ZGFN*, no. 5, 1986, p. 12.
51 For example, *NMRB*, 12 June 1986, p. 2.
52 Interview with Zhang Fengyu, head of Huairou County Women's Federation, 6 September 1989.
53 Interviews with rural women in Xindu, Jinniu and Wenjiang counties, Sichuan, October 1989.
54 Interviews with Ran Moying, Research Office of the Sichuan Women's Federation, and Li Dongshan, Institute of Sociology, Sichuan Academy of Social Sciences, October 1989.
55 Interviews with rural women and cadres, Beijing, Shandong and Sichuan, 1989
56 *FNGZ*, no. 9, 1984, pp. 14–15.
57 *Zhongguo Renkou Nianjian (Almanac of China's Population)*, Beijing, Shehui Kexue Wenxian Chubanshe, 1986, pp. 314–15.
58 *NMRB*, 12 November 1988, *Renkou yu Jingji (Population and the Economy)*, February 1988, p. 2, and *Zhongguo Funü Bao*, 8 April 1988, p. 1.
59 These differences also relate to a heavy/light dichotomy: men predominate in heavy industry while women are concentrated in light industry and services.
60 *NMRB*, 27 November 1986, p. 4.
61 *Zhongguo Nongmin Bao*, 29 April 1984, p. 1.
62 *Zhongguo Funü Bao*, 16 October 1987, p. 1.
63 *NMRB*, 11 January 1989, p. 3.
64 Leung Wing-yue, *Smashing the Iron Pot. Workers and Unions in China's Market Socialism*, Hong Kong, Asia Monitor Resource Center, 1988, pp. 151–4.
65 Ibid., p. 152.
66 *SWB*, 25 August 1988, FE/0239/B2/1. A similar situation is to be found in the labour intensive export industries of southeast Asia. See Noleen Heyzer, 'From rural subsistence to an industrial peripheral workforce:

an examination of female Malaysian migrants and capital accumulation in Singapore', in Lourdes Beneria, ed., *Women and Development. The Sexual Division of Labour in Rural Societies,* New York, Praeger, 1982, pp. 179–202, and Rachel Grossman, 'Women's place in the integrated circuit', *Southeast Asian Chronicle,* no. 66, January–February 1979, pp. 2–17.

67 For example, *Zhongguo Funü Bao,* 5 October 1987, p. 1 and *RMRB,* 15 October 1988, p. 4.

68 Wang Shuhui, op. cit., pp. 20–9.

69 Interviews with twelve young rural women working as nannies in Beijing, August 1989.

70 *Hunyin yu Jiating,* no. 5, 1986, p. 13.

71 *NYJJWT,* no. 10, 1986, pp. 16–18.

72 Shi Chenglin 'Lun xiandai nongcun funü zai laoli zhuanyi zhong de diwei he zuoyong' ('A discussion of the status and function of rural women in the present movement of labour'), *Fujian Luntan: Jingji, Shehui Ban* (Fujian Tribune: Economy and Society Edition), no. 9, 1987, pp. 54–6.

7

A CONFLICT OF INTERESTS

Current problems in educational reform

Zhang Ning

On 22 December 1978, educational reform was launched as one of the strategic tasks for the modernization programme and for economic reform in China. The communiqué of the Third Plenary Session of the Eleventh Central Committee emphasized the importance of strengthening scientific and educational work to meet the needs of modernization.[1] Since that time, educational development has been repeatedly stressed and a series of policies and regulations have been adopted to revive the education system crushed by the anarchic forces of the Cultural Revolution. On 20 October 1984, the Third Plenum of the Twelfth National Congress of the CCP adopted a further major decision on the economic reforms, in which educational development was again stressed as one of the urgent strategic tasks. The decision said

> Science, technology and education play very important parts in the development of the domestic economy. With the economic reforms, science and technology systems and the educational system are becoming strategic tasks which need to be addressed urgently.[2]

The Chinese leadership sees the development of science and technology and the development of education as decisive for modernization programmes, and, of these, education is the foundation.[3]

In May 1985, the Central Committee held a national conference on education. At this conference, a decision was made to reform the educational structure and to invigorate the educational system at all levels. Deng Xiaoping, in his address to the conference, said the rationale for this reform was that China's overall strength, as well as its economic growth, increasingly depended on the skills of its workers and the quality of its intellectuals.[4] He also pointed out that

144

education should be geared towards modernization, the world and the future.[5] These ideas have become the guiding principles of educational reform.

Ten years have passed. The situation in China's education, however, is not the ideal it was expected to be. Many old problems remain and new problems have emerged. China still has 220 million illiterates,[6] and over 2 million new illiterates are added each year.[7] There is a great shortage of education funds; the country invests only 3.7 per cent of its GNP in education, less than 120 other countries.[8] Schools and universities (especially schools) are poorly equipped; books and resource materials are in great shortage. Teachers are the country's third worst paid group, earning less than factory workers and most peasants.[9] Many teachers have no incentive to stay in teaching and have been leaving their jobs or seeking second occupations. The devaluation of knowledge and the belief in the uselessness of education (*dushu wuyong lun*) that prevailed in China during the Cultural Revolution have gained ground again in people's minds. More than 30 million children dropped out from primary and secondary schools between 1980 and 1987,[10] and the drop-out rate rose over the years 1988–89. Thousands of college students and postgraduate students have followed suit. Universities' enrolment plans do not satisfy the requirements of the economy.[11] Courses are offered according to what is available, not what is needed, and graduates become unemployed or cannot find ideal jobs while many employers or institutions are eager to get qualified personnel but cannot find them.[12] The list of problems goes on and on.

These problems have many causes, but the most basic is that people and all levels of leadership do not believe in the importance of education in social and economic development. The idea that the economy comes first and education last still predominates in many people's minds.[13] They are more interested in making instant returns.

At the beginning of 1989, Deng Xiaoping and other state leaders were forced to admit that education had been the biggest failure of the decade.[14] This chapter will examine why that has been so. It will discuss problems in four major aspects of education in China, educational funding, teaching staff, basic education and higher education. It will conclude by examining the consequences of those problems for the reforms.

EDUCATIONAL FUNDING

In the ten years between 1978 and 1988, educational funding increased considerably. In 1988, the state education budget was 32.1 billion yuan, 3.2 times the 1978 figure. A further 6 billion yuan was invested from other sources, such as educational contributions and taxes from industrial enterprises, capital construction funds outside the plan, profits made by school- and university-run enterprises and donations from individuals or collectives. Altogether education received about 38.1 billion yuan.[15] It was anticipated that in 1989 the figure would rise to around 44.1 billion yuan.[16]

However, these funds could not cover all the necessary expenses. China has 228 million students at all levels.[17] Average expenditure is therefore less than 200 yuan for each student. For tertiary education, educational funding is 2,300 yuan per student year, for secondary education 140 yuan and for primary education 60 yuan. In reality, more than 50 per cent of the budget goes on the pay roll of staff members in tertiary institutions and over 80 per cent covers the salaries of school teachers and other staff members. Very little money is left for expenditure on teaching activities. According to one survey, in some areas of the country there are only 5 yuan per student year for secondary schools and only 1 yuan per child year for primary schools.[18] High inflation also devalues the funds. At present there is a shortage of 75 million square metres of school buildings and 13 million sets of school desks and chairs. In addition, 45 million square metres of school buildings which are currently in use are on the point of collapse.[19] Many schools do not have basic teaching equipment. Only 47 per cent of secondary schools and 6 per cent of primary schools are equipped with laboratories. Less than 10 per cent of primary and secondary schools are fully equipped according to teaching requirements.[20] Higher educational institutions are also faced with serious accommodation problems. The majority of universities do not have enough equipment for both teaching and research, and what they do have is usually out of date.[21]

The reasons for the lack of educational funding are mainly ascribed to the fact that all aspects of society need money for reconstruction, while China's economic basis is weak.[22] This is an undeniable fact. One may well ask, however, whether more could not have been done to increase educational funding. Lack of resources is not a new problem that emerged only after the Cultural

Revolution. In China, education has never been given priority.[23] Nobody wants to give priority to education when planning state or provincial budgets because they see education as public welfare, from which little profit can be gained. With economic development given priority, the authorities will invest more money in the areas where they can see immediate results. The statement 'industry and telecommunications come first, finance and commerce second, make what is left do for culture and education'[24] reflects the reality of how education is perceived.

When discussing education as a form of investment, Hough points out

Education leads, or should lead, to a more productive, more efficient, and more usefully employable person and it is therefore clearly of an investment nature.[25]

Education and economic growth are thus closely related. A powerful country with advanced technology and high living standards is characterized by the high level of education of its people. Hough also quotes the mammoth study by Denison of the growth of the economy of the USA for the period of fifty years to 1960. He says

[Denison] derived aggregate production functions (mathematical relationships between economic inputs and outputs) and then examined the remaining or 'unexplained' portion of economic growth in relation to a number of factors, including education. The ensuing calculations arrived at the finding that over the period 1930–60 education contributed as much as 23 per cent of total economic growth, which was more than any other source except for the increase in the labour force in whom the effects of the education were incorporated. When the incidence of population growth was discounted and the result expressed as a per capita basis, the contribution to economic growth from the education system increased to the quite remarkable figure of 42 per cent.[26]

This example cited the USA but economically developed countries in Asia have had similar experience. In Japan, for example, education has attracted a great deal of attention from government and society. This was particularly evident during the early phase of Japan's modernization. After the Sino-Japanese War of 1894–95, the Chinese Qing government was forced to pay compensation of 200 million *liang* (1 *liang* = 50 grams) of silver to the Japanese government. The Japanese Emperor ordered that all the money be spent on education, and that even the most remote country area should have a good school.[27]

Clearly China's government is not prepared to make a similar investment, despite its official view of the importance of the relationship between education and economic growth. And while the excuse might be that China does not have a large sum of compensation from any other country and that there is not enough money to go around, the following figures suggest that to some extent the real position of education in the minds of China's leaders is quite different from the rhetoric and that this may be a more important constraint than the lack of funds.

In the period between 1981 and 1986, about 20 billion yuan (in foreign currency) was spent on imported cars. In 1987, more than 53 billion of public money was spent on entertainment expenses and other benefits and 66.5 billion was spent on luxury consumption items such as cars, televisions and video cameras. In recent years, 1,300 billion has gone on buildings, hotels, and the like.[28] Such large expenditure contrasts with the 38.1 billion yuan spent on education in 1988. Furthermore, even that small amount of funds was not totally spent on education. According to China's Statistical Bureau, in 1986, 420 million yuan of educational funding was diverted by local governments and departments.[29] Some local governments spent large sums of money building modern hotels, theatres and department stores, leaving many school buildings on the point of collapse.

Therefore, the shortage of educational funding in China is not solely a matter of capital shortage. More importantly, it shows the lack of real commitment in tackling educational problems. Although state leaders have repeatedly stressed the importance of educational development for the success of economic development, there is no practical action to achieve it.[30] State government and party leaders have appealed to the whole country to pay attention to educational development, but at the local level many do not see the importance or are not willing to spend money on education when they can make immediate profits in other ways.

China has a very large population and a poor economic base. Sectors like industry, agriculture, transport, telecommunications and municipal works all badly need capital for development. In the circumstances, it is next to impossible for the government to provide a large increase in educational funding.[31] Both government and educationalists agree that educational funding should come from many sources. First, governments at all levels should increase educational budgets along with the development of the economy. This should constitute the major source of educational funding. Local authorities should be allowed to levy extra charges for education. Second, there is a great need to revise social consumption patterns and to encourage more investment in education. State-owned enterprises, public organizations and individuals should be encouraged to run schools. Third, educational structures should be adjusted to achieve the highest return on investment. Schools and universities should make profits from running enterprises on condition that they guarantee their teaching qualities. Finally, students and parents should pay a reasonable amount in administration fees, while students from poor and disadvantaged areas and from low-income families could have subsidies.[32] Whatever measures are to be taken, however, legislation is the most important. Otherwise, their effectiveness is not guaranteed.

TEACHING STAFF

After the Cultural Revolution, there was a great shortage of teachers at all levels. During the Sixth Five-Year Plan period (1979–84) there was an increase of 700,000 teachers. In 1987 the number of staff members in China's educational institutions reached 13,222,000, of whom 10,102,200 were full-time teachers. Compared with the 1978 figures, there was a 2,041,000 increase in staff members, of whom 830,000 were full-time teachers.[33] Various types of teacher training programmes have been conducted. In 1986 national teacher training programmes were started using satellite television. During the Seventh Five-Year Plan period (1985–89) the State Council set aside 1.3 billion yuan for the development of teacher training colleges and schools. At present there are around 490,000 students at some 270 teacher training colleges and normal universities, and these constitute 24 per cent of all tertiary students in China. There are also 1,065 teacher-training schools at senior secondary level with 680,000 students.[34]

However, staffing is still a very big problem. Many schools lack qualified teachers and some remote areas do not have any. Teaching is an unattractive occupation. Teachers do not have the incentive to stay in education, and teacher training universities are more enthusiastic about producing scientists and engineers than

149

teachers. Students at these universities also aspire to non-teaching jobs. They will try every means to avoid working in education, especially teaching at schools. Over the past ten years teacher training universities and schools have failed to attract enough students whose results in the entrance examination was of a sufficiently high standard. Zhejiang Normal University, for example, planned to recruit 550 undergraduate students in 1989, but only about 100 candidates reached the required level. In Hubei province even fewer people applied to enter teacher training colleges or schools.[35]

In many provinces thousands of school teachers have been leaving their posts to go into business. For example, in 1989, 400 teachers in Zhongshan city and over 800 teachers in Dongwan city, both of Guangdong province, left their jobs. In one area 148 schools had to be closed temporarily because teachers had left. As a result about 3,000 children had no school to go to.[36] In Shanghai in 1988, 200 school teachers went overseas as private students and 400 school teachers went into other business. Many of them were key teachers in their schools. According to a random survey in Tianjin, 57 per cent of teachers are not enthusiastic about working in schools.[37] From 1984 to 1987 teachers' colleges and normal universities graduated 120,000 students and over 70,000 secondary school teachers received in-service training. Secondary schools should therefore have had around 200,000 new qualified teachers. However, the numbers of teachers who left their jobs and graduates from teachers' colleges who were not assigned to teach in secondary schools during those three years reached 130,000. During the same three years, vocational schools trained 250,000 people to be junior secondary school teachers and another 250,000 junior secondary school teachers obtained certificates through in-service training. However, the number of teachers who left their jobs and teachers' school graduates who were not assigned to teach in junior secondary schools reached 170,000.[38]

The staff problem is mainly caused by two factors: teachers' incomes and living conditions, and their social status. Although the government has increased average teachers' annual salaries from 582 yuan in 1978 to 1,423 yuan in 1988[39] and tried to improve teachers' living conditions by providing more housing, teachers are still at the bottom of the social order. Salary levels have improved only from the worst to the third worst, and teachers' housing problems are still serious. In Beijing, tertiary pay scales range from about

62 yuan a month for a beginning assistant lecturer to about 300 yuan a month for a full professor. However, a middle-income lecturer earning roughly 140 yuan a month cannot support a family of three at current prices without a second income in the family.[40] School teachers earn much less than tertiary staff members. According to one survey, at the end of 1987 an average household in a higher educational institution had 36.6 square metres of living space, much less than the standard of 56 square metres set by the government. Some 29.7 per cent of tertiary teacher households were waiting for residences to get married or had no residence after getting married and 63.5 per cent of households were overcrowded or not up to the standard.[41] According to a 1988 survey, primary and secondary school teachers in counties, towns and cities had only an average of 29.51 square metres per household, much less than the average of 42.24 square metres per household in the urban population; and 15.42 per cent of teacher families had no residence of their own at all.[42]

For several years, the government has been promising a rationalization of the salary system to improve the payment to those who do mental work compared to those who do manual labour. Educational professionals are supposed to receive substantial increases under this proposal, but there has been no indication of when the new system might be put into effect.[43]

In practice, the improvement of the social status and material income of teachers is in the hands of local authorities. Although central funding is provided for a partial pay rise, local governments have moved very slowly in improving teachers' living standards. Pessimism about the improvement comes from the fact that schools are non profit making, whereas in production units a bonus often constitutes the largest part of one's income. Both central and local governments fear that an improvement in teachers' salary will result in the demands for pay rises by other groups, such as workers, and lead to higher inflation.[44]

One important issue which needs to be mentioned here is the difficulties experienced by teachers in schools run entirely by local people, the so-called *min-ban* teachers. In China there are over 3 million *min-ban* teachers. Of these, 2,894,000 work in rural areas, many of them in very poor and remote regions. These teachers receive much less welfare from the government than state-employed teachers.[45] It is assumed that they will earn more by farming contract land, but as they carry a heavy teaching load, they have no time to farm. Conversely, if they spend time farming they will not have sufficient time and energy for teaching. Many of the *min-ban* teachers are very concerned because their jobs are not secure and they do not enjoy a retirement pension or other benefits received by state teachers. As a result many of them are leaving their posts and this in turn greatly exacerbates the problem of teacher shortages in rural areas.[46] The government is aware of this problem and programmes are now in place to raise the income of *min-ban* teachers and to reduce the ratio of *min-ban* to state teachers.[47] Until the problem is solved, however, the quality of rural education, particularly in remote areas, will continue to suffer.

Teachers' lower social status not only stems from the social perception that teachers' financial income is low, but also from the general view that teaching is simply repetitive skilled work and not a form of specialized creative work. 'Anybody can teach' is a view held by many.[48]

This misconception is not unfounded. After the Cultural Revolution there was a great shortage of teachers. Many newly-employed teachers had not undertaken any professional training and did not even have adequate academic qualifications. In 1988, 11 per cent of teachers in higher institutions did not have the required qualifications. In senior secondary schools 58.7 per cent of the teachers were unqualified, in junior secondary schools 64.4 per cent, and in primary schools 31.9 per cent. Of the 5,940,000 rural primary and secondary teachers, 2,500,000 were not qualified.[49]

Since 1978 teacher training has been one of the government's main efforts to revive education. From 1980 to 1988 over 100,000 tertiary teachers out of a total workforce of 393,200 received training. From 1987 to 1988, 24,000 tertiary teachers were sent overseas to study and 20,000 returned. In September 1986 an examination system for primary and secondary teachers was adopted. By 1988, 68.1 per cent of primary teachers and 35.6 per cent of junior secondary teachers had obtained appropriate academic qualifications.[50] However, there is still a large proportion of unqualified teachers, and, as teaching is an 'iron rice bowl', it is very hard to eliminate them. At the same time, their presence makes it difficult for schools to allocate more qualified teachers. Consequently they still have to teach in classrooms.

In fact student–staff ratios in China are quite low. The existing pupil-teacher ratios, according to World Bank 1985 statistics, were 25:1 in primary and 17.6:1 in junior secondary schools.[51] By 1988 the number of primary and secondary students had decreased, but primary school teachers had increased by 67,500 and junior secondary school teachers by 89,200.[52] This has lead to an even lower student-teacher ratio. Nevertheless, little attention seems to have been paid to this issue. Educational and planning departments continue to send graduates from teachers' colleges to over-staffed schools, whereas remote areas are crying out for teachers and getting very few. As living standards in some rural and remote areas are much lower than those in cities and townships, nobody wishes to be assigned to work there for life. The result, however, is a great waste both in terms of money and time.

Solutions put forward to deal with this problem include practical planning for recruitment and allocation of graduates from teacher training colleges or schools, training more local people to be teachers in rural or remote areas, and encouraging teachers from cities or townships to go and teach in rural areas for a fixed term by raising their salaries and improving their living conditions. It is also believed necessary to create a competitive environment for over-staffed schools in cities. The 'iron rice bowl' should be broken and teachers paid according to their achievements. In some schools, like Beijing No. 8 Secondary School, experiments with this have already been undertaken.[53] It has resulted in more enthusiasm and initiative among teachers. The problem remains, however, that schools cannot dismiss or transfer unqualified teachers and this requires government action.

The evidence indicates that to stabilize teaching staff and to improve teaching quality, the most important thing is to improve teachers' social and economic status. Only when these problems have been solved can teaching become an attractive occupation and can teachers become fully devoted to their careers.

BASIC EDUCATION

The May 1985 Central Committee decision to reform the educational structure laid great stress on the reform of basic education, that is education in primary and junior secondary schools. A target of introducing nine-year compulsory basic education was subsequently adopted by the National Peoples' Congress.[54]

The nine-year compulsory education programme divides the country into areas according to three categories based on their economic and educational conditions. Different timetables have been set for achieving nine-year compulsory education in each of the three types of areas. The first category comprises cities, economically developed areas in the coastal provinces and some parts of the interior. It covers one quarter of the country's population. Junior secondary school education was already universal in most of these areas, while the remainder were required to make it universal by 1990 in accordance with set standards for quality and quantity. The second category is composed of economically semi-developed townships and villages where about half of the country's population resides. These areas must first of all make primary school education universal and bring it up to standard. At the same time, they must prepare to make regular junior secondary school education or junior secondary vocational and technical education universal by around 1995. The third category is made up of economically underdeveloped areas where one quarter of the country's population resides. These areas must, as economic development permits, introduce a variety of measures to spread basic education. The state will do its best to assist these areas in their educational development. The decision emphasizes very strongly that the power for the administration of basic education belongs to local authorities.[55]

Four years later there had been some improvement. According to one report,[56] in 1988 there were 793,300 primary schools with 125,357,800 children. Altogether 1,326 counties out of a total of over 2,000 have been certified by the provincial governments as having universal basic education, a 7 per cent increase over the 1987 figure.[57] In 1990, the figure reached 1,459.[58] Furthermore, some 69.4 per cent of primary school graduates continued their studies in junior secondary schools, a 0.4 per cent increase over the 1987 figure, and a 1.4 per cent increase over that of 1981.[59] In 1990, the proportion of primary school graduates advancing to secondary schools was anticipated to be 74.6 per cent, up 3.1 per cent from 1989.[60]

However, just as many school teachers are trying to leave their jobs, thousands of school children have also been dropping out of schools. In 1988, 4,280,000 children dropped out of primary school. The drop-out rate was 3.3 per cent. Some 2,870,000 students dropped out of junior secondary schools. The drop-out rate was 6.9 per cent.[61] The problem is more serious in country areas, where one-fifth of school-age children are not at school – three times as many as in the cities.[62] New illiterates are thus increasing in number.

Obviously the compulsory education law has not been carried out effectively, and there are two main reasons for this. First, the average person's sense of their legal obligations is weak. Parents regard their children's education as their personal business. Leaders in local areas also have not taken compulsory education seriously. They do not take action against the drop-outs and their parents, and, as noted above, even break the law themselves by diverting educational funds.[63] Some departments even occupy school buildings and students have to study in old and poor buildings. *Zhongguo Jiaoyu Bao* reported in 1985 and 1987 that the leaders of a village in Zhejiang Province sold the village's primary school building and students were forced to study in an old mill. The mill collapsed, six people were killed and sixteen injured.[64] Such examples provide further evidence that in many areas local officials pay no attention to education. Furthermore, there is no system or legal organization to supervise the implementation of the law on nine-year compulsory education.

The second main reason for the failure of the nine-year compulsory education programme is that it is too unrealistic to be implemented.[65] The lack of funds, teacher shortages and many other problems cannot be solved within a short period of time. Without such inputs it will be impossible to realize the programme.

Failure in the implementation of compulsory education and the increasing number of drop-outs from schools also have a number of social causes. The emphasis on money-making that has accompanied the reforms has encouraged people to concentrate on what they can earn. Many parents, especially in country areas, keep their children fully engaged in productive labour, apprenticeships or other work. Some local enterprises run by townships, villages or private entrepreneurs, and businesses run by individual proprietors (*getihu*) violate the law and employ under-age workers. For example, an enterprise in Shenzhen recruited 1,024 teenage workers in one month from the Yulin area in Guangxi. Among them 556 were from secondary school and 468 from primary schools. The youngest worker was only ten years old.[66] In China many peasants still believe that women are inferior to men. Of the 220 million illiterates, women constitute 70 per cent. The *Renmin Ribao* reported that in 1987 there were over 2.7 million school-aged children who did not enter school and that 83 per cent of them were female.[67] Females who start school also drop out later in large numbers. In Gansu, for example, 80 per cent of female students did not finish primary school in 1986, and most of them were from the country areas.[68] In one district in Jiangxi, 85 per cent of child peasants and child businesspersons under fifteen years old were female. The parents of these children usually hold the view that no matter how much schooling a female has, she will be married to another home, so it is not worth educating her. They would rather keep their children home and let them do housework or make money by working in the fields or in business.

The devaluation of knowledge and the phenomenon that 'the more knowledge one has, the poorer one is'[69] also mean that many people do not see the benefit of schooling. A survey in Shanghai revealed that in 1986, the average monthly income of professional and technical personnel was 109.33 yuan – 23.39 yuan lower than the average monthly income of the wage earners of the city.[70] Thus the view that it is better to start making money early than to have more education has become common.[71]

Dropping out is also due to problems within schools. As most schools' major objective is to guarantee that more graduates continue their studies at higher educational institutions, teachers focus their teaching on how to make their students achieve higher marks or better results in the university entrance examinations. The content of learning is usually irrelevant to real life situations or to the students' future careers. This problem is more serious in the countryside. As the general level of teaching is low there, very few children can pass national entrance examinations. Peasant parents do not see any benefit in sending their children to schools, especially children who have little chance to get into colleges, universities or vocational secondary schools. Students who are set unattainable goals soon lose confidence in themselves and interest in studying.[72]

Compulsory education should mean that students do not have to pay tuition fees, but in some areas, especially the poorer ones, schools try to collect funds by making all sorts of charges. It is not uncommon for a primary school child to pay 40 yuan, a junior secondary school student to pay 80 yuan and a senior secondary student to pay 100 yuan each semester.[73] An ordinary family cannot afford to pay so much money. People complain that what their children learn at school is useless in practice and that what children need to learn is not taught at school. Thus, sending children to school, especially at such high cost, is a waste of both money and time.

In discussing the task of education, Hough quoted the Crowther Report as follows:

The task of education in the technological age is thus a double one. On the one hand, there is a duty to set young people on the road to acquiring the bewildering variety of qualifications they will need to earn their living. On the other hand, running through and across these vocational purposes, there is also a duty to remember those other objectives of any education, which have little or nothing to do with vocation, but are concerned with the development of human personality and with teaching the individual to see himself in due proportion to the world in which he has been set.[74]

These two purposes of education are both compelling and important, and China is no exception in the emphasis laid on both dimensions.

For many years China's educational goal has been to train workers with both socialist consciousness and culture. But because basic education in the rural areas has never attracted enough attention and investment, the general educational level of peasants in China remains very low and there is a great shortage of specialized and technical personnel in the countryside. Since 1949, 1,040,000 people have graduated from agricultural colleges or schools, but only 400,000 trained agricultural specialists are employed in agricultural work. Of these 260,000 work in various government institutions and only 150,000 people in production.[75] Economic reforms need more technology and scientific skills. Agricultural production is no exception. In developed countries, 60–80 per cent of agricultural production increase depends on new technology. It is estimated that during the Sixth Five-Year Plan period, the application of science and technology accounted for only 30–40 per cent of the total production increase in China.[76] It is also argued that 70 per cent of the new agricultural technology presently available cannot be popularized. The major reason is that peasants do not have enough knowledge to apply it.[77]

In 1984 a village in Sichuan province had 427 specialized households (*zhuanyehu*) with an average annual income of over 700 yuan per head. Among those households, 30.7 per cent had at least one member with senior secondary school education, 38.6 per cent junior secondary school education and 31.2 per cent primary school education. There was not one household in which all members were illiterates. By contrast, of the 28 poor households (*pinkunhu*), 22 (78.5 per cent) were illiterates or semi-illiterates.[78]

Economic reform makes it more and more important for people to be educated. In the country areas, a large number of peasants are moving away from farming and into construction, transportation and other enterprises. They desperately need knowledge and skills to develop their business. In cities and townships, there are millions of young people waiting for job opportunities. They need special skills to establish their own business or to find employment. Many self-employed people have expressed their eagerness for knowledge in order to develop their business and to survive amid severe competition.[79]

Basic education, therefore, has become very important, and it must meet the needs of social and economic development. In rural areas, in particular, teaching should be adapted to peasants' needs. Vocational and technical subjects which are relevant to the local economic situation will bring benefits. In fact, there is evidence that most parents would be willing to spend money on their children's education if they believed it brought real benefits.[80]

As noted by Hough above, however, basic education is not only to serve the needs of the economy but also has other purposes. In his speech at the National Conference on Education in 1985, Vice-Premier Wan Li said:

> The fundamental aim of the (educational) reform is to raise the quality of the nation and train more qualified people. By 'qualified people', I mean people needed by the new period. Our country is now in a new historical period when another revolution is being carried out to eliminate poverty and backwardness, greatly strengthen democracy and the legal system and build a powerful socialist country with a high level of civilization and democracy. People needed by the new period should have lofty ideals, moral integrity, education and a sense of discipline.[81]

Some Chinese educationalists argue that in recent years the importance of education was often addressed in relation to economic development, but it was ignored in terms of spiritual civilization (*jingshen wenming*). This is also seen as one of the reasons for the failure of educational reform.[82] An economy built on such a basis cannot last in the long run.

The success of China's political and economic reforms depends on the entire Chinese people, not only academics and intellectuals. In this respect, basic education is more important than any other level of education. Unfortunately, the universalization of basic education cannot be realized by an educational system alone; it is related to the total environment. Only when people see that education is closely related to more income and a better life will it be sought after, and only when people's educational levels are raised, can their quality be improved. As discussed below, however, that quality depends not only on whether they receive education but also on how they are educated.

HIGHER EDUCATION

In the past ten years, higher education in China has gone through major changes. The economic reforms have provided unprecedented incentives for the development of universities. In 1988, the number of higher educational institutions reached 1,075, 477 more than in 1978, with 2,066,000 undergraduate students (1.5 times 1978), 113,000 post graduate students (9.4 times 1978) and 635,000 correspondence and evening university students. Including adult educational institutions, there were altogether 4 million students in higher education.[83] From 1978 to 1988, 3,250,000 students graduated; this exceeds the total number of about 3 million graduates during the first 30 years after 1949.[84]

Like basic education, reforms in higher education are also important for economic development. The argument is put that universities in China should have three functions: teaching, research and economic activity, and that institutions of higher learning are obliged to provide the community with advice and the most current information.[85]

Rigid control over such things as personnel, funding, student enrolment, job assignment, capital construction, and foreign academic exchange, however, is an obstacle to such functions. Therefore in 1985 the National Conference on Education decided that higher education should be given autonomy in these areas.[86] This flexibility provided many opportunities for university development.

Before the reforms, universities and colleges were run by either the national or provincial governments. National institutions, which are located in different parts of the country, were financed and administered by the central ministries. They recruited students nationally and graduates were in turn allocated work all over the country. Provincial institutions recruited students from their respective provinces and graduates were assigned within the province.

In 1985, the National Conference on Education gave authority to key cities to establish universities and other tertiary institutions. A key city meant a recognized city and its surrounding counties. The latter form a kind of satellite structure with the city as the main commercial centre.[87] The emergence of city-level tertiary institutions is to a large extent a consequence of economic reform. Provincial universities are not meant to serve the needs of specific cities and counties. City-level institutions, which are locally funded for the most part and completely controlled by local governments, can meet the booming demand for skilled personnel brought about by the growth of local economies resulting from the economic reforms. As a result, the number of these institutions increased rapidly. In the years between 1983 and 1987, the number of universities and colleges grew at the rate of one new institution each week.[88]

Before the reform, university enrolment was planned by central and provincial governments. There was no financial advantage in taking on additional students. Since universities and colleges have gained autonomy, apart from recruiting a certain number of students as planned by the government, they can enrol commissioned students (*dai pei sheng*), and fee-paying students (*zifei sheng*). A 'commissioned student' means that the university is commissioned to train students for particular work units. The unit may pay 1,800 yuan per student per annum over a four-year degree programme. Commissioned students are bonded to their sponsoring work unit.[89] 'Fee-paying students' are the students admitted beyond the state-planned enrolment quota. Unlike the quota, they pay tuition fees which cover a part of the teaching costs.[90] Students in this category are not guaranteed employment, but they usually obtain employment as they have generally studied subjects in high demand, such as foreign languages, accountancy or statistics.[91] Universities and colleges may also run correspondence or evening courses which attract thousands of people who cannot enter universities or colleges for a full degree course.[92]

Autonomy in enrolment has several advantages. First, it can solve some funding problems. Commissioned and fee-paying students bring extra money to the institutions, even though the number of enrolments is small (usually around 10 per cent of the total).[93] Second, universities and colleges can serve the needs of the local economy. Employers are able to obtain qualified personnel, especially for rural and remote areas and for those institutions which cannot get graduates from state job assignment.[94]

The university boom stimulated by the economic reforms has, however, also led to criticism. There is an argument that higher education is expanding too rapidly and that its growth should be co-ordinated with economic development, the important thing being to raise the quality of higher education, not the quantity.[95] Some educationalists argue, for example, that 'too many college students are being turned out at these when China's greatest economic growth has been taking place in small-scale county enterprises . . . Such industries need intermediate level technicians, not university graduates.'[96] In this view the ratio between students in vocational and professional training schools and those in universities and colleges is inappropriate. In 1986 the ratio of undergraduate to vocational and professional students was 100:56, and of undergraduates to vocational secondary school students 100:40.[97] Furthermore, in 1989 the ratio of postgraduates to undergraduates was 1:10.9. This situation is seen by many to be totally inappropriate for China's social and economic needs. As a result, postgraduates become unemployed or have to do jobs more suitable for ordinary graduates or even vocational secondary school graduates.

Some Chinese educationalists argue that given China's economic situation, the ratio of postgraduates to undergraduates should be 1:20, and the ratio of undergraduates to vocational and professional secondary school students should be 1:4.[98] They advocate reducing higher education enrolments[99] and developing vocational and professional education.[100] Changes during 1990 reflected this shift in emphasis. Postgraduates enroled in colleges and universities declined by 8.2 per cent and undergraduates by 0.9 per cent compared with 1989. By contrast there was steady development in vocational and technical education.[101]

As economic development occurs, China needs more scientists with applied scientific knowledge, more social scientists with modern management techniques, more engineers who can turn designs into practice, and more medical scientists with clinical expertise. Such demands cannot be met in the short term, and if problems are not solved in the universities, not even in future. At present, courses are taught not according to social needs but according to the teachers available. The major reason for this is the poor administration of academic staff employment. Although the reform decision stipulated that individual universities have the

161

power to appoint staff, it is difficult to dismiss anyone. For many years after 1949, China's higher education followed a set pattern and remained static. New sciences and disciplines were not introduced and developed. In addition, the Cultural Revolution caused considerable disruption. At present it is hard to bring together complete teams of qualified university staff able to meet the demands of social and economic reforms.

In most universities, the situation is as follows.[102] Old faculty members have good basic knowledge and theory and are experienced in teaching and research. For reasons of age and training, however, they are not able or not willing to equip themselves with new knowledge and theories or to change into new disciplines. They find it hard to teach new and urgently needed subjects or to carry out research in new areas. Nevertheless, most of them still play a major role in teaching and research because they will lose the opportunity for promotion if they leave their positions. Middle-aged academics were deprived of opportunities during the Cultural Revolution. They do not have a solid foundation in either theory or practice, and do not have the ability to teach new and most needed subjects. They feel insecure when the university adjusts the subjects or disciplines to be taught. Some university leaders say these people should 'be taken care of'.[103] This means they should be given teaching and research positions even though they are not able to teach the most needed subjects or to carry out research in such areas. Young faculty members are more enthusiastic about learning new theories, but they lack experience or interest in teaching. This is partly because of the decline in interest in teaching in an increasingly materialistic society, and partly because of the rigid seniority system in the universities. Young academics who have both ability and enthusiasm thus find it difficult to give full play to their talents and skills.

Another big problem in universities is teaching methodology. This problem has been addressed under the national programme of educational reform. In 1985 Vice-Premier Wan Li pointed out,

China's traditional educational thinking and ossified teaching methods have a long history and are deep-rooted . . . The pattern of thought formed under the guidance of this kind of traditional education theory is totally incompatible with modern science and technology development. Scholastic forced feeding throttles wisdom and prevents the emergence of talented people who can make great progress in science and technology. We need large numbers of these talented people . . . Now we have too few talented people. This has much to do with traditional educational thinking and teaching methods.[104]

To varying degrees, the force-feeding method is still used in schools and universities. The students are required to listen to their teachers in class and memorize what they are taught. They have to rely on mechanical memorization to pass examinations.[105] In addition, students are usually trained too narrowly.[106] Zhang Mengwei, Deputy-Director of the Department of Teaching of Qinghua University, says, 'Some students at Qinghua University, a highly selective institution, "don't know how to fish".'[107] Graduates cannot adjust themselves quickly to the new working environment when they get a job and employers are not satisfied. In 1987 and 1988, about 5,000 graduates who were assigned jobs were returned to universities or colleges by employers.[108] Some graduates remain unemployed, and one reason is the incompatibility of education with economic and social needs. Although higher institutions have reduced specialized disciplines from 1,343 to 671[109] with the aim of broadening students' knowledge, there is still a long way to go in the reform of learning content and teaching methods.

The new policy that graduates are not guaranteed jobs (although not yet universally practised) also has problems.[110] One of them is that many people are worried about job-market fairness. They do not believe that fair competition is possible. One reader of *Zhongguo Qingnian Bao* wrote: 'In finding employment, there is only equality on the surface, but not underneath.'[111] Many Chinese agree that the major difficulty is that the best job opportunities have been reserved for male graduates from big cities whose parents have the right 'connections'.[112] Needless to say, female graduates face larger problems than male graduates in finding employment opportunities.

In order to find work, many university and graduate students and their parents devote much effort to establishing connections and seeking the help of influential people. Parents and students have to offer large 'bribes' to get an ideal job or even just to be assigned a job in big cities. Many parents now feel that the burdens of sending their children to senior schools and on to college or university are too great, and the monetary rewards are too small.[113]

163

Students currently studying at colleges and universities have low morale. Despite the lack of facilities, many campus study halls were reported to be empty in the evenings in 1988. At Zhongshan University in Guangzhou, 46 per cent of students responding to a survey said that there was nothing wrong with cheating on examinations.[114] Many students have no confidence in the future and pay little attention to their studies, being seen by some to fall into four groups: the mahjong players, the TOFEL testers, the disco dancers and the tourists.[115]

In autumn 1988, a sharp drop in the number of applicants for senior secondary schools and universities occurred for the first time since the end of the Cultural Revolution, while at the same time technical and vocational schools had many more applicants for limited places. The declining interest in academic careers is mainly attributed to the low-paying jobs given to many university graduates and the move to end both tuition-free higher education and guaranteed job assignments.[116]

CONCLUSION

China's educational reform was seen as essential for economic growth and modernization. However, it has failed to achieve the goals set and many problems still exist. This chapter has identified a number of issues now crucial for the reform.

First, one of the biggest problems for educational development is educational funding. Although the education budget has increased, it is still much too small. Basic education urgently needs funding. Even the small amount of funding available is not completely and appropriately used in educational development. There is, however, no direct and immediate solution for this problem. A number of suggestions have been put forward.[117] First of all, it is felt important to make leadership at all levels realize the importance of investment in education. In 1989, Deng Xiaoping pointed out 'We must try every means to solve the problems in education, even if we have to slow down the speed of development in other areas.'[118] Although it is argued that education should be given priority in the state budget, any increase in funding is not likely to be much while the three-year retrenchment plan (1988–91) drafted by the State Planning Commission is in force. This places emphasis on reduction in investment, in the budget deficit, in consumption and in non-state economic activity. It is suggested that industrial institutions, social groups and collectives should be encouraged to donate funds for education. In economically developed areas, students should pay a reasonable amount of their tuition fees. Schools and universities can also make a profit by running their own enterprises on condition that their normal teaching activities are not negatively affected. Without legislation to control spending, however, there is no guarantee that education can be developed properly, no matter how much money might be available. Furthermore, as many educationalists argue, basic education should attract the largest increase in funding, as it is more crucial for the whole educational reform and for long-run economic development.[119]

The second important issue is the difficulty with staffing. The low social and economic status of teachers, their low morale, their lack of qualifications and their efforts to move to other jobs are major problems for the improvement of teaching quality and the universalization of basic education. Solutions can be sought by improving teachers' income and living conditions and by running more teacher training programmes. Only when teachers' incomes depend on their qualifications and performance and are at average or above average level will there be some hope of improving teaching quality and solving staffing problems.

Another important issue discussed above is teaching method and learning content. There is a conflict between traditional educational thinking and new ideas. Greater individual creativity is required by economic and social development. The traditional force-feeding method which dominated Chinese classrooms for centuries is still practised in today's schools and universities. Learning content is also irrelevant to social and economic needs. This is one of the reasons for the revulsion against education and the increasing number of drop-outs from schools. Although this problem has been addressed in the educational reform programme, it is very difficult to solve within a few years. Many teachers cannot easily change their curriculum and teaching methods. It will take years to train new teachers and to establish qualified teaching teams.

Apart from difficulties with staffing, the structure of education is also important for economic development. For many years, China's basic education aimed at sending students to higher education, and higher education's goal has been to meet the requirements of the planned economy. This structure is no longer compatible with the effects of economic reform. Basic education, especially in rural areas, should include more vocational and professional content to suit local economic situations. There should be more vocational and professional training at senior secondary school level.[120]

The aim of education is not only to train people to obtain adequate skills for economic growth but also to develop their moral integrity and personality. The latter task has always been regarded as more important in China. If traditional educational thinking has dominated China's classrooms in science and technology learning, it is even more the case in ideological education. One of the purposes of China's educational reform was to change such an approach. As one Chinese leader said, people trained in this way can only be 'worshippers of books and authority' and 'we advocate training students in independent thinking and the spirit of being bold in making innovations'.[121] The open-door policy and economic autonomy require open educational thinking. Since the reforms began, a great challenge for the Chinese government has been how to have more openness while at the same time continuing to enforce limitations. It is reluctant to be liberal in the political and ideological fields. Conservative forces regularly reassert themselves within the Communist Party, carrying out drives against 'spiritual pollution' and 'bourgeois liberalization'. This has caused much confusion in the educational reforms, and Chinese academics and educationalists feel threatened when such drives occur. The major changes in the political climate after the June 1989 incident in Beijing inevitably intensified such problems. Political and ideological education have regained priority in schools and universities. The Chinese government has stressed repeatedly that schools and universities should not neglect ideological education, that higher education should strengthen its education in Marxism, Leninism and Mao Zedong thought, and that high schools and primary schools should carry out education in socialism and communism.[122] Obviously, party control is being re-emphasized and the separation of party and administration which was advocated before has been halted.

In all, China's educational problems have many complex political, economic and educational causes. As political reforms move very slowly and there have been regular attempts to reassert party controls over education, academics and students feel unsettled and lose confidence. Economically there are enormous conflicts between the demands of society and the content of education, between the need for expertise with open knowledge and privilege in job allocation, between rural needs for graduates and urban privileges, and between the need for basic vocational education and the university boom. In educational terms, there are still many problems in structure, learning and content. These problems in turn hinder the economic reforms. In many ways, therefore, the process of educational reform still faces major obstacles. The consequence of this for both economic reform and economic growth are likely to be profound.

NOTES AND REFERENCES

1 *PR*, no. 52, 29 December 1978, p. 11.
2 *RMRB*, 21 October 1984.
3 *RMRB*, 4 January 1990.
4 *BR*, no. 21, 27 May 1985, p. 6.
5 *BR*, no. 24, 17 June 1985, p. 20.
6 *ZGJYB*, 28 March 1989 and Ai Hua, 'Zhengshi Zhongguo de jiaoyu weiji' ('Give serious thought to the crisis of China's education'), *October Review*, vol. 16, no. 2, February 1989, pp. 14–16.
7 Jasper Becker, 'Where learning comes last', *Guardian*, 14 May 1989.
8 *GMRB*, 19 April 1989.
9 *ZGJYB*, 28 March 1989.
10 Becker, op. cit.
11 *ZGJYB*, 28 June 1989.
12 *GMRB*, 19 April 1989.
13 *GMRB*, 6 January 1989.
14 *GMRB*, 31 March 1989.
15 *ZGJYB*, 18 March 1989.
16 Ibid.
17 *ZGJYB*, 28 March 1989.
18 Ibid.
19 *ZGJYB*, 18 March 1989.
20 Ibid.
21 Ibid.
22 *ZGJYB*, 28 March 1989.
23 *GMRB*, 6 January 1989.
24 *JYQBCK*, 20 August 1984.
25 J. R. Hough, *Education and the National Economy*, New York, Croom Helm, 1987, p. 48.
26 Ibid., p. 52.
27 *GMRB*, 29 March 1989.
28 Ibid.
29 Ibid.
30 *GMRB*, 31 March 1989.
31 *ZGJYB*, 28 March 1989.
32 *ZGJYB*, 18 March 1989 and He Dong-chang, 'The program of reform of the educational system of China', in *Educational Reform and Development in China*, compiled by Wu Wei, edited and translated by Chen Shu-ching, Shu Hang-li and Wu Yen, State University of New York at Buffalo, 1987, p. 4.

33 *ZGJYB*, 26 June 1989.
34 *ZGJYB*, 18 March 1989.
35 Zhang Chengxian, 'Yao xia juexin wending shizi duiwu' ('We must stabilize teaching teams'), *ZGJYB*, no date 1989.
36 *ZGJYB*, 26 June 1989.
37 Zhang Chengxian, op. cit., 1989.
38 Ibid.
39 *ZGJYB*, 18 March 1989.
40 Suzanne Pepper, 'China's university leaders nervous about future as government seeks to control failing economy', *The Chronicle of Higher Education*, 26 October 1988, pp. A1 and A50.
41 *ZGJYB*, 18 March 1989.
42 Ibid.
43 Pepper, op. cit.
44 Cheng Kaiming, 'China's recent education reform: the beginning of an overhaul', *Comparative Education*, vol. 22, no. 3, 1986, p. 259.
45 Wang Jingzong, 'Yingdang zhongshi de jige wenti' ('A few problems which should be addressed'), *RMJY*, no. 1, 1989, pp. 16–17.
46 Ibid.
47 Zang Aizhen, 'Min-ban jiaoshi tongyang shixing jiaoshi zhiwu pinrenzhi' ('Min-ban teachers should also have a teacher employment contract system'), *RMJY*, no. 1, 1989, p. 19, and no author, 'Yao zhubu tigao gong-ban jiaoshi de bili' ('We must gradually increase the proportion of state-employed teachers') (extracts from the Central Committee and State Council 'Decision on several issues concerning universal primary education' of 3 December 1980'), *RMJY*, no. 1, 1989, p. 19.
48 *GMRB*, 12 April 1989.
49 Bao Guoqing, 'Jiaoyu yu jingji xianghu cujin de shexiang', ('New thoughts on the interaction between education and economy'), *JYYJ*, no. 12, 1989, p. 6.
50 *ZGJYB*, 18 March 1989.
51 Cheng Kaiming, op. cit., p. 259.
52 *ZGJYB*, no date 1989.
53 Tao Zuwei, 'Gaohao neibu jizhi shenru jiaoyu gaige' ('Vitalize the internal system and deepen educational reform'), *RMJY*, no. 1, 1989, pp. 13–14.
54 *Law of the People's Republic of China on Compulsory Education in Beijing*, Beijing, 1986.
55 Cheng Kaiming, op. cit., p. 256.
56 *ZGJYB*, 28 June 1989.
57 In 1987, there were 1,240 counties with universal basic education, ibid. In 1984, there were only 393 counties, Cheng Kaiming, op. cit., p. 258.
58 *SWB*, 25 February 1991, FE/1005/C1/6
59 *ZGJYB*, 28 June 1989.
60 Ibid.
61 *ZGJYB*, 18 March 1989.
62 Ai Hua, op. cit.
63 Article 16 in the law on compulsory education is 'No organization or

individual shall appropriate, withhold or misuse the funds earmarked for compulsory education . . . ', *Law of the People's Republic of China on Compulsory Education in Beijing*, Beijing, 1986.

64 Xue Huanyu, 'Dui dangqian woguo zhong-xiaoxuesheng liushi wenti de tantao', ('An enquiry into the present problem of school drop-outs in China'), *JYYJ*, October 1989, pp. 49–53.

65 *GMRB*, 26 March 1989.

66 *ZGJYB*, no date 1989.

67 *RMRB* (overseas edition), 6 April 1989.

68 Ibid.

69 *ZGJYB*, 28 March 1989.

70 Ai Hua, op. cit.

71 *ZGJYB*, no date 1989.

72 *GMRB*, 26 March 1989.

73 Ibid.

74 J. R. Hough, op. cit., pp. 9–10.

75 Wang Mingda, 'Nongcun xuexiao jiaoyu bixu gaige' ('Education in rural schools must be reformed'), *Renmin Jiaoyu*, no. 12, 1987, pp. 3–4.

76 Ibid.

77 Ibid.

78 *JYQBCK*, 20 August 1984.

79 Zhang Gengfu, 'Geti qingnian de liu da xuqiu' ('The six major needs of self-employed youth'), *ZGQN*, no. 3, 1988, p. 46.

80 *JYQBCK*, 20 August 1984.

81 *BR*, no. 24, 17 June 1985.

82 *GMRB*, 31 March 1989.

83 *RMRB*, 3 January 1990.

84 *RMRB*, 26 March 1990.

85 John F. Cleverley, 'The concept of enterprise and the Chinese university: a cautionary tale of profit and loss', *Comparative Education*, vol. 23, no. 3, 1987, pp. 345–53.

86 Han Yanming, 'Zhongguo daxue guanli tizhi gaige jinkuang shu yao' ('A brief account of the current reform of the administrative system in China's universities'), *Han Sheng (Chinese Culture)*, vol. 24, January 1989, pp. 38–9.

87 Cheng Kaiming, op. cit., p. 263.

88 Robert L. Jacobson, 'Expectations rise for higher education in China as reform temper begins to take hold', *The Chronicle of Higher Education*, 28 October 1987, pp. A40–2.

89 Cleverley, op. cit., p. 348.

90 Cheng Kaiming, op. cit., p. 264.

91 Ibid, p. 265.

92 Cleverley, op. cit., p. 349.

93 Ibid.

94 *ZGJYB*, 24 September 1988.

95 Jacobson, op. cit. 28 October 1987.

96 Robert L. Jacobson, 'An unprecedented pact, China and Carnegie Foundation will join in a "comparative study" of higher education', *The Chronicle of Higher Education*, 16 November 1988, pp. A39–40.

97 *GMRB*, 29 March 1989.
98 *GMRB*, 18 April 1989.
99 Jacobson, op. cit., 16 November 1988.
100 Jacobson, op. cit., 28 October 1987.
101 *SWB*, 25 February 1991, FE/1005/CI/6.
102 Zhao Rui, 'Wo xiao jiaoshi duiwu jianshe de jige wenti' ('A few problems in staff development in our university'), in Liao Yuandi, ed., *Putong Gaoxiao GuanLi Tizhi Gaige Yanjiu* (*Studies on the Reform of the Administrative System in Ordinary Higher Institutions*), Beijing, 1988, pp. 285–93.
103 Ibid.
104 *BR*, no. 24, 17 June 1985.
105 Ibid.
106 Jacobson, op. cit., 28 October 1987.
107 Pepper, op. cit.
108 *ZGJYB*, 18 March 1989.
109 Ibid.
110 Pepper, op. cit.
111 Robert L. Jacobson, 'Goals of China's campuses range from "open Marxism" at People's University to Shenzhen's "socialistic capitalism"', *The Chronicle of Higher Education*, 11 November 1987, pp. A43–6.
112 Pepper, op. cit.
113 Ibid.
114 Ibid.
115 *RMRB*, 19 May 1989.
116 Pepper, op. cit.
117 *RMRB*, 3 January 1990.
118 *GMRB*, 12 April 1989.
119 Jacobson, op. cit., 16 November 1988.
120 *GMRB*, 10 April 1989.
121 *BR*, no. 24, 17 June 1985.
122 *RMRB*, 6 April 1990.

8

THE MANAGEMENT OF THE RURAL ECONOMY

The institutional parameters

Andrew Watson

Who now manages production at the basic level in the Chinese countryside?[1] How do they manage it? What are the institutional, political and social consequences of China's new rural development strategy? How are the new social relationships created by changes in the distribution of economic wealth and power articulated? How do these consequences feed back into rural economic growth? The profound changes in the Chinese countryside generated by the reforms over the past ten years have raised a wide range of issues which are still in the process of being resolved. To a large extent, questions of this kind still require consideration of the major role played by state institutions, rural cadres and party organizations. These set the parameters for rural economic activity. Their economic and administrative decisions influence the way peasant households behave and the way social relationships function. After ten years of economic reform, however, the face of the countryside has changed. The decisions of local government and village cadres are premised on a different economic system, characterized by decentralization and growing market forces. The freedoms granted to the peasants have created a generation of rural entrepreneurs who are forging new social and economic relationships. The economic and geographic mobility of ordinary peasants has created fresh ambitions and different forms of behaviour. The relative prosperity of the countryside has transformed peasants attitudes and led to demands which did not exist a decade ago. The peasants have not only developed a new sense of their own interests in contrast to those of government and urban society but also are experiencing new social realignments among themselves based on such things as accumulation of wealth, entrepreneurial and technical skills, and shifting channels of patronage. All of these changes have raised new questions about the nature of China's rural society and its direction. This chapter attempts to address some of the issues involved.

One of the central issues in the political economy of economic development is the relationship between economic growth and institutional structures. No matter whether the process is one of capitalist accumulation through market exchange or socialist construction through government planning, no matter whether it focuses on industrialization, technological change, social welfare maximization or efficiency of resource use, it inevitably involves changes to institutional structures and to the social relations they embody. Such changes are both a condition for and a consequence of economic growth. It can be argued, for example, that without the introduction of appropriate institutions to manage changing economic relationships, development will be constrained or slowed down. The absence of either administrative mechanisms or integrated national markets for capital, labour and other factors of production may place constraints on the efficient transfer of resources between sectors and thereby increase the costs of development. As growth occurs the relationship between the different factors of production changes and, depending on the capacity of those factors to respond, the returns to the different groups in society who control them also change. The resulting disequilibrium between the established social order and the new social reality will then require political and institutional changes to achieve a new balance. The supply of such change may, in turn, reflect either the political power of the different social groups involved or the potential to innovate outside of or in conflict with the established order. Such changes may be evolutionary or revolutionary. Clearly this process is complex and the causal linkages can be seen as flowing in both directions between economic growth and institutional structures. Furthermore, analysis has to take account of such things as technical and scientific innovation and cultural and ideological patterns, which may be seen as endogenous or exogenous to the economic process taking place.

Writing in 1985, Hayami and Ruttan argued that rapid growth in agriculture requires economically and ecologically viable agricultural technology, the dynamic adjustment of resources and adaptive cultural, political and economic institutions.[2] Reviewing the evolution of development theory from the classical economists onwards, they argue that there is an integrated relationship between economic forces, the emergence of new technologies, and institutional innovation. Ultimately, they argue, it is the role of the latter two which is pivotal in the achievement of successful economic development. They thus see an inevitable process of institutional change as economic growth takes place:

> The disequilibria in economic relationships resulting from technical change represent a major source of institutional change. . . . Anticipation of the latent gains to be realized by overcoming the disequilibria resulting from changes in factor endowments, product demand and technical change is a powerful inducement to institutional innovation. Institutions that have been efficient in generating growth in the past may, over time, come to direct their efforts primarily to protecting the vested interests of some of their members by maintaining the status quo and thus becoming obstacles to further economic development. The growing disequilibria in resource allocation resulting from institutional constraints generated by economic growth create opportunities for political entrepreneurs or leaders to organize collective action to bring about institutional changes.[3]

As Hayami and Ruttan acknowledge, general features of this argument are shared with earlier generations of economists, including Marx. In various forms, it is also shared by other such as Schultz,[4] and Johnston and Kilby.[5] Hayami and Ruttan's particular focus, however, is their emphasis on technical and institutional change as an endogenous aspect of the rural economy.

In China, institutional change has also long been seen to be central to the process of rural development. Sun Yat-sen made redistribution of ownership a major goal of his economic programme. From the 1920s onwards, Mao Zedong evolved an integrated vision for rural development which linked social, political and institutional change to economic growth. After 1949, that vision grew to embrace a total transformation of systems of ownership, marketing and pricing and social morality. Until the reforms began, therefore, China's rural development strategy was built around the replacement of individual farming and market linkages by governmental regulation, collective ownership and management, and administrative distribution. The emphasis was placed on collective accumulation and investment as a means of meeting state production goals, transforming rural technology through planned inputs, removing economic and social differences based on ownership of land and other assets, and equalizing the share of the benefits to be obtained from rural economic growth. This strategy was developed not only as a reaction against the perceived failings and inequities of the traditional small peasant economy but also to realize the potential that was assumed to lie in collectivization.[6]

The reforms have highlighted the economic costs of that strategy which included poor managerial efficiency, low incentives to producers, a bias towards urban areas, rigidity in planning and management, and low rates of growth. The social consequences were also profound, with entrenched regional inequalities,[7] a low social status for peasants which left them with minimal geographical mobility,[8] and low levels of income, especially by comparison with urban areas. While the collective institutions enabled some types of accumulation and investment to take place and provided a channel for new technical inputs, the weaknesses of attempting to manage in a centralized way agricultural production, which requires on-the-spot decision making and a long seasonal perspective, eventually created a tension between the institutional framework and the nature of the production process.

Under this policy, village life was profoundly affected by the pressures of central policy as interpreted through the ambitions of village cadres, some of whom sought to obey to the letter party and government policies and some of whom sought to interpret those policies in ways to benefit best their local constituency.[9] These social and economic shortcomings shaped peasants' attitudes towards the collective system. In many, if not most, areas they generated a reservoir of resentment and grievances which boiled over once the reforms began. Peasant rejection of the strategy thus contributed to the rapid unravelling of the collective farming system. To some extent, therefore, the path the reforms have taken must be seen as a process of institutional adaptation in a situation where the existing framework could not meet the needs of rural development.

By contrast with the situation before 1978, the new strategy for rural development is not fully articulated and defined. It has set the general goals of improving living standards, accelerating rates of growth, and diversifying rural production through specialization. These aims are associated with a return to household farming, price incentives and market relationships. The nature of this strategy, however, has emerged from a series of pragmatic adjustments and from reactions to the consequences of those adjustments. It has also been constrained by the remaining influence of central planning and collective institutions. This is particularly the case in systems of rural administration and governmental management, in the pricing and marketing of some key commodities and in attitudes to further changes in systems of ownership. The reforms have to be implemented by transforming existing structures and through personnel working according to long-established procedures. This institutional inertia inevitably colours the way policies work.

Overall, the new strategy focuses on quite different goals to its predecessor. It gives primacy to the development of local comparative advantage and specialization as the mechanisms for accelerating rates of growth. It relies on greater commercialization of production and of the supply of inputs as a means of achieving efficiency of allocation. It promotes competition and inequalities as production incentives. It seeks to transform the structure of rural production by encouraging a major shift of labour and other resources out of agriculture. It also calls for less direct governmental intervention in production, for the separation of economic and administrative powers, and for the primacy of producer interests in production decisions. In Marxist terms, such changes inevitably entail changes in the relations of production and changes in the social power and status of different actors in the production process. In institutional terms, they demand a new framework for managing the rural economy, for the provision of inputs and technology, for the links between the household and the state, and for the role of government. In social terms, they lead to new relationships between different social groups with different economic functions, such as between cadres and peasants, between producers, providers of services, middlemen and consumers, and between the owners of capital and labour and the users thereof. Such changes must take place if the potential for further growth through the market system is to be realized. The way those issues are resolved will therefore have major implications for the next phase of economic development in the countryside.

In analysing the series of questions raised at the outset and their implications for China's rural development, therefore, this chapter examines the nature of rural government and administration and the structure of rural economic management. It concludes with some observations on the way these institutional factors and their social consequences are now shaping economic growth in the Chinese countryside.

RURAL GOVERNMENT AND ADMINISTRATION

Under the commune system, the key actors in the countryside were the county government, the brigade and team cadres, and the household. Except in the minority of rich areas, where collective accumulation had given real economic content to the commune level of administration, commune cadres often played little more than an intermediary role between village and county. Indeed, in some poor areas the role of brigade-level cadres was similarly constrained. The county administration set the economic targets and distributed the inputs. The brigade cadres assigned those targets and inputs to the teams and managed co-ordinated equipment and projects, while the team cadres organized agricultural production and kept the accounts. The households simply supplied their labour to the collective. This was their major source of income, supplemented by work on their private plots. Collective sidelines might be owned and managed at team or brigade levels.

Between 1979 and 1984, the household production responsibility rapidly eroded this structure. Du Runsheng saw this as the first phase of agricultural reform, centring on the dismantling of the communes and the emergence of household management of production.[10] In place of the commune, a new set of relationships evolved.[11] The brigade and team levels ceased to play a major managerial role in agricultural production, and decisions over the use of land, labour and other inputs passed to the household. The key relationships became those between the county, the village and the household. The county still set the major production targets and distributed state-controlled inputs. The village became the owner of the land and the manager of any residual collective services. The household, subject to tax and sales obligations, gained the freedom to act as an independent agricultural producer.

As Jean Oi has noted, however, this did not mean that the role of the rural cadres was totally undermined.[12] They continued to use their authority over the distribution of inputs, their links to systems of administration and their knowledge of market opportunities to sustain an important social position. Meanwhile, as rural production diversified and labour moved out of agriculture, the economic functions of the township (formerly commune) and village (formerly brigade) changed. The growth of non-agricultural enterprises, owned and managed at those levels, gave the village cadres a new economic identity, especially in the more developed areas, and generated a new relationship between their economic and administrative functions. In other words, the changes in the institutional structure of the countryside and the introduction of different and profitable economic activities presented the cadres with the opportunity to carve a new basis for their social and economic power based on their entrepreneurial skills and their established network of social connections. In many areas, therefore, they were able to retain significant social authority over the local villagers. The basis of that authority, however, was no longer primarily their role in the administrative hierarchy. It was founded on their skills in expanding the local economy and their linkages to networks of patronage and distribution.

Against the background of these innovations in the first phase of reform, the major goals of the second stage since 1984 have been described as the perfection of new types of market linkages, further clarification of ownership and usage rights, and the establishment of new administrative mechanisms to promote the growth of the commodity economy. In this process, the role of government at county, township and village level has become a major issue. In particular this involves the functioning and nature of the agricultural management system, now summed up as 'a combination of unity and division with management at two levels' (*'tong-fen jiehe, shuang ceng jingying'*). Both the role of local government and management structures in this combination and of the household and the private entrepreneur need clarification, as does the nature of the relationship between them. Furthermore, discussion of these issues in China has been obscured by the fact that much of the framework for analysis is structured in terms of the transformation of the old collective system, whereas, as noted above, the way local leadership actually functions is already responding to quite different economic forces.

PALACE ECONOMIES

The impact of the reforms on *county-level* administration has been profound.[13] The decentralization of administrative powers, which has been a distinctive feature of the reforms, has done much to strengthen the independence and initiative of county governments.[14] As discussed by Findlay and Jiang above, one of the crucial factors in this respect has been the development of financial contracting and the strong sense of local economic identity this has created. According to this system, county governments agree with the next level up to meet defined income and expenditure targets. Any additional revenue is shared according to a ratio set out in the financial contract. Excess expenditure outside the stipulations has to be met by the county. Surplus and extra-budgetary income can be used at its discretion. One of the major aims of this reform was to improve the efficiency of financial management at county level. Large numbers of counties had operated with a budget deficit for many years, and the new system generated powerful incentives to reverse that situation. Nevertheless, an important by-product of the change is that the upper levels of government have lost some of the direct controls they once had over county government behaviour. The changes have also generated friction between the counties and their superiors, as they try to increase their autonomy, to maximize the funds under their control, and to promote their local economy regardless of more general concerns. Inevitably this has led to emphasis on local industrial and commercial development, which is the major source of county-level income. The increases in county income which have resulted have then led to greater expenditure on infrastructure, cadre and urban incomes and county services.

In effect, each county is developing its own 'palace economy'. In Wendeng county, Shandong, for example, local government investment in fixed assets grew at a rate of 56.4 per cent per year from 1983 to 1985, with by far the most going to industrial and urban construction.[15] Furthermore, apart from its direct control over investment, the Wendeng government was also able to use indirect influence on bank loans to promote economic activity according to its priorities. Since agriculture is much less significant for county income, county governments as whole have less incentive to promote agricultural investment. This has therefore declined and even those funds originally intended for agriculture are put to other uses.[16]

While all these changes have created alternative employment for peasant labour, increasing total local output and incomes, they have created problems in crop farming. The net effect is that pressure is put on agricultural producers to supply those commodities required for county industry, while county industrial enterprises are given administrative protection in the supply of raw materials and against outside competitors.[17] The development of non-agricultural sectors, which can be seen as a gain to the rural economy as a whole, is thus influenced by an institutional system which favours local protectionism and the subordination of economic efficiencies to administrative priorities. In this situation, there is a growing consensus that the solution has to be found in further institutional reforms to separate administrative and economic systems and to change tax administration, with a division of revenue and expenditure responsibilities between levels of government.[18]

LINGXIAN 'INCORPORATED'

An example of the impact of these factors on the relationship between the county government and producers can be found in Lingxian, a county in the northwest of Shandong province, north of the Yellow River and close to the border with Hebei.[19] Formerly notorious for its poverty, Lingxian's per capita income rose from 47 yuan in 1978 to 545 yuan in 1986, above the average for the country as a whole. The reason for this turn-around began with major irrigation projects implemented in the early 1980s and continued, both because of the incentives the reforms have given to individual peasant producers and because of the strong sense of integrated purpose in the county's economic policies. The priorities set by the county government influence the choice of investment made at township and village level, the flow of funds through the county budget and banking system, and the arrangements for supply and marketing.

Since the county is an important cotton-producing area, cotton processing is given major emphasis in investments at all levels. The flow of cotton and cotton products between the county, townships and villages takes place through both planned allocation and through the market. The county also encourages townships and villages to invest in cotton processing by helping with credit and with access to technology and training. Clearly the county government is aiming to promote development by realizing local comparative advantage and by maximizing the returns to it from the resources under its control. Given that all major cotton-producing areas are experiencing the same pressures, it is no surprise to find that in 1989 and 1990 the danger of a 'cotton war', the latest in a series of commodity wars in which processors compete for supplies of raw materials, had emerged.[20] The economic imperatives of the institutional structure in the county was thus affecting the way the local economy developed and had knock-on effects into the functioning of national markets and industries. At the same time, however, it also meant that the relationship between county- and lower-level cadres and between village cadres and peasant households and private entrepreneurs was not shaped by market forces but was based on a network of patronage directed towards county-level ends. The county thus, in part, had the character of an integrated economic entity, competing with the outside.

Cotton processing is not the only industry developed in Lingxian in this way. The promotion at township and village levels of animal husbandry, the dairy industry, and fruit and vegetable cold stores are other examples of how the county government has set economic priorities and used its control over investment and contracts to influence the behaviour of its subordinate units. And those subordinate units, while conscious of their own interests against other townships and villages, clearly benefit from the process, provided they are willing to conform to the local pattern.

In contrast to its earlier poverty, Lingxian is now representative of the richer counties along the coast and in suburban areas. In many other parts of China, however, counties are less integrated and successful. Nevertheless, the economic and institutional pressures at county level would tend to provoke similar administrative responses, depending on local resources and skills, and this has led to a renewed interest in China in the nature of the county as an administrative and economic entity and to discussion of the appropriate models to adopt for its future evolution.[21] This discussion has addressed a number of significant issues. It has stressed the need for counties to encourage agricultural development and for new incentives to develop an appropriate strategic balance between agriculture and other sectors. Concerned by the fact that county economic systems are still characterized by a linkage between administrative and economic roles, the discussion also calls for a simplification and decentralization of administrative procedures so as to avoid the old problems of rigid hierarchies and inflexible administrative boundaries (*tiaotiao, kuaikuai*). Many observers stress that counties should adopt different models of economic management and growth according to local circumstances. They also advocate the acceptance by county governments of open market linkages with the outside, rather than the adoption of local protectionism. The status of the county as an intermediary between the macroeconomic policies of the state and the microeconomic behaviour of the peasant producers is thus very significant.

This situation is complicated by the fact that county economies are no longer composed of communes and local state enterprises subordinate to a hierarchy of administrative controls. Instead there is a mix of producers ranging from households to enterprises owned and operated by both private and collective entrepreneurs. Management of this mixed system and the relative economic strength of the different components varies substantially across the country, yet a common attribute is that the local administration is often able to manage its economy as a discrete, autonomous cell and to influence the way it relates with the national economy. This, in turn, means that counties tend to have 'administrative' rather than 'economic' methods of management. All of these factors serve to emphasize the prominent role of county governments in local economic development.

The problem facing further economic reform is that that role is commonly interpreted as a means of promoting local interests against total interests. A strong local economy means a strong local budget, and enlarged local bureaucracies, with higher incomes and services and booming county capitals. These pressures are reflected in the relationships between the different arms of national government, banking and services within the county area. Given that personnel, wages and rationed goods such as fuel and housing are commonly supplied through local government allocation, the county leadership is able to bring strong pressures to bear to ensure conformity to its goals. The poor counties of the interior, for example, can be expected to want to protect their interests against those on the coast and to maximize both local employment and local value-added, preferring to keep their raw materials for their own use. By contrast, counties with rich resources can be expected to want to extract maximum value from them and to use them as a lever to obtain other advantages from outside. No wonder one Chinese commentator in 1988 saw the situation as one where:

> feudal lords contend, regions set up blockades, trades practise monopolies, and wars are continuous, where there is 'official speculation' and loss of control, and administration and economic enterprises are not separate, and where a form of privileged exchange in the selling of 'batch goods' is mixed in with normal market exchange.[22]

Although the deflationary policies of 1989 and 1990 worked to take much of the steam out of the conflicts inherent in the institutional framework described above, they did so through economic pressures. The lack of capital and the collapse of consumer markets removed the economic incentives for local investment. The institutional and administrative systems which created the situation, however, have yet to change. Until that happens, the stage is still set for a continuation of the type of local economic development that characterized the second half of the 1980s. In terms of the issues discussed at the opening of this chapter, the problem remains one of changing institutional and administrative systems, both to enable the development of more open economic relationships across administrative boundaries and to ensure that local government sees its role as providing producers with the incentives, services and technological inputs to develop production efficiently and in a sustainable way, rather than bolstering its social and economic power through administrative intervention to protect its own interests.

THE ROLE OF THE TOWNSHIP

With the disappearance of the communes, the *township* became the lowest level of governmental administration. As yet, however, the township is the least formalized of the administrative structures in the countryside.[23] Its commune functions have disappeared, but its administrative and economic relationship to the county is still being defined. In areas where township enterprises are relatively underdeveloped, the township government is little but a hollow shell. The status of its cadres as locally-appointed officials or as subordinates of the county hierarchy also remains undecided. The nature of its budget, the sources of its revenue and the range of its expenditure is far from standardized. The fact that, as the successor to the commune level of administration, it still plays a role as a collective economic unit, with a strong residual notion of collective ownership in the area it administers, has led to a continued overlap of functions between administration and direct economic management. In fact, in discussion with rural cadres the words 'commune' and 'brigade' are still commonly used when referring to townships and villages, indicating the sense of continuity with the past. This is particularly the case in respect of the rural enterprises which commonly form the main source of local revenue to support both township administration and to pay the wages of township cadres.

A good example of the problems involved is provided by the status of technical extension personnel from the County Agricultural

Bureau stationed at the township level in Lingxian.[24] The Bureau provided them with technical and professional guidance but their salaries and their actual work was assigned by the township. Their everyday needs, accommodation, fuel and so forth were also provided by the township. When contradictions over policy and work arose between the county and the township, the extension workers tended to obey the latter since they depended on them for their day-to-day livelihood. By 1988, this had become a major issue for the Bureau. It was grappling with the problem of how to ensure the local personnel followed its technical guidance. In effect there was a misalignment between economic activity and administrative mechanisms. The organization of the agricultural extension system still followed the old pattern. Originally the extension people working at commune level got their wages from the Bureau, and the funds were handed to the commune to pay out. The reforms now meant that 'you belong to whoever pays your wages'. As a result, the townships no longer wanted to be responsible for the living expenses of these technical personnel and argued that their superiors should bear the costs. The townships, for example, didn't want to supply them with fuel. The Bureau, on the other hand, couldn't supply them because they were widely scattered across the county and there was no means to deliver coal to each of them. As a result, the extension workers were unable to work effectively and securely, and there was a dispute between county and township, focusing on the costs of administration. Though in some ways a minor example, the issue demonstrates the larger proposition that the reforms have created new economic relationships but this has not been matched by the introduction of appropriate institutional and administrative structures. Given their important role in technological change and economic growth, the net effect on agricultural development could not have been helpful. Clearly a solution would eventually be found and the administrative system was being forced to adjust to handle such problems, but until the process has worked itself out across the full spectrum of such institutional issues, the full logic of the reforms cannot be realized.

THE SIGNIFICANCE OF TOWNSHIP ENTERPRISES

Although the lack of a budget system and of a clear set of administrative procedures means that in many, if not most, areas of China the township government remains relatively weak, one dimension in which the role of township cadres is significant is the management of rural enterprises. In this respect, the position of township and village cadres is much the same, and the current institutional position of both is the product of their former role in the collective hierarchy. Rural enterprises may be operated collectively, privately or in various forms of contractual linkages between local government, villages and private entrepreneurs. There are also many different models of management, ranging from those with a strong collective focus in Jiangsu[25] to the purely private system of Wenzhou in Zhejiang.[26] Among the many issues this development has raised is the nature of administration of these enterprises and, in particular, the role of township and village cadres.[27]

Apart from the role of the cadres in resolving the conflict with agriculture for resources which the growth of rural enterprises has generated,[28] one of the major problems is the definition of enterprise ownership. According to former members of the now-abolished Rural Development Research Centre of the State Council,[29] the ownership of rural enterprises and the legal status of that ownership are not defined. It is not clear, for example, who is responsible in case of bankruptcy (and since the mushroom growth of these enterprises has been largely based on credit, the debt level is very high). Is it the head of the township or village or all the peasants who are nominally the collective owners? Since the township is the successor to the commune, it retains the character of an area-based collective economic unit. In theory, all the peasants living in an area are the collective owners of the enterprises. In most cases, however, the peasant owners do not draw an economic return from their enterprise, except indirectly where enterprise income is used to finance administrative services, welfare and agricultural inputs (*yi gong bu nong*). If peasants leave their village, there is no way they can realize their share of the collectively-owned assets. Furthermore, most of the income from the enterprises is used to pay cadre wages and administrative costs, and to finance further enterprise developments. Among the consequences of this are excessive profit levies by township cadres which threaten enterprise viability, indiscriminate transfer of resources between enterprises by administrative decision, and little direct economic benefits for the peasants. Hidden among these economic and administrative issues is also the fact that the social and kinship linkages within townships and villages mean that the cadres and managers both receive and express social demands and obligations in the way they administer the enterprises, appoint the staff and distribute the income. If not, they face the jealous 'red eyes' of the people with whom they interact.

The fact that the enterprises have neither ownership independent from local administration, whereby questions of profit and loss should establish viability, nor fully established systems of regulation also means that issues of scale and location are decided administratively. Every township or village wishes to develop its own enterprises as a source of income. This leads to duplication and support for what otherwise might be seen as marginal investments. In addition, the scattering of enterprises across the countryside creates problems in the provision of infrastructure, with waste of capital and land. Once again this leads to enlarged demand for credit and labour, pushing up average costs. The large demand for energy, transport and construction materials exacerbates competition with the state system for scarce commodities. Furthermore, the combination of scattered location and poor management also generates many problems of environmental pollution. Indeed, the issue of pollution was used as an argument by the central government in its efforts to control these enterprises and to slow down the economy after June 1989.[30]

Ultimately, in responding to the economic incentives to develop local enterprises and income, the dual role of the township cadres, combining functions of administration and ownership, has had a number of managerial, social and economic consequences. These consequences have also influenced private entrepreneurs, who have to rely on the goodwill of the local administration. Not surprisingly, the result has been a strong argument that rural enterprises should be separated from township government through the development of a shareholding system of ownership. Nevertheless, the regulations concerning rural collective enterprises adopted in June 1990 did little to clarify the situation.[31] In effect, the more conservative approach to economic policy evident after the political upheavals of 1989 led to a reassertion that 'the property of an enterprise belongs to the entire peasants' collective within the scope of the township or village where the enterprise is located'. The new regulations thus failed to address the economic problems inherent in the existing institutional framework.

THE VILLAGE

As indicated above, the *village* level of administration shares many features in common with the township. The sources of cadre income, the overlap between economic and administrative functions and the powers village leaders have in the distribution of inputs, combine to ensure that, even though they no longer directly control production by households, they retain a significant role in many parts of the Chinese countryside. An example of how important that role can be in some cases is provided by Zhangxilou village in Lingxian.[32] The village has retained a strong collective identity and its head, Zhang Wanze, was also the former leader of the brigade. During the early 1980s, Zhang was instrumental in obtaining loans from the county bank to begin developing village enterprises. In 1983 the village was among the first to build a large brick kiln and it thereby benefited from the surge in rural and urban construction. The following year, it obtained another loan to build a cold store and, thereafter, Zhang became involved in long-distance trade in apples and garlic sprouts. Local produce is bought up at harvest, stored and then sold in distant cities when prices are high. As a result, Zhang spends a considerable amount of time travelling outside the village to establish trading contacts and subscribes to a wide range of economic papers to keep abreast of market developments. His role has thus become that of village economic entrepreneur. His village-level investments have also stimulated household activity. A number of peasant households have invested in transport and sub-contract the carriage of bricks and fruit. By 1986, per capita income had climbed to around 1,300 yuan. During 1988–89, the village launched a new phase of development, with a large investment in cotton spinning and weaving. This enterprise meshed with county-level plans to expand cotton processing. It involved a large loan from textile enterprises in Hangzhou in return for guaranteed supplies of raw materials and local arrangements with the county government for the supply of cotton and yarn. Per capita income in 1989 had risen to nearly 1,400 yuan, and it was hoped that full production in 1990 would generate 1,700–1,800 yuan.

Several aspects of the development of Zhangxilou stand out. First, the established relationship between Zhang Wanze and the county administration helped to ensure the supply of credit, technology and other inputs for village development. The network of personal and administrative ties which was created during the collective system thus clearly remained important in this case. Second, the village's collective economic system is expressed through Zhang's management of collective resources. Zhang's personality is pivotal and he plays the dominant role in all key managerial and investment decisions. In effect, he is the managing director of the village corporate identity. Third, there is a linkage between the economic activities of households and the collective economy. Households are able to invest in the knowledge that some of the risk is offset by their relationship to the village economy as a whole. Fourth, though retaining a strong collective character, the village acts as an independent operator in respect of the outside. It has contractual and other links with the county and competes with other villages for inputs. It also competes in the market outside the county. This is particularly the case in its cold store operations. Its investment in cotton processing, however, underlines that it remains strongly influenced by the economic strategy of the county. Finally, there is an identity of interests between the success of the village economy and the status and authority of the village leadership. While that suggests that the institutional framework may encourage technological change and efficient investment, the potential for distortion because of the confusion of administrative and economic identity remains. In effect, the model of development represented by Zhangxilou still owes much to the previous collective system. It incorporates many of the transitional features associated with the mixture of plan and market and of collective and private ownership created by the reforms.

Nevertheless, it must also be recognized that Zhangxilou is far from typical of China's villages. The national conference on basic level rural administration held in July 1989, for example, reported that only 30 per cent of China's villages had good organizations, 50 per cent were 'ordinary' and around 20 per cent had ineffective or slack leadership. Many rural cadres 'could no longer use the old methods and hadn't mastered the new'.[33] Presumably this judgement applies at both township and village levels. The situation was summed up by one observer as follows:

> The rural reforms begun ten years ago have smashed the old tradition of purely using administrative methods to organize production and management. The basic organizations in the countryside have begun to build up their conception of the

commodity economy and openness. However, because the basic administrative organizations in the countryside in abandoning their traditional management methods have not yet grasped new methods, because the reform of the system of management has been delayed, and because of the negative reaction of the cadres and peasants against the long years of administrative control of production, the management functions of the basic administrative organizations in the countryside have been greatly weakened. In some places, not only are administrative functions weak but economic and social functions have been abandoned.[34]

The evidence suggests, therefore, that the abandonment of the commune system has left many uncertainties in the structure and functions of village-level administration which have yet to be resolved. In some areas, as in Zhangxilou, the old collective system has retained a great deal of influence. In others there is a vacuum. The adoption in mid-1988 of the new law on village committees put forward at the end of 1987[35] does not appear to have resolved the problem. This is in part, one suspects, because the law clearly reflects the origins of the committees in the team structure of the communes. It calls for a separation of economic and administrative functions. Such a call conflicts, however, with both the rural land law and the rural collective enterprise law which clearly vest ownership in the village collective. The potential for conflict between an emerging system of market relationships and an ownership system based on area-defined collectives thus remains strong.

DUAL LEVEL MANAGEMENT

The administrative structures discussed above in many ways represent an adjustment of the collective management system in an attempt to adapt to the existence of market relationships and independent household production. Many observers in China have thus come to see a dual level of management, with a balance between village or collective/co-operative management and household management as the appropriate model for sustaining rural development.[36] The argument is based on the view that the single household is too small a unit to maintain all of the operations needed for rural economic growth. While it can manage agricultural production efficiently in response to economic incentives from the market, there are many things it cannot do. These, it is argued, include the provision of services before, during and after crop production, the maintenance of local infrastructure, and the development of non-agricultural undertakings. The conclusion is that these things can be provided by township and village levels, whose functions are, as described above, bolstered by their continued ownership of economic resources. In effect, the model suggests a way of preserving some of the functions of collective management.

The issue, however, remains the subject of debate. Some observers believe that the idea of a 'dual level' reflects what is actually happening in the rural areas, and they argue that, at the present stage, attention should focus on the role played by the collective as the upper level. After June 1989, this appeared to become the favoured official position as reflected by State Council member Chen Junsheng.[37] Chen argues that the functions of the upper level include: strengthening technical guidance and promoting production; improvement of peasant human resources; consolidating the relationship between cadres and peasants, and building up township and village government. In other words, he focuses on the provision of inputs and services which provide joint benefits to households and argues that these functions should be vested in some kind of restructured collective management.

Against this position, others have argued that the idea of 'dual operation' has become the barrier to the healthy development of a co-operative economy. They suggest that the concept of 'unified operation' is vague and may lead to the unconditional implementation of the directives from above, contrary to the principles of producer independence. In addition, they suggest that dual level management implies joint action, while in fact most operations in rural areas belong exclusively either to the collective or to the household. In this view, the development of a market-oriented economy requires a more complex structure with many different levels of management and organization. The concept of dual level management is thus seen as a retrograde step and primarily a reassertion of collectivist principles.

An example of this argument was put forward by Ran Mingquan before 1989.[38] Ran argued that the ideal solution to the institutional problems of the countryside is the development of new types of independent co-operatives which correspond to the way the economy functions. He stated that the idea of dual level management is in part a politically-inspired attempt to sustain the collective and in part a recognition that the remnants of collective organization can fulfil some social functions while new structures are developed. Nevertheless, the logic of household production extends beyond the boundaries of the collective and requires many different vertical and horizontal services. To support this view, Ran cited one peasant survey which reported the great majority of peasants looked towards outside government departments and the market for those services rather than to their village. Ran concludes that it is only government institutions and cadres who wish to promote the revival of collective operations through the dual level system, primarily because it is in their interests. He suggests, therefore, that such a system should only be transitional while a new form of co-operative organization evolves.

COLLECTIVES VERSUS CO-OPERATIVES

While this debate reflects the problems of institutional adaptation in the face of new economic forces, it also raises some significant questions about the underlying nature of collective and co-operative organizations in rural development. The old collective economy was built around a definition of the collectivity as a geographical area. In effect, it consisted of the families 'belonging' to a particular area of land. The collective ownership of the land and the other assets of that area and the disposal of the income therefrom was expressed through management by the cadres at the level concerned. The transfer of labour and resources across the geographical boundaries between teams and brigades was often criticized as an expression of excessive egalitarianism. In this situation, the peasants born into a particular community automatically became members of that collective. They were very unlikely to change that status for the rest of their lives. Institutions or people outside the geographical area could not become part of the collective, and the few peasants who did move to urban employment did not retain ownership or income rights in their village. In the view of some Chinese observers,

> Although in name the collective ownership of the communes meant that all assets belonged to the commune members, they did not belong to any member in particular. Collective ownership rights were expressed through a small number of commune and brigade cadres who played both an

190

administrative and an economic management role. Because of this lack of clarity in the ownership rights over collective assets . . . peasant rights were eroded. . . . The peasants' concept of ownership of collective assets was shaken. They became indifferent towards collective management and economic efficiency. Their enthusiasm for labour productivity was not high, and collective economic development lacked an internal momentum.[39]

One of the key features of the rural reforms has been to try to break this nexus between a geographical area and economic activity or economic rights. As part of that process, a major goal has been the separation of governmental administration and economic management. As discussed above, however, the goal has not been realized in practice, since local cadres depend on collectively-owned undertakings for their revenue. The result, in some areas, has been the introduction of new types of economic organizations at township and village levels which, under the banner of dual level management, attempt to retain aspects of collective management in new forms. Such organizations are often known as co-operatives, joint co-operatives, or companies, and, like their predecessors, they can be conceived of as collective organizations since they are based on the same community of peasants living within defined geographical boundaries. In essence they are still area-defined economic entities, nominally owned by all the members of the community and managed on their behalf by the local cadres. Such a solution to the problem of establishing new systems of economic management is to be expected, given the inertia of the collective structures upon which the new systems had to be built. To the extent that such organizations do provide pre- and post-production services to their village communities, they can be seen to fulfil necessary economic functions. To the extent that they serve the revenue needs of the local administration, they can also be seen to play an important role.

These collectively-inspired organizations now exist alongside a bewildering variety of private enterprises and co-operatives established voluntarily and according to quite different principles. Some of them are traditional peasant co-operatives based on sharing of tasks among a related group of families.[40] Others are more like shareholder co-operatives, with peasants offering differing combinations of labour, capital and skills as their share contribution and receiving appropriate dividend payments. Some are based on different stages of the production process, including production, processing, services and transport. Others are more vertically integrated. Many cross the former administrative boundaries and build new links between town and countryside. In areas where the level of economic development is low, such organizations may be few. Along the coastal regions, where many opportunities for diversification and specialization exist, they are many and varied. The economic relationships between these new types of co-operatives are determined not by administrative controls and quotas but by economic contracts. Such changes have raised many practical problems for local government. They have also raised a plethora of theoretical and analytical issues. Chinese economists have had to redefine the nature of the rural economy and its co-operative basis.[41]

Some scholars have argued that the concept of a 'co-operative economy' means specific economic units based on voluntary co-operation among labourers and, as a result, only particular types of co-operatives can be so defined. Others have debated whether it forms an economic system based on public ownership of land and encompassing the entire rural economy, or whether it is simply a system of economic management. Some have suggested it is an elastic concept, embracing a variety of forms of co-operation and ownership. Some have argued that the concept subsumes the old idea of the collective, and others have argued the reverse. Still others have seen them both as quite different concepts. Nevertheless, it is accepted that co-operatives could have many different functions, operating in or across different economic sectors, having different degrees of specialization, crossing old administrative boundaries, and involving participants from many different social groups.

The social and institutional implications of these two strands of collective and co-operative organization are, however, quite distinct. Within those which have grown from the collectives, rights of ownership and distribution are still nominally shared by all peasants, even if they are exercised by township and village cadres. The main issue of debate is whether those rights should be expressed through some form of shareholding. In the other types of co-operatives, relationships are defined through ownership rights and contractual linkages, involving owners of assets, and employees, and they are subject to the rigours of the market. The problem facing China is that of which types of institutions are most suited to the development of an economy which is increasingly based on market relations and all that that entails. The official emphasis on dual level management reflects a political and institutional inertia which attempts to preserve some of the vested interests of the previous system. A shift to co-operatives based purely on economic linkages, however, would require further changes to ownership and property rights. Until that is resolved, the rural reforms will remain in an uncertain, transitional stage.

CONCLUSION

The foregoing discussion has focused primarily on governmental and administrative structures and their relationship to economic growth and change. While not the centre of discussion here, it is important to bear in mind that these issues have an important social dimension which will also affect the rate and nature of institutional change. The development of the household economy has meant that household economic income and power is now a function of accumulated assets, technical skills and entrepreneurial ability. The way households inter-relate and the way they respond to village cadres is therefore quite different from the collective past. The emergence of private enterprises and new types of co-operatives, subject to market forces, needing to make a profit and with linkages which cut across administrative boundaries, has meant that the aims of many rural entrepreneurs may conflict with those of the village leadership and the local government. In other words, new sets of economic interests have evolved, and they are pressing for expression in the administration and management of the local economy and society. The recognition in the debate over dual level management that some means has to be found to provide these independent economic entities with the joint services that they need is a partial recognition of this new relationship between the local administration and the independent producers. The way the issues are finally resolved, however, will not be a simple choice based on economic efficiency. They must inevitably also reflect the changing balance of social power between households and new economic enterprises generated by the reforms.

The basic argument of this chapter has thus been that the collective institutional structure built up in the Chinese countryside after 1952 was profoundly undermined by economic forces set in motion in 1978. The price increases for agricultural products and the changes in labour management and marketing introduced at that time initiated a process of diversification and specialization in production. Once begun, that process further changed the economic relationships between the factors of production (land, labour and capital) in ways that encouraged producers to become sharply aware of the opportunity costs they faced and also led to changes in social relationships and to demands for further institutional reform. In the words of Hayami and Ruttan cited at the outset, 'the disequilibria resulting from changes in factor endowments [induced] institutional innovation'.

As the reforms evolved, therefore, the momentum for institutional change came as much through demand from below as through innovation from above.[42] One Chinese observer noted that, especially in the period from 1979 to 1984 when the communes disappeared, the formula used to introduce change was invariably expressed as 'you may do "a", you may do "b", and you may also do "c"' (*keyi, keyi, ye keyi*). The interpretation was

> Everything after 'you may do' was considered correct at the time and should be implemented. But things after 'you may also do' could not yet be affirmed, needed further consideration and were only allowed for limited trial. The things in this last category were not yet agreed upon or even the subject of fierce debate.[43]

Yet, as the author goes on to point out through a careful analysis of key reform statements, it was these 'also mays' that were most rapidly adopted by the peasants and became the norms. This process of reform, almost by sleight of hand, also tends to bear out Hayami and Ruttan's argument that 'institutional innovations will be supplied if the expected returns from the innovation . . . exceeds the marginal cost of mobilizing the resources necessary to introduce the innovation'.[44] In the late 1970s and early 1980s, the political costs to the leading reformers of attempting a direct reform of the commune system would have been very high. Allowing experimental institutional innovation from below tended to reduce the political costs and encouraged changes that accommodated the economic pressures being felt by producers. The problem facing China's leaders is that the trend of economic development now requires some clear decisions about fundamental issues of ownership and control. Sleight of hand is no longer possible.

If the problems of the relationship between local government and economic enterprises, systems of ownership, village management, and co-operative organization are not resolved, economic distortions will continue. In social terms, solutions to these problems will, however, lead to conflict over the economic and political interests of those involved. Nevertheless, as the discussion in this chapter has demonstrated, the current structure of rural institutions in China illustrates that there is a tension between economic forces, the adoption of further technological change and the transitional arrangements in place. The fluctuations in agricultural production, the growth of 'palace economies' and the series of commodity wars since the mid-1980s have reflected these tensions. The efforts to reassert centralized controls and to re-emphasize collective economic activity since June 1989 have, however, done little to resolve the underlying problems. Institutional innovation remains at the top of the agenda in the countryside, and the pressures for institutional adaptation in the face of economic and technological change identified by Hayami and Ruttan continue to work.

NOTES AND REFERENCES

1 This chapter draws on research funded by the University of Adelaide and the Australian Research Council. Thanks are due to Christopher Findlay and Greg O'Leary for comments on an earlier draft.
2 Yujiro Hayami and Vernon W. Ruttan, *Agricultural Development: an International Perspective*, Baltimore, John Hopkins University Press, 1985, Introduction, pp. 1–10.
3 Ibid., pp. 94–5.
4 Theodore Schultz, *Transforming Traditional Agriculture*, New Haven, Yale University Press, 1964.
5 Bruce F. Johnston and Peter Kilby, *Agriculture and Structural Transformation: Economic Strategies in Late Developing Countries*, New York, Oxford University Press, 1975.
6 Michael Ellman, 'Agricultural productivity under socialism', *World Development*, nos. 9/10, 1981, pp. 982–8; and Alec Nove, *The Economics of a Feasible Socialism*, London, Allen & Unwin, 1983, p. 85 ff.
7 Mark Selden, 'Income inequality and the state', in William Parish, ed., *Chinese Rural Development*, New York, M. E. Sharpe, 1985, pp. 193–218.
8 S. Potter, 'The position of peasants in modern China's social order', *Modern China*, vol. 9, no. 4, October 1983, pp. 465–99.
9 For an analysis of the complexities of these relationships in one village in south China see Anita Chan, Richard Madsen and Jonathan Unger, *Chen Village: the recent history of a peasant community in Mao's China*, Berkeley, University of California Press, 1984.

10 'Du Runsheng tan nongcun di er bu gaige wenti' ('Du Runsheng talks about problems of reform in the second stage of rural reform'), *Xinhua Yuebao* (*New China Monthly*), no. 7, 1986, p. 86, cited in Reeitsu Kojima, 'Agricultural organizations: new forms, new contradictions', *The China Quarterly*, no. 116, December 1988, pp. 706–35. For further discussion of the differences between the first and second stages of rural reform see Wu Xiang, 'Nongcun gaige de huigu yu zhanwang' ('The past experience and future prospects for rural reform'), *Zhongguo Nongye Nianjian 1987* (*China Agricultural Yearbook 1987*), Beijing, 1987, pp. 1–6, and the volume of essays from the 1986 conference of the Young Agricultural Economists Forum, Nong-mu-yuyebu Zhengce Fagui Si, ed., *Nongcun Jingji Di Er Bu Gaige Tansuo* (*An Exploration of the Second Stage of Rural Reform*), Jiangsu, Jiangsu Kexue Jishu Chubanshe, 1987.

11 See Andrew Watson, 'New structures in the organization of Chinese agriculture: a variable model', *Pacific Affairs*, vol. 57, no. 4, winter 1984–85, pp. 621–45 for a discussion of the early phase of these changes. Reeitsu Kojima, op. cit., analyses the evolution of these structures over the period up to 1986.

12 Jean C. Oi, 'Peasant households between plan and market: cadre control over agricultural inputs', *Modern China*, vol. 12, no. 2, April 1986, pp. 230–51.

13 For a further discussion of these issues see Christine Wong, 'Between plan and market: the role of the local sector in post-Mao China', *Journal of Comparative Economics*, no. 11, September 1987, pp. 385–98 and C. Findlay and A. Watson, 'Risk and efficiency: contracting in the Chinese countryside', mimeograph, University of Adelaide, April 1989.

14 The following discussion draws on He Daofeng *et al.*, 'Dui xian-ji zhengfu xingwei de chubu fenxi' ('A preliminary analysis of county-level government behaviour'), *NYJJWT*, no. 2, 1987, pp. 19–22; Gu Xiulin, 'Xian-ji jingji tizhi gaige he caizheng bao gan wenti' ('Reform of the county-level economic system and the question of financial contracting'), *Nongcun Fazhan Yanjiu* (*Rural Development Studies*), no. 1, 1986, pp. 67–82; and interviews with the Finance Department of Ling county, Shandong, September 1988. A study of changing systems of county budget management and the growth of independent local resources can be found in Vivienne Shue, 'Beyond the budget: finance organization and reform in a Chinese county', *Modern China*, vol. 10, no. 2, April 1984, pp. 147–86.

15 He Daofeng *et al.*, op. cit.

16 *NMRB*, 7 March 1987, p. 1; and Shi Bing, 'Guanyu nongye xuyao zengjia touru wenti de tantao' ('An exploration of the need for an increase in agricultural investment'), *NYJJWT*, no. 1, 1987, pp. 6–9.

17 The example of how this has affected wool production is analysed in A. Watson, C. Findlay and Du Yintang, 'Who won the "wool war"?: a case study of rural product marketing in China', *The China Quarterly*, no. 118, June 1989, pp. 213–41.

18 Wan Shaofei, 'Zhongyang he difang caizheng guanxi de mubiao moshi'

196

('The target model for central and local financial relations'), *Caimao Jingji (Financial Economics)*, no. 6, 1988, pp. 22–7.

19 The following is based on research carried out in Lingxian in September 1987, August–September 1988 and September 1989, funded by the Australian Research Council and assisted by the Rural Development Research Institute of the Chinese Academy of Social Sciences.

20 *Jiefang Ribao (Liberation Daily)*, 30 March 1989, p. 1. See also Tian Jiyun's speech at the conference on cotton marketing, 7 August 1990, *JJCK*, 8 August 1990, p. 1.

21 Wang Peng, 'Xian jingji fazhan zhanlüe diwei, mubiao yu moshi' ('The role, targets and models for county economic development strategy'), *NYJJWT*, no. 9, 1986, pp. 28–31; Xiao Zhenyuan, 'Qian tan xian-ji jigou shezhi de shang-xia duikou wenti' ('A brief discussion of hierarchical linkages in county organisational structures') *NYJJWT*, no. 9, 1986, pp. 26–7; Hubei Social Sciences Academy, *Zhongguo Xian Jingji de Gaige yu Fazhan* ('The Reform and Development of the County Economy in China), Beijing, Jingji Guanli Chubanshe, 1987, and Jiang Hong and Qin Yongnan, 'Wo guo xian jingji de zhongguan tezheng he xian-ji zhengfu jingji zhineng de zhuanbian' ('The intermediate characteristics of the county economy in China and the evolution of the economic functions of county-level government'), in Guo Shutian and Niu Ruofeng, eds, *Biange de Tansuo (Explorations of Transformation)*, papers presented at the 1985 Young Agricultural Economists Forum conference, Zhongguo Nongye Jingji Xiehui, 1985.

22 *Zhongguo Shangye Bao, (China Commercial Paper)*, 23 August 1988, cited by Chen Wenhong in *Xianggang Jingji Ribao (Hong Kong Economic Daily)*, 6 September 1988.

23 For a discussion of the many issues involved see Guangdong Province Survey Group on County Reform, 'Xian-ji caizheng tizhi gaige de zuofa' ('Ways of reforming financial administration at county level'), *NYJJWT*, no. 3, 1986; pp. 41–3; Su Ming, 'Wo guo xiang caizheng jianshe wenti chu tan' ('An initial discussion of problems of building up financial administration at township level'), *NYJJWT*, no. 12, 1985, pp. 49–52; Liu Wenshao, 'Nongcun shiyanqu dui zhengzhi tizhi gaige de yaoqiu' ('The requirements in rural experimental areas for reform of the governmental system'), *NYJJWT*, no. 10, 1987, pp. 13–15; Yi Yannong, 'Dingzhou shi jian zheng fang quan, jiaqiang xiang (zhen) zhengquan jianshe de diaocha' ('A study of the simplification of administration, transfer of authority downwards and the strengthening of governmental authority at township (town) levels in Dingzhou City'), *ZGNCJJ*, no. 8, 1987, pp. 44–6 and 54; Zhou Fuyuan, 'Lishun tiao-kuai guanxi, shixing fen ji guanli' ('Smooth the relationship between lines and branches, implement administration by levels'), *ZGNCJJ*, no. 8, 1987, pp. 48–51; and Fan Conglai and Li Fusheng, 'Xiangzhen jingji zuzhi xitong de chongxin gouzao' ('The reconstruction of the systems of economic organisation in townships'), *ZGNCJJ*, no. 6, 1988, pp. 1–7.

24 Interviews, August 1988.

25 Sun Guogui, '"Sunan moshi" tansuo' ('An exploration of the Southern Jiangsu model'), *NYJJWT*, no. 9, 1986, pp. 13–15.

26 Li Renxu, 'Xiangzhen gongye jingying geju tansuo – Wenzhou moshi de yaoyi yu shijian' ('An exploration of management patterns in township industry – the meaning and practice of Wenzhou'), *NYJJWT*, no. 4, 1986, pp. 8–12.

27 Cao Guoying, 'Xiangzhen qiye jiceng guanli tizhi gaige tantao' ('A discussion of reform of the basic level administration of township enterprises'), *NYJJWT*, no. 12, 1986, pp. 18–21; Wu Zhikang, 'Ru he dui xiangzhen qiye jinxing guanli' ('How to administer township enterprises'), *NYJJWT*, no. 12, 1986, pp. 21 and 24; Chen Qingyu, 'Xiangzhen zhengquan yu xiangzhen qiye fenpei' ('Township governmental authority and economic distribution in rural enterprises'), *NYJJWT*, no. 6, 1986, pp. 40–2, and Wang Jianhua, 'Xiangzhen qiye de suoyouzhi wenti' ('Problems of the system of ownership of township enterprises'), *NYJJWT*, no. 8, 1985, pp. 14–16.

28 Jiang Yu, 'Xiangzhen gongye yu wo guo nongye xietiao fazhan wenti: taolunhui jian jie' ('A brief introduction to the conference on the co-ordinated development of township industries and China's agriculture'), *NYJJWT*, no. 5, 1986, pp. 50–2.

29 Interview, August 1988. The following discussion also draws on Chen Chunlai, Andrew Watson and Christopher Findlay, 'One state – two economies: current issues in China's rural industrialisation', mimeo, Chinese Economy Research Unit, University of Adelaide.

30 See the Central Committee, 'Decision on further rectifying economic order and deepening reform', 9 November 1989, published in *RMRB*, 17 January 1990, pp. 1–2.

31 *RMRB*, 11 June 1990, p. 2. Translated in *SWB*, FE/0793/B2/6–10, 18 June 1990.

32 The following discussion draws on interviews conducted in 1987, 1988 and 1989.

33 *RMRB*, 13 July 1989, p. 1. See also *SWB*, FE/0512/B2/7, 19 July 1989.

34 Ding Guohua, 'Lun nongcun jiceng zuzhi jianshe' ('On building up basic organisations in the countryside'), *ZGNCJJ*, no. 10, 1989, p. 11.

35 See *Nongcun Caiwu Kuaiji (Rural Finances and Accounting)*, no. 1, 1988, pp. 18–20 for the text of the law.

36 The following discussion is based on Zhang Luxiong, 'Lun shuang ceng jingying tizhi de keguan biranxing' ('The objective necessity for the dual level management system'), *ZGNCJJ*, no. 4, 1988, pp. 40–5; Xia Ying, 'Nongcun shuang ceng jingyingzhi de chuangxin jiazhi' ('The creative value of the rural dual level management system'), *NYJJWT*, no. 7, 1988, pp. 45–8; Tang Shengqi, 'Wanshan shuang ceng tizhi shi shenhua nongcun gaige de jichu gongcheng' ('Perfecting the dual level structure is the basic project in deepening rural reform'), *ZGNCJJ*, no. 3, 1989, pp. 23-7; Zhang Shiyi, Liu Xuesheng, Li Baowen and Yang Zeting, 'Shuang ceng jingying shi nongye lianchanchengbaozhi de fazhan fangxiang' ('Dual level management is the development trend of contracting related to output'), *Zhongguo Shehui Kexue* (Social Sciences in China), no. 1, 1989, pp. 33-46 and 'Yutian xian nongcun jiaqiang shuang ceng jingying de chubu xiaoguo' ('The initial results of strengthening dual level management in Yutian County'), *Zhongguo*

Shehui Kexue, no. 2, 1990, pp. 151-6, and Chen Junsheng, 'Guanyu jianli he wanshan nongcun shuang ceng jingying tizhi wenti' ('On the issue of establishing and perfecting the rural dual level management structure'), *JJRB*, 9 April 1990, p. 2.

37 Chen Junsheng, op. cit.

38 Ran Mingquan, 'Chongjian nongcun hezuo zuzhi: lixiang he xianshi de chongtu' ('Rebuild rural co-operative organisations: the conflict between the ideal and the reality'), *Gaige (Reform)*, no. 4, 1988, pp. 97–103, reprinted in Renmin Daxue Shubao Ziliao Zhongxin Fuyin Baokan Ziliao, F2, *Nongye Jingji (Agricultural Economics)*, no. 8, 1988, pp. 63–9.

39 Jiang Li *et al.*, 'Shi lun nongcun hezuo jingji jiti suoyouzhi guanxi de gaige' ('The reform of collective ownership relations in the rural co-operative economy'), *NYJJWT*, no. 7, 1987, p. 3.

40 Ran Mingquan sees these traditional forms built around social obligations as an obstacle to the development of co-operatives based on economic principles, op. cit., p. 66.

41 See, for example, Zhang Lin, 'Yi nian lai guanyu nongcun hezuo jingji de taolun zongshu' ('A summary of discussion on the rural co-operative economy during the past year'), *JJYJ*, no. 3, 1986, pp. 76–80, and Wang Dai and Guo Lulai, 'Quan guo nongcun hezuo jingji xueshu taolunhui guandian zongshu' ('A summary of viewpoints at the national conference of studies on the rural co-operative economy'), *NYJJWT*, no. 2, 1988, pp. 56–9.

42 For a further discussion of this point see Andrew Watson, 'The family farm, land use and accumulation in agriculture', *The Australian Journal of Chinese Affairs*, no. 17, January 1987, pp. 1–27.

43 Liu Huazhen, 'Always remember that the wishes of the peasants must not be violated' ('Qie ji bu yao weibei nongmin de yiyuan'), *NYJJWT*, no. 6, 1989, pp. 9–15 and 21.

44 op. cit., p. 107.

9

A MASS-LINE WITHOUT POLITICS

Community policing and economic reform

Michael Dutton

It is a fundamental tenet of Chinese Marxist textbooks on law that socialist transition involves the gradual elimination of crime.[1] This is because communism .pre-supposes the absence of any form of criminality.[2] Whatever one may think of this utopian notion, one thing is certain: it has suffered as a result of China's economic reform.

The spectacular economic growth which has been witnessed from the beginning of the economic reform period in 1978 is said to have been shadowed by a similarly spectacular growth in the rate of crime. Indeed, the increases have been such that one could well argue that crime now constitutes one of the big 'growth industries' of the reform period. Reports suggest that crime has not only increased but also that the underlying motives for crime have changed. Crime is no longer said to be primarily of a political nature. Instead, it now covers a wide spectrum of activities from prostitution to drug running.[3] In short, criminal activity in recent years is said to have developed a new profile. This in turn has forced the Chinese Public Security Bureau to institute a series of reforms modifying its own past policing practices. It is some of these changes instituted in the domain of community policing that constitute the object of this study.

Generally, reforms within policing have involved greater levels of specialization. No longer is policing simply a matter of implementing the 'mass-line'. A new division of labour has been introduced, whereby key units are trained to fulfil specialist roles. With this professionalization of the force, the days of 'barefoot policing' have come to an end.[4] A Peoples' Armed Police has been formed,[5] well-equipped mobile patrol units have been instituted, and anti-terrorist squads established.[6] China has even joined Interpol.[7] Yet despite all these important changes, when it came to the key area of community policing the reforms in policing strategies have led to a strengthening rather than weakening of mass-line style policing.[8] It is this re-emphasis and redeployment of the mass-line in community policing – albeit in modified and augmented forms – which is my main focus here.

This ambiguous and specialized re-emphasis of the mass-line under the rubric of reform has been missed by many western studies of the Chinese legal system. Such studies have tended to treat policing as either a sub-plot of discourses on reforms in the legal arena or as an example of the socialist system's intrinsically totalitarian nature.[9] These two quite different approaches have similar effects in that both underplay the importance and relative autonomy of policing. The same can also be said of the more theoretical debates within Chinese legal studies. Structured around a search for the origin of law or the essence of legal form in the works of Marx, they dismiss the importance of theoretical specificity. Consequently, policing strategies are, if dealt with at all, regarded as little other than 'effects' of legal discourse. In dismissing the theoretical and 'practical' specificity of policing, Chinese legal scholars inadvertently left all strategies in this domain in the hands of the policing units themselves. They in turn redeployed in a modified form the mass-line formula of pre-reform days.[10] Such redeployments, I would argue, do not constitute a willed political action on the part of a 'conservative' or 'leftist' police force. Rather, they are the result of certain accepted knowledges and social structures being redeployed to address very new and very different problems. The police response, then, was from within a discourse of policing dominated by a political concept known as 'the mass-line' and it was the 'operationalization' of this which constituted the police response to a perceived rise in street crime in the reform years. An examination of these issues, however, requires us to turn our attention to the predominant western discourses on Chinese law, policing and the state.

WESTERN APPROACHES: POLICING AS A SIDE-SHOW

Given the level of interest western studies of China have shown in the closely related issues of law and the state, why has the question of policing been all but ignored? Briefly, the answer is found in the nature of the discourses deployed in western readings of the

Chinese state. For those who suggest China is a totalitarian state, the role and operation of the police is largely 'transparent'. Policing is the means by which the despotic state sits above, controls and ultimately crushes the self-activity of civil society. Policing, then, is little other than the repressive arm of the totalitarian communist state which unreflexively does its bidding.[11] With this as an *a priori*, any evidence suggesting the relative autonomy of policing is dismissed as 'inessential'.

The implicit bifurcation of the social into state and civil society upon which this reading is based is important to note for it operates to foreclose the possibility of taking a form of specificity which seriously cuts across this divide. Despite this limitation, this sort of division has been central to western political philosophy and sociology for a very long time. Genealogically, the state/civil society divide can, at the very least, be traced back as far as the eighteenth century when it was deployed in the works of both Kant and Humbolt. The second thing to note is that it is not politically anchored. That is to say, the state/civil society divide is as much a part of the liberalism of Constant as it is the anarchism of Godwin. Even Marxist texts have utilized it in attacking the 'inhumanity' of capitalism.[12]

This latter point goes some way to explain the reason why the totalitarian school's essentialist reading of the state is methodologically not that far removed from the logic of the radical left.[13] The Chinese radicals, after all, had suggested that a strong all-round proletarian dictatorship was the basic guarantee of the transition process.[14] In suggesting this the radicals were, of course, inverting the logic of the totalitarian school. With the radical reading, it was a politically advanced state structure which would liberate (not oppress) civil society and aid the process of transition. The totalitarian school's dystopian inversion of this utopian Maoist reading has obvious political effects. Nevertheless, in both accounts policing is portrayed as an unreflexive instrument of some form of dictatorship. In both accounts the specificity of policing is unimportant, for its autonomy is limited.

More liberal western 'realist' accounts tend to present a very different picture. The conception of China as an unchanging totalitarian state is replaced by a model of a dynamic state propelled forward by economic reform. Much is made of the enormous legislative changes undertaken in the reform period which are seen as signs of the fact that due legal process is taken seriously and that the state is beginning to operate on the basis of law.[15] In this respect, the liberal 'realist' accounts appear to move away from the 'grand theory' of both the totalitarian and radical models and to offer the opportunity to take the specificity of policing seriously.

Unfortunately, this is not the case. As with works which rely on a model of totalitarianism, liberal accounts essentialize the actions of the state and, as a result, policing is read as an 'effect' of legislative reform rather than as a domain of action in its own right. Unlike works written within the totalitarian model, however, policing in more liberal western accounts becomes an 'effect' of a socialist state which was, until recently at least, moving toward a normative model organized around the dual concepts of the rule of law and due legal process. Contrary evidence which could potentially disrupt this reading is treated either as an effect of a 'time lag' between legislative action and its implementation within the police force or the 'spoiling' actions of conservatives trying to roll back the reform process. At times it is even treated as an effect of both.[16] In any case, policing becomes little other than a side-show in someone else's carnival. It either 'lags' behind the dominant legislative domain and catches up only eventually, or it is the pawn of the conservative forces in their continuing battle over reform. Yet again, the specificity of policing strategies is dismissed as marginal. This tendency within western scholarship to work from 'grand theory' and ignore the specificity of policing is also an all too common tendency within Chinese legal studies.

CHINESE LEGAL STUDIES AND POLICING

Generally, Chinese legal scholars have attributed the recent rise and diversity of crime in China to the decline in respect shown for the law. This is attributed partly to the continuing influence of Lin Biao and the 'Gang of Four' which has eroded respect for the law, partly to the increasing influence of 'decadent' capitalist value systems brought on as a result of the open door policy, and partly to the effect of negative 'feudal' values and superstitions.[17]

Having assessed the various causes of crime, legal scholars have generally agreed that the remedy lies in the formulation of a strong, stable legal code. By having such a code, it is argued, the 'legal nihilism' which has characterized the period of radical rule throughout the Cultural Revolution period could be overcome, morality re-established and unhealthy tendencies successfully combated.[18]

Although legal scholars have been unanimous in their critique of the harmful effects of this legal nihilist tendency, what is actually meant by the term 'legal nihilism' has never really been made clear. This has allowed the term to be appropriated by all factions and used for a variety of ends. This 'flexibility' is evidenced by the fact that, while the early attacks upon legal nihilism emanated from the liberal Marxist perspective, after the June 1989 massacre, the attack upon nihilism resurfaced to be used against the pro-democracy movement.[19]

This current attack upon the nihilism of the pro-democracy movement contrasts sharply with previous attacks. The earlier, more liberal attacks upon legal nihilism centred upon a defence of a strong, autonomous domain of law. This was then counterposed to the more orthodox Marxist view that law was simply a class tool. To view law as a class tool, the liberals suggested, would be to reintroduce a form of 'legal nihilism'. This was because the 'class tool' view of law failed to take into account the complexity of the legal domain and, instead, reduced it to a mere epiphenomena of power.[20] If law were reduced to a question of power, then 'socialist' law must involve populist interpolations thus bringing in notions such as 'popular indignation' and mass involvement. For the liberals, however, such notions undermined due legal process and thereby negated the very basis of law itself.[21] Such a populist approach, it was argued, caused a diminution of legal, administrative and enforcement procedures and this in turn meant that law could no longer guarantee, specify or enforce citizen rights.[22]

Just how important these debates were to the practices of the law enforcement agencies is fairly questionable. Indeed the texts written by the agencies themselves tend to suggest that a very different set of considerations were central to their agenda. First, the principle of the autonomy of the legal domain – so central to the liberal Marxist schema – was not at all important in the formulations of the law enforcement agencies. It was not the independence of law that they sought, but rather the speedy arrest and prosecution of criminal elements. Rather than contributing to this process, the reforms advocated by the liberals caused a diminution of police power and therefore, in the eyes of the public security organs, hindered the work of law enforcement. What was needed was not a separation of powers but more co-ordination. The police, the procuratorate and the courts should be carefully co-ordinated and their actions unified to ensure maximum effect. To do otherwise, it was suggested, would be to promote the very 'legal nihilism' the more 'liberal' voices had hoped to combat.[23]

Second, and contrary to the views of the more liberal Marxist legal theorists, it was suggested that recourse to populist rhetoric and institutional forms was of great value in aiding law enforcement. Popular indignation was not always to be ignored in the determination of sentence, and the mass-trial format could not simply be dismissed as a pre-legal historical relic. Indeed, the procuratorate went to great lengths to stress the educative value of the mass judgement meetings in the maintenance of social order. For more liberal Marxists, however, the mass judgement meeting constituted an abrogation of due legal process and a 'feudal relic' to be abolished.[24] That such practices remained, it was argued, was indicative of the fact that 'criminals are treated in the same way as they were under feudalism. They are not treated as people with human dignity or political rights.'[25] Despite this argument, the organs charged with the task of enforcing the law have insisted upon maintaining the mass judgement meeting in their armoury of responses to crime. The reason for this is simple: they constitute an effective means by which to police serious crime. Such meetings, the people's procuratorate suggested, were 'of use in that they frighten the criminal, encourage healthy trends, give publicity to the legal system and educate the masses'.[26]

THE CONSIDERATIONS OF THE PUBLIC SECURITY UNITS

What is clear in all these debates over the role of law is just how differently structured scholarly argument is from that of the enforcement agencies. Most arguments put forward by the legal scholars (about the class nature of law, the rule of law or the rule of 'man' and so forth) led away from questions about the 'operationalization' of the law and centred instead upon a dialectically based search for the origin of law or the essence of legal theory within the Marxist classics.

Such issues were far from the concerns of the units charged with policing the law. In other words, the debates within legal theory were generally conducted at the level of principle or abstract theory rather than at the level of policy formulation. Consequently, they proved to be largely irrelevant in terms of policing strategies and actually being able to guarantee rights.

Neither the theoretical accuracy of any particular reading of Marx nor the teleological trajectory of law has been responsible for the changes in policing and punishment strategies in the reform period. Policing strategies are not the effects of the deployment of grand theory – be that the theory of the dictatorship of the proletariat or the rule of law. Rather, they are the outcome of a series of developments in which inherited policing strategies, knowledges and institutions have been augmented, transformed and redeployed, largely in a piecemeal manner, to counter a perceived increase in the levels and diversity of crime which economic reform is said to have brought in train. While emphasizing the piecemeal and contingent nature of such redeployments, it is important to stress that such operations and technology are not without a theoretical and ethical dimension. Rather, it is to suggest that the political, theoretical and ethical dimensions of these strategies are inscribed in the technologies themselves. Moreover, the decision to redeploy certain technologies (rather than others) is in itself, in part at least, an ethical decision based upon certain theoretical and discursive assumptions.[27] Thus, while Chinese legal scholars debated the dialectic of law, its class nature, the rule of 'man', the rule of law, and so forth, the law enforcement agencies set about their business, instituting policies and programmes on the basis of the politico-ethical technologies inherited from the pre-reform past to deal with an ever increasingly difficult and different criminal situation. The perceived nature and difficulty of the problem the police faced is evidenced by the statistical information they have released.

TOWARD A NEW TYPOLOGY OF CRIME

Throughout the 1960s no more than 0.04 per cent of the population were ever convicted of common criminal activity. By the early 1980s convictions were double those of the 1960s,[28] and while the publicly-released figure suggests a rate well below world standards, it is, even on that figure, still very high indeed by Chinese standards.[29] The studies carried out to analyse this rising rate of crime pointed not simply to a 'crime wave' but to an altogether new type of criminal activity committed by a new generation of criminals.

Studies suggested that it was from the very classes the Communist Party claimed to be defending that the majority of the new criminals were being drawn. In one survey of prison inmates' class backgrounds conducted in 1983, it was discovered that almost 95 per cent of offenders came from worker or peasant family backgrounds.[30] Moreover, the types of crimes that these criminals committed were also very different from those of the past. Up until the June 1989 crack-down on political dissent, economic and 'moral' crimes were far in excess of those committed for political reasons.

In the cities, in particular, a new criminal form seemed to be taking shape. Armed robberies, rapes and violent hoodlum activities were the new 'problem crimes' of the early 1980s.[31] In relation to the issue of social order, 'street crimes' carried out by 'hoodlum elements' now tended to predominate.[32] The new street criminals were far more violent than the political criminals of the past.[33] In addition, they were also far younger. The decline in the age of the criminal has been an on-going process ever since the beginning of the Cultural Revolution, although it has now reached 'plague-like' proportions. In 1965, youth crime in many big and medium sized cities accounted for some 30 per cent of all crimes. By 1975 that figure was 60 per cent.[34] The figure today is still growing and by the early 1980s in some cities it was as high as 80 per cent.[35] It was under these new conditions that the police began to resort to the old Maoist political technique of the 'campaign'.[36]

THE RECIDIVIST AND THE TRANSIENT CRIMINAL

The decrease in the age of criminals and their class composition were not the only questions which needed addressing. The other major concerns of the police were the predominance of recidivist and transient criminal elements who are now said to be responsible for somewhere between 20 to 30 per cent of all crime.[37] In cases of major crime such as armed hold-ups or drug running and so forth, recidivists and transient criminals are responsible for somewhere between 30 per cent to 40 per cent of all crime.[38] The problem of recidivism did not end here. Investigations into recidivism and its role in youth gangs suggested that the recidivists often constitute the main 'backbone elements' of hoodlum gangs, planning their crimes and playing a leading role in their execution.[39] Recidivists, then, not only contributed to the general level of criminality by involving themselves in new crime but also contributed greatly to the education of a new generation of criminals.[40] Recidivism, in the language of economic reform, could be said to have had a very large 'multiplier effect'.

As a consequence, recidivism has become a major area of concern for the police.[41] Wang Zhongfang has suggested that the recidivism rate 'in recent years' is, on average, about 15 per cent.[42] He notes elsewhere, however, that 'in recent years' it has also risen by about 15 per cent. Indeed, in some units and workplaces, he suggests, it has increased by as much as 20 to 30 per cent.[43] In such a situation, then, the reform through labour prison system can be said to be in trouble. It has simply failed to address the changing nature of the criminal.

The response of the reform through labour units to this new challenge has been to restress the punitive dimensions of their work. In particular, they have adopted policies to force criminals to remain at the site of reform if they are classified as still in need of reform. There is nothing new in this policy. The same sorts of restrictions have been operative in varying degrees since the mid-1950s.[44] What is new in the reform period is the level of specificity which has emerged and the use of community based household registration policing laws to enforce these new restrictions. In the past, such measures were used somewhat indiscriminately and were instituted *ad hoc* by the prisons themselves. Today, however, they are increasingly used as a specialized means to target particular types of criminals and rely less upon internal prison regulations and more upon a manipulation of existing laws relating to the community. In relation to targeting certain groups the issue is clear. On 11 June 1981, for example, legislation was passed by the Standing Committee of the People's National Congress which clearly targeted urban recidivists. By December, an internal notice from the Ministry of Public Security added more target groups to this list.[45] The way in which they were targeted for banishment demonstrates the new-found co-ordination that existed between community police and the prison authorities. In most cases, it was the automatic right of urban residency which was revoked and this was made possible by a modification of the household registration laws. This was made clear in a classified 'Notice Concerning the Cancellation of the Household Registrations for those Undergoing Labour Education' (document 172) which was circulated jointly by the Ministry of Justice and the Ministry of Public Security in 1984. This notice stipulated the conditions under which certain types of (principally urban-dwelling) prison inmates could have their rights of residency revoked.

These recent measures, then, have largely addressed the problem of social order in urban areas. Indeed, in the 1984 notice it was the urban youth, rounded up in the 1983 anti-street-crime campaign in the cities, who were the target.[46] The key question this notice sets out to address is how to halt the re-emergence of crime in the cities once these criminal elements have been released. The answer that was settled upon was to delay prisoners' release and, in some cases, banish certain types of offenders. From 1984 onwards, all criminals who had previously lived in cities of more than 30,000 people were eligible to have their household registration permanently revoked.[47] To avoid this fate, prisoners from urban areas needed to demonstrate that they had 'absolutely' reformed. Having demonstrated this, their previous work unit, their district police station, and the department in charge of grain allocations for their area had to be consulted and had to agree to their return. Only after this would their urban household registration be restored.[48] For the rural resident, no such stringent conditions were set.

City based recidivism was 'solved', then, not by a major alteration of the reform through labour programme but by various forms of banishment based upon a manipulation of the household registration system.[49] The unreformed were unrecoverable and would simply disappear from sight. While questions still remain regarding the effectiveness of such measures, they have nevertheless proven useful enough to be subsequently re-employed.[50] There are reports, for example, that similar sorts of measures were introduced against political dissidents in the immediate aftermath of the 1989 pro-democracy demonstrations.[51]

In many respects, the household registration system also proved flexible enough to help in combating the other major criminal type, the transient. As noted above, the alarming increase in the recidivism rate has been accompanied by an equally alarming rise in the rate of transient crime. Increases in this particular form of crime are demonstrated by the massive increase in the amount of crime committed on trains. Of the 1,403 convictions for criminal activity on trains in 1985, 632 cases or 45 per cent were committed by transient criminals. This was an increase of 15 per cent over the previous year.[52] Since that time, transient crime on trains has continued to rise. In the first quarter of 1989 alone, 1,600 cases of criminal activity on trains were reported, prompting the Minister of Railways to say that China now faced the worst criminal situation on trains since the revolution.[53]

The problem of transient crime is not simply restricted to in-transit crime. Communities, too, have been hit by a new wave of crime in which transient criminal elements play a significant part. Xu

Miaofa conducted a study of crime and the transient population in 1987. His conclusion was that any substantial increase in the temporary population within a community led to an increase in the crime rate. This was because:

> mixed in with the outsiders are criminal elements who take advantage of economic activity and become part of the mobile population moving hither and thither committing crime. From an examination of various large, important and particularly vicious cases it can be seen that there has been a very sudden increase in the number of outsiders committing these types of crime.[54]

To demonstrate this, Xu examined the court records of a number of southern Chinese cities. In one local level court in Hangzhou in 1987, for example, of 55 criminal convictions, 87 per cent involved outsiders. In another in Wenzhou in 1986, the proportion was 35 per cent, while in Fuzhou, of the 627 convictions registered throughout the city in 1987, 31 per cent involved outsiders. These figures suggest not only the mobility of the 'new' criminal but also the problems faced by the state in trying to respond. Local level policing in contemporary China has always turned on a stable population held in place by a tight system of household registration. What Xu's study concludes is that things have changed so much in the period of economic reform that when it comes to criminal activity, 'one can no longer simply look at the permanent household register'.[55]

In this changed environment, occasioned by economic reform, many of the old mechanisms previously central to both policing and punishment proved ineffective. Consequently, a new specialized form of policing developed whereby police adopted specific strategies to counter specific types of crime. While this response promoted a new professionalism for police designated to fight certain types of crimes (international terrorists, drug racketeers and so forth), in relation to community policing, the revisions generally led away from this model. For community policing, specialization meant strengthening and redefining the mass-line style of work and greater reliance upon mass-line organizations. The problem was, in a period of economic reform, how could policing based on the mass-line operate without disrupting the conditions necessary to promote the market?

TECHNOLOGIES OF POLICING IN NEED OF REFORM: THE ROLE OF THE HOUSEHOLD REGISTER AND THE SECURITY COMMITTEE

Nowhere was this contradiction more keenly felt than in relation to the fight against transient crime. Transient crime could flourish in the reform period because economic reform required large-scale social movement to the newly-constituted markets and employment centres. Pre-reform policing strategies, on the other hand, had always turned upon a demographically stable population. With increased population movement, the pre-reform policing strategies based upon the static household register were found wanting. Transient crime thus began to flourish in the fissures opened by the reform process.

In the past, policing relied upon the household registration system which recorded details of all household members and any movements between households. Registration was both compulsory and necessary. The entire state welfare system in China was underpinned by this register. Until the economic reform period, without registration papers a citizen could not get housing, work, health care, education and grain, cotton or pork allocations. This meant that the household register also constituted a good basis upon which to calculate population distribution, skills, sex ratio and age. Indeed, the register constituted the basis of all census work from the time of the second census in 1964 onwards.[56] In this way, the register provided the statistical material essential for the efficient operation of a centralized state economic plan. Because it was so central to planning and therefore needed to be as accurate as possible, prior to economic reform, great efforts were made to separate the household registration system from the systems of community policing.[57] After 1955, the household registration police were no longer charged with tasks relating to civil affairs. These areas of responsibility became the preserve of street, neighbourhood and village committees.[58]

Since economic reform, however, this has not been the case. Because of the demands of the birth control programme and the deteriorating local crime situation, the policing of local populations as well as transients has meant that the household registration police have been increasingly dragged back into civil affairs. The problem is that the registration police have been asked to fulfil a whole series of new demands at a time when they are least able to cope.

One of the clearest indications of the failing nature of the registration system lies in the fact that it is no longer as accurate as it once was. The positive benefits which once existed only for the registered citizen and thereby virtually guaranteed a registered population are now almost all available through the free market.[59] The implications of this for local level policing are great. At the very time when criminal activity is said to be increasing and becoming more mobile, the technologies of policing are breaking down.

Temporary registration is a case in point. As was pointed out earlier, in the past the structure of the household registration system was largely geared to the policing of a stable population. The registration of temporary residents was a subsidiary task within this system that police were required to perform. Prior to economic reform, temporary registration was manageable because movement was less common. With economic reform, all this changed. Population movements to market or employment centres dramatically increased the size of the population in need of temporary registration. This, in turn, put great strains on the household registration police who found it increasingly difficult to register this segment of the population accurately. An indication of just how serious this problem has become can be gauged by the flow of temporary residents into Beijing. In 1957 an unusually large influx of peasants into Beijing prompted a study into the problems of the city's temporary population. This study calculated the total transient population of Beijing at 150,000 people and it suggested that urgent measures were necessary in order to regulate the 'immigration' flow.[60] This figure pales in comparison to more recent statistics. In 1985, the number of 'permanent' temporary residents in Beijing was 660,000. This meant that temporary residents in Beijing constituted 12.6 per cent of all residents.[61] By 1988, the floating population of Beijing had reached 1.15 million,[62] and it was no longer simply a problem of the major cities. By this time the problems Beijing faced were ones common to all Chinese cities and towns.[63] Almost all were recording record influxes of rural labourers. In 1989 the floating population throughout China was estimated to be approximately 60 million people, 70 per cent of whom were thought to be unemployed rural workers migrating into the cities and towns in search of work.[64]

Faced with this major crisis in the policing of the mobile population, the state responded with sweeping reforms which culminated in the introduction of the identity card system in June 1984.[65] Where once a register of the static population would suffice there was now clearly a need for a new type of policing based less on territory and more on individual identity.

Yet, the identity card system was introduced to supplement rather than replace the household registration system. Indeed the various details given on the identity card are drawn from the household registration files in every local police sub-station.[66] The aim of this new system was to introduce a means of policing for a population in-transit. Previously, most policing had been conducted at the points of departure and arrival through the household registration system. Checks on train passengers and travellers had relied upon such non-standardized documentation as work unit identity cards, household transfer documents and letters of introduction. With the introduction of the identity card system, China now had a uniform system by which to monitor efficiently and effectively the moving population.

It seems clear that the identity card system is designed for the convenience and flexibility of those with the legal right to travel while increasing the level of surveillance over those without. Nevertheless, this identity card system does not address some of the other problems the overburdened household registration system has encountered. It does not, for example, aid the household registration police in the work of registering the high numbers of temporary residents. Moreover, and this is a far more serious problem given the relationship between the floating population and crime, it only partly contributes to the detection of those wishing to avoid registration. To deal with this group, other measures were necessary.

Xu Miaofa, after conducting an extensive survey of the reforms necessary to make the household registration system effective in a period of economic reform, concluded that the move away from a purely territorially based policing system which the introduction of the identity card programme heralded was, in itself, insufficient to maintain social order effectively. In addition to this, he argued, a much closer relationship needed to be forged between those 'organs which were the backbone of public security' and the 'work of investigating, checking, verifying and registering the temporary resident population'.[67] Xu recommended that offices be set up through village or street committees which would then carry out the tasks of registering and verifying registration. Furthermore, contract systems should be instituted whereby local landlords and hotel managers would be responsible for the good order of their registers and would be liable for any irregularities discovered in documentation.[68] These recommendations not only returned the registration system to its pre-1955 role but also established systems of mutuality not unlike the pre-modern system of household registration.[69] In many respects, such a re-emphasis and redeployment of mass-line organizations was inevitable given the structure and organization of policing in China.

Table 9.1 Public security personnel in 1987

Nature of personnel	Number ('000)
Total	1,200
1) Professional police	600
Of which: Public security administration police	320
Police dealing with criminal matters	150
Other	130
2) People's Armed Police	600

Source: Wang Zhongfang, op. cit., p. 481

One of the legacies of the pre-reform 'mass-line' in policing was a remarkably low ratio of police to population. In China, there are currently only 6.03 police per 10,000 people, which is well below world standards.[70] Additionally, only half the regular force has been assigned community or crime oriented police work. The remainder have been deployed in the para-military People's Armed Police (see Table 9.1). The consequences of this are that community based policing has become structurally reliant upon the village and street security organizations and systems. An indication of just how reliant the police are upon these organizations can be gleaned from Table 9.2. In terms of the human resources available to augment the regular police force in the task of community policing, the neighbourhood security network cannot be overlooked. Moreover, at a time when the police are themselves faced with increasing workloads and ever increasing problems, it is to these organizations that the Public Security Bureau has turned to gain some relief.

Table 9.2 Public security committees and small groups in 1986

A) Public security committees				
	Total	Internal*	City and town	Village
Committees	1,174,456	291,548	154,984	728,824
Personnel	5,305,447	1,580,426	858,943	2,866,078
Retired cadres	328,002	44,298	248,967	34,737
B) Public security small groups				
Committees	3,049,759	407,763	394,300	2,247,696
Personnel	6,743,436	1,312,576	1,083,385	4,347,475
Retired cadres	444,979	45,195	359,985	39,799

* Internal refers to those within an enterprise or work unit

Source: Wang Zhongfang, op. cit., p. 485

In this respect, it is therefore less than surprising to discover that Xu Miaofa's recommendations for closer co-ordination between the police and the mass-line organizations were being taken up in many parts of the country.[71] The Public Security Bureau has long advocated such an approach and has been successful in promoting the idea of public security pacts (*zhi'an gongyue*) in a number of provinces and rural regions. Such pacts invariably contained 'citizen pledges' which involved the community in the tasks of maintaining order and actively combating transient criminal elements. They were organized around the household register and it was the responsibility of the household head to contribute to them.[72] It is this system of policing which is now said to offer an effective form of control in rural regions.[73] The question is, whether such a system of criminal control could be effective in the cities where the transient populations are much larger and where the problem of youth crime is more pervasive. The argument put forward by those advocating this style of policing was that it could, and a whole series of reports on successful security committee activities in city areas were published to substantiate such claims.[74]

One model adopted by the Qinghe Street Committee of Heping District, Tianjin, was said to have been particularly successful, leading to seven 'crime free' years in an area previously renowned for its high rates of crime.[75] The system adopted in Tianjin centred upon the street committee setting up a public security committee which would then recruit retired workers and old women of the area to take charge of patrols, to check on local security and to ensure that the neighbourhood ran in an orderly manner. In addition to this, however, they were also charged with the task of running educational programmes for the young people of the district. During the holiday breaks the youths would be organized into small groups and given lectures on the 'Lei Feng spirit' and the need to obey the law. In addition, they would be sent down to local industries to work alongside the labouring people.[76] This combination of small group activity centring upon both education and labour was designed to counter the emergence of youth crime and to strengthen the ideological commitment of the young to socialism. This combination of work and education was clearly modelled on the transformation practices adopted by the units charged with the re-education of criminals in the reform through labour system.

Like the reform through labour system, the emphasis upon collective activity is not simply designed to facilitate control but is also said to have a didactic function. The 'collectivity' of prison life is but a coercive model of the collectivity which constitutes the basis of socialist morality. It is this form of morality which is pitted against the 'bourgeois individualism' of the criminal and the wayward youth. It is the rejection of this individualistic and hedonistic morality of the criminal in favour of a collective morality of socialism which can be said to constitute the basis of both the reform through labour programme and the contemporary community policing strategy of redeploying the security committees. From this it is clear that, while there were important structural and human resource questions at stake in this redeployment of the mass-line, the operation was not without an ethical dimension. Nevertheless, the redeployment was neither the further extension of totalitarian communism nor the triumphant march forward of socialism. Instead, the mass-line is redeployed as a result of a crisis in policing. In short, while it cannot be said that either punishment or policing lacks a theoretical dimension, it should be pointed out that such a dimension cannot be 'read off' totalitarian or socialist 'grand theory', any more than it can be seen as a distillation of the legal codes. Rather, the 'theory' within the regimes of policing and punishment is a 'theory' structured into the politico-ethical technology deployed.

This current re-emphasis upon the role of the public security committees in the 'training' of youth so as to prevent them from turning to crime, upon the use of education and work programmes based around the small group organization and upon the tendency for registration systems to be utilized in a direct policing role all point to the way in which erstwhile 'revolutionary' technologies, albeit in modified forms, have been pressed into the service of economic reform and utilized to redress current problems in social order. Yet these are not the only mechanisms of the mass-line which have been redeployed.

CAMPAIGN-STYLE POLICING

The strengthening of mass-line organizations to police the community was but one aspect of the revival and redeployment of Maoist 'revolutionary strategies'. From 1983 onwards, policing units were resorting to more coercive and draconian means in order to rein-in what they perceived to be a burgeoning crime rate. The campaign against street crime launched in that year was to set the trend for future actions. Apart from the usual panoply of populist enforcement mechanisms being utilized against the criminal, this campaign involved actually changing the law so as to facilitate easier arrests, detentions and prosecutions. Sections of the criminal code were suspended, the sentences for certain types of crime increased dramatically and the trial procedures were speeded-up.[77] The right of defence was seriously limited as a result of legislative changes enacted to facilitate this campaign, as was the right of appeal. This seemingly popular campaign against street crime did have the desired effect and led to a temporary decline in the rate of crime.[78] Its long-term effects, however, were to include a serious erosion of civil rights.

First, it is questionable whether the 100,000 or so detainees[79] in this campaign were given fair trials.[80] Second, the summary provisions of the 1983 legislation have proven to be 'flexible' enough to use in other circumstances as in the current campaign against pro-democracy demonstrators.[81] Similarly, the campaign against corruption followed the same path as the campaign against street crime. Draconian legislation increasing the penalties for those involved in corrupt activities was first introduced in 1982 and later augmented by even harsher measures passed in January 1988.[82] Such tough legislation was a signal to the police that greater effort was to be made in pursuing this type of criminal and this, in turn, resulted in a greater number of arrests. Between January and June 1989, 64,584 cases of corruption were exposed, 15,165 of which were processed by August and 10,172 people punished.[83] The police were advised that a flexible approach to the law was acceptable in such cases.[84] Generally, then, as the situation in law and order has deteriorated in the 1980s, one way in which the police have responded was by redeploying the politico-ethical campaigns which were once so much a part of the Maoist political mobilization strategies.

CONCLUSION

Some western scholars regard the debates within legal theory and the increasing amount of legislative enactments in the economic reform period as signs of an ever increasing respect for the law. By stressing legislative and legal debate, there has been a tendency among them to conceive of populist policing technology as a relic of a bygone era which would eventually be swept away as economic reform advanced. As the economy developed, however, there were rises and changes in the rate of crime and this, in turn, led to demands for more effective forms of policing. Under this pressure the police responded in a number of ways, one of which involved the selective redeployment of many of the populist techniques of the mass-line period. This is most evident in three of the strategies adopted. First, the police reintroduced the campaign style of policing. In so doing they reinvested the force with all the populist symbols and technologies of the mass-line. In the reform period, however, it was a mass-line strategy without an overtly political core. It is this campaign style of policing which has come to the fore in the aftermath of 4 June 1989.[85] Second, there has been a modification and strengthening of some of the more mundane technologies of the mass-line. The residency identity card system has been devised to strengthen and augment the old household registration system. Third, community police units have begun to re-emphasize the value of the neighbourhood committees, the local security committees and the work unit in policing and educating the population.[86] Since the 1989 pro-democracy demonstrations and crack-down which followed, enormous efforts have been made to boost the status of these local level policing and sub-policing units, and the value of model citizens involved in these activities has been extensively canvassed.[87] While all these mechanisms and modifications have so far failed to dent the gradual increase in crime rates, their re-emphasis, even before 4 June, signalled one of the more ambiguous lessons of the reform period.

It is important to re-emphasize the piecemeal nature of these redeployments. It is not the essential totalitarianism of the system breaking through the 'sham' legalism of the reform period which has inspired such methods. Rather, these redeployments have taken place in an effort to redress certain localized problems of policing. Whether such mechanisms will work successfully in the reform period is highly problematic. What is less problematic, however, is that the redeployment of such mechanisms will lead to a further erosion of citizens' rights.

NOTES AND REFERENCES

1 The author gratefully acknowledges support provided by the Australian Research Council.

2 Examples of this type of argumentation can be found in Wang Tiefu, 'Shilun woguo jianyu de zhineng' ('A tentative discussion of the function of our nations prisons'), *FX*, no. 10, 1983, p. 17 and also Yang Xiangguang, Huang Changying and Lu Yongkang, 'Laogaifa zai falü tixi zhong de diwei' ('The status of the reform through labour law in the legal system'), in Zhou Mingdong, Xu Zhangrun and Zhu Ye, eds, *Laodong Gaizao Faxue Gailun Cankao Ziliao (Reference Material Outlining the Legal Study of Reform through Labour)*, Beijing, Zhongyang Guangbo Dianshe Daxue Chubanshe, Beijing, 1987, p. 60.

3 One must treat such Chinese assessments with at least a degree of scepticism for they are, in part, derived from changes in the methods of statistical measurement utilized in the reform period. In the past, for example, there was a far greater tendency to label a crime 'political'. Despite this, it is fair to add that the changes described above are not purely a statistical invention. They emerged long before the reform period began. They were, in fact, first noted in the Cultural Revolution period. For a re-examination of these tendencies in that and the following period see Zhao Mingzheng and Lan Jie, 'Shilun woguo gege lishi jieduan fanzui de tedian ji qi yu jieji douzheng guanxi' ('A tentative examination of the special characteristics of crime in each period of our nation's history and its relationship to class struggle'), in *Fanzuixue Cankao Ziliao (Criminology Reference Material)*, vol. 1, Beijing, Zhongguo Zhengfa Daxue Laogai Fajiao Yanshi, 1984, p. 108.

4 For a brief overview of this trend see Dorothy H. Bracy, 'Police training and professionalism in the People's Republic of China', *The Police Chief*, May 1985, pp. 36–8.

5 The People's Armed Police came into existence in 1983, taking over many of the duties previously carried out by the army. While being called a police force these units are actually under the Ministry of State Security which is a relatively new Ministry formed in June 1983. See

Shao-Chuan Leng and Hungdah Chiu, *Criminal Justice in Post-Mao China; Analysis and Documents*, Albany, State University of New York Press, 1985, p. 77.

6 Tai Ming Cheung, 'Crackdown on Crime', *Far Eastern Economic Review*, 3 November 1988, p. 23.

7 China joined the International Police Federation in 1982 and Zhu Entao, the Deputy-Director of the International Cooperation Department of the Ministry of Public Security, was elected an executive member of that organization. See 'New Minister discusses security problems', *BR*, 30 December 1985, p. 17.

8 By far the clearest example of this renewed stress on the mass-line in community policing is to be found in the police handbook *Gong'an Gongzuo Gaishu (The General State of Public Security Work)*, Beijing, Qunzhong Chubanshe, 1984.

9 For a more detailed examination of the various methodologies employed in examining Chinese systems of justice see James P. Brady, *Justice and Politics in People's China*, London, Academic Press, 1982, pp. 5–12.

10 Such technologies as the neighbourhood security committee system, the campaign style of policing and the welfare system organized around the household register are examples of this mass-line style of community policing. It is these which will be examined in this chapter.

11 The classic example of this approach is to be found in the cold war literature on 'totalitarian' communist policing and punishment practices which had its heyday in the fifties. For a typical example in the field of Chinese legal studies see Dorothy Thompson, 'The People's Tribunals: the antithesis of justice', *American Bar Association*, Baltimore, Chicago, vol. 40, April 1954, pp. 289–92. Such readings are far from being a thing of the cold war past. For a more recent and more sophisticated rendition see Geremie Barmé and John Minford, eds, *Seeds of Fire; Chinese Voices of Conscience*, Hong Kong, Far Eastern Economic Review Ltd, 1986. In their introduction Barmé and Minford refer to '"Proledic" – the Dictatorship of the Proletariat, whose organs (the Security apparatus) are in effect the "other China", the Chinese Gulag, the ever-present (but often intangible) tentacles of which reach into every work place, enfolding the lives of every member of society' (p.xvii).

12 See Pasquale Pasquino, 'Theatrum politicum: the genealogy of capital – police and the state of prosperity', *Ideology and Consciousness*, no. 4, autumn 1978, pp. 41–54.

13 Here, we can also include elements of the left in the west as well as China. James Brady, for example, works on a similar division between state/civil society in his examination of policing and justice. For Brady there are two traditions of justice in China, one 'bureaucratic' the other 'popular'. Using bureaucratic justice, the deformed or pseudo-workers' state attempts to crush civil society. Contrary to this, popular justice operative in a true workers' state forges a dialectical unity with civil society and pushes the society forward. It is this unity which is at the heart of the Chinese mass-line and socialism. See James P. Brady, 'The transformation of justice under socialism: the contrasting experiences

of Cuba and China.' *The Insurgent Sociologist*, vol. X, no. 4–vol. XI, no. 1, summer-fall 1981, pp. 14-18. See also James Brady, *Justice and Politics in People's China*, London, Academic Press, 1982, pp. 57 ff.

14 Zhang Chunqiao's works on the all-round dictatorship of the proletariat is a classic example of this approach. See Chang Chun-chiao, 'On exercising all-round dictatorship over the bourgeoisie', *PR*, vol. 18, no. 14, 4 April 1975, pp. 5–11.

15 A recent example of this was Jerome Cohen's post-massacre retrospective account which highlighted just how far the legal reforms had gone in making China a nation governed by the rule of law and just how much had been lost as a result of the recent crack-down. See Jerome Alan Cohen, 'Law and leadership in China', *Far Eastern Economic Review*, 13 July 1989, pp. 23–4.

16 Shao-Chuan Leng and Hungdah Chiu's work offers a recent example of an approach which combines the two. Shao-Chuan Leng and Hungdah Chiu, op. cit., p. 78. Alternatively, see J. D. Brewer, A. Guelke, I. Hume, E. Moxon-Brown and R. Wilford, *The Police, Public Order and the State*, London, Macmillan Press, 1988, p. 212, where they conclude by stating that draconian legislation introduced in the period of economic reform suggests that 'the oriental tail is still capable of wagging the modernization dog'.

17 See Wei Pingxiong, 'Jianjue guanche zhixing yi fa cong zhong cong kuai chengfa de fangzhen' ('Firmly implement the policy of swift, severe and legal punishments'), *Fanzuixue Cankao Ziliao (Criminology Reference Material)*, vol. 3, Beijing, Zhongguo Zhengfa Daxue Laogai Fajiao Yanshi, 1984, p. 110.

18 See, for example, Chen Shouyi, 'Xin zhongguo faxue sanshinian yi huigu' ('A review of new China's research in law during the past thirty years'), *FXYJ*, no. 1, 1980, pp. 6–7.

19 Examples of how this was used can be found in *RMRB*, 31 July 1989 and 28 August 1989.

20 See Zhou Fengju, 'Fa danchun shi jieji douzheng gongju ma? Jianlun fa de shehuixing' ('Is law purely a tool of the class struggle? Some thoughts on the social character of law'), *FXYJ*, no. 1, 1980, p. 39. For further discussion on the nature and problems of legal nihilism see Ning Hanlin, 'Fandui xingfa kexue zhong de falü xuwuzhuyi qingxiang' ('Oppose the tendency within criminal science toward legal nihilism'), *Beijing Zhengfa Xueyuan Xuebao (The Journal of the Beijing Political Science and Law Institute)*, no. 1, 1979, p. 8.

21 An example of this type of critique is given in Ge Ping and Wang Honggu, 'Tan sixing' ('A discussion of the death penalty'), *FXYJ*, no. 1, 1980, p. 70.

22 Zhou Fengju, op. cit., pp. 39–40.

23 Zeng Longyao, 'Jianchi "gongjianfa" de huxiang peihe he huxiang zhiyue' ('Persist with the mutual co-ordination and interaction of the public security forces, the procuratorate and the courts'), *FXYJ*, no. 1, 1979, p. 43.

24 Chen Pengsheng, 'Tichang zhaokai "wenming fangshi de xuanpan dahui"' ('Advocating the convocation of "civilized forms of mass

judgement meetings"'), *Faxue Zazhi* (*Legal Studies Magazine*), no. 2, April 1982, p. 48.

25 Ibid., p. 49.

26 *Jiancha Yewu Wenda* (*Questions and Answers about the Professional Work of the Procuratorate*), Beijing, Falü Chubanshe, 1986, p. 28.

27 Although in a quite different field, I have found the work of Ian Hunter useful here. In relation to the emergence of the discipline of English, Hunter notes both the ethical and piecemeal nature of the deployment of certain technologies of government. See Ian Hunter, *Government and Culture*, London, Macmillan Press, 1989, pp. 67–9.

28 'Woguo qing-shaonian fanzui de qushi he yufang' ('The trends in juvenile delinquency in China and its prevention'), *Zhongguo Qingshaonian Fanzui Yanjiu Nianjian – 1987* (*Yearbook on Chinese Juvenile Delinquency Studies – 1987*), Beijing, Chunqiu Chubanshe, 1988, pp. 41–2.

29 The publicly-released figure for the number of people involved in crime is below 1 per cent of the population, whereas in France it is 3.9 per cent, in the Federal Republic of Germany it is 4.3 per cent, in the USA it is 4.8 per cent and in the UK it is 5 per cent; 1985 figures quoted in *China Daily*, 20 December 1985, p. 1.

30 Zhao Mingzheng and Lan Jie, op. cit., p. 108. Here again it is important to stress that this study neither endorses nor disputes the statistics generated by public security units. It is about policing strategies generated by perceived threats, not the veracity of the threat. Additionally, it should be added that, while statistics are not fabrications, they are nevertheless 'coloured' by policing strategies which may, for example, pick up on street crime but not cadre crime. For further discussion of this problem see Jock Young, 'Left idealism, reformism and beyond: from New Criminology to Marxism', in Bob Fine, Richard Kinsey, John Lea, Sol Picciotto and Jock Young, eds, *Capitalism and the Rule of Law: From Deviancy Theory to Marxism*, London, Hutchinson, 1979, pp. 20–1.

31 Wei Jiuming and Jiang Hong, '1981 nian qing-shaonian fanzui qingkuang de fenxi he yufang gongzuo de fazhan' ('Developments in the prevention work and analysis of the youth crime situation in 1981'), *Fanzuixue cankao ziliao*, vol. 1, p. 275. To characterize the situation in this way is, of course, to leave aside the issue of corruption which is also rampant. This, however, cannot be dealt with here as it is not the preserve of community policing.

32 Xu Xuewei conducted a detailed survey of street gang's in Shanghai in 1984 and discovered that somewhere between 40 per cent and 50 per cent of crime could be attributed to 'hoodlum elements' and that 45.8 per cent of convictions in most district courts were of this type. See Xu Xuewei, 'The special characteristics of the city's criminal hoodlums and preventative counter-measures' ('Chengshi liumang fanzui de tedian yu fangfan duice'), *Legal Studies* (*Faxue*), no. 7, 1986, p. 22.

33 Zhao Mingzheng and Lan Jie, op. cit., p. 102.

34 Ibid., p. 96. Recently released figures by Cheng Weiqiu, the head of the Department of Law at China's Political Science and Law University,

indicate that the problem of youth crime which used to be city-centred is now a nation-wide problem. He pointed out that the number of crimes committed by young people in 1988 accounted for 60 to 70 per cent of China's total number of crimes. See *SWB*, 26 October 1988, FE/O292/B2/3.

35 'The Tendency of Development of Juvenile Delinquency in China and Its Prevention', op. cit., p. 41.

36 It was under these conditions that the 1983 campaign against 'street crime' was launched. This campaign was said to have been a particularly effective weapon. See ibid., p. 47.

37 In 1987 just over 30 per cent of all crime committed was attributed to one of these two categories. Transients alone constituted 10 per cent of all arrests in that year. In 1987, 55,843 transients were arrested and charged, a 20.5 per cent increase over the previous year. Wang Zhongfang, *Zhongguo Shehui Zhi'an Zonghe Zhili de Lilun yu Shijian* (*The Theory and Practice of Comprehensive Management of Public Order in China*), Beijing, Qunzhong Chubanshe, 1989, p. 148.

38 Zhao Mingzheng and Lan Jie, op. cit., p. 103.

39 Zhang Zhongjiang and Huang Wenjun, 'Leifan, guanfan zai qing-shaonian fanzuituanhuo zhong de zuoyong' ('The role played by recidivists and habitual offenders in juvenile criminal gangs'), *Zhongguo Qing-shaonian Fanzui Yanjiu Nianjian – 1987*, p. 177.

40 This is also evident in their role in the reform through labour camps themselves, where the presence of recidivists in a labour team has been shown to have a major negative influence upon the team's reform progress. See Dong Chunjiang, 'Tigao gaizao zhiliang, yufang he jianshao chongxin fanzui' ('Raise the standard of reform to prevent and reduce recidivist crime'), *FXYJ*, no. 1, 1987, p. 54.

41 Recidivism (*chongxin fanzui*) is defined by Chinese sources as being crime committed by ex-convicts within three years of their release from a penal institution.

42 Wang Zhongfang, *op. cit.*, p. 28.

43 Ibid., p. 207.

44 From the mid-1950s onwards, policies decisions were taken to ensure that certain elements remained on the prison farms as 'free' labour. Initially these policies were quite sweeping, as in the case of the *duoliu shaofang* (many stay and few are released) decision of the second reform through labour conference convened in December 1953. Since that time, however, the policies of forcible detention after the completion of sentence have been greatly refined and made far more specific. For a detailed discussion of these measures see Michael Dutton, *Policing and Punishment in China: From Patriarchy to 'The People'*, Cambridge University Press, 1991.

45 There were five categories of criminal eligible to have their urban based household registration rights revoked. These were: 1) those who within three years of their release from a reform through labour education unit re-commit crimes; 2) convicted escapees who, within the five-year period of their extended sentence at the reform through labour education unit commit further offences; 3) those who underwent reform

through labour and who, following release, committed further offences; 4) those who have had their period of custody at a labour education unit extended for a year but who, in that time, commit a criminal offence, and 5) those undergoing labour education who have had their terms extended but still try to escape. A further category is those criminals undergoing labour education who are deemed by the reform units to be difficult to reform. This notice is quoted in Zhang Qingwu, *Huji Shouce (A Handbook on Household Registration)*, Beijing, Qunzhong Chubanshe, 1987, p. 88.

46 Ibid., pp. 88–9.

47 Ibid., p. 89.

48 Ibid., pp. 88–9. What Zhang means by full reform is never made clear.

49 For those city based prisoners – especially those from Beijing, Shanghai and Tianjin – who have proven difficult to reform and who are forced to remain as 'free' labourers within the prisons there are recommendations that they be sent out from the city prisons to other prison units in the outlying provinces and autonomous regions. Xu Juefei, Shu Hongkang, Shao Mingzheng and Yu Qisheng, *The Study of Reform Through Labour (Laodong Gaizaoxue)*, Beijing, Qunzhong Chubanshe, 1983, p. 237.

50 Discussions with public security personnel from the Public Security University, Beijing, in February 1990 indicate that at least some sections of the public security ministry and justice ministry were not happy with these measures. Quite apart from any ethical considerations, they stressed that such measures were counter productive. For household registration police, who have gone to great lengths to present their work as scientific and welfare-oriented, such measures undercut their position and their credibility. Prison guards were also critical of these measures. For them the task of securing the good order of the prison was undermined by this type of legislation. Urban-dwelling prisoners, believing they had little chance of returning home, became disruptive elements within the prison. It was suggested that such measures were therefore invariably short lived and were abandoned once a campaign against the target group died down.

51 See the document allegedly drawn up and passed by the CCP Central Committee and National Peoples' Congress which was reprinted in the dissident magazine *Zhongguo zhi Chun (China Spring)*, no. 1, 1990, p. 77.

52 'Tielu liucuan fanzui huodong fenxi' ('An analysis of the activities of transient criminals on trains'), dated May 1986, *Zhongguo Qingshaonian Fanzui Yanjiu Nianjian – 1987*, pp. 365–6.

53 *RMRB* (overseas edition), 26 April 1989, p. 1.

54 Xu Miaofa, 'Cong renkou liudong kan huji guanli tizhi de gaige qushi' ('Examining the reform trends in the household registration management system from the viewpoint of population movements'), *Shehui Kexue (Social Sciences)*, (Shanghai), no. 2, 1989, p. 38.

55 Ibid.

56 For a detailed analysis of the relationship between census work and the register see Zhang Qingwu, op. cit., pp. 168–89.

57 For further elaboration of this point see my article: 'Policing the Chinese household: a comparison of ancient and modern forms', *Economy and Society*, vol. 17, no. 2, May 1988, pp. 216–19.

58 H. Yuan Tian, *China's Population Struggle: Demographic Decisions of the Peoples' Republic 1949–1969*, Columbia, Ohio State University Press, 1973, p. 77.

59 This point is exemplified in the words of one peasant-turned-trader who told the *New China News Agency* journalist that: 'You need residence registration in order to get grain and coal rations. We buy grain and coal at negotiated prices. We have no use for residence registration. Even though we do not have residence registration, we have money and we are far better off than you are.' The report goes on to comment that such peasants form 'a special group that is virtually subject to no one's jurisdiction and thereby poses a threat to family planning efforts'. Xinhua, 3 March 1989, quoted in *SWB*, FE/O412/B2/5.

60 *RMRB*, 27 November 1957.

61 *Beijing Wanbao (Beijing Evening News)*, 6 August 1985.

62 *RMRB*, 26 February 1989 quoted in *SWB*, FE/0397/B2/1.

63 One other example is Tianjin with a permanent population of 8.5 million but a floating population in 1989 of 800,000. In 1985 the floating population in Tianjin was only 200,000. Interview with the head of the Tianjin household registration police, Tianjin, 12 January 1990.

64 Of these 60 million people, 40 million are said to be permanent temporary residents in cities and towns and 20 million are regarded as being 'in-transit'. This information comes from interviews with scholars from the Population Research Unit of the China Public Security University, Beijing, 17 January 1990.

65 *Zhonghua Renmin Gongheguo Jumin Shenfenzheng Shixing Tiaoli (Trial Regulations for the Residence Identity Card of the People's Republic of China)*, Beijing, Falü Chubanshe, 1984.

66 Zhang Qingwu, op. cit., 1987, pp. 168–89.

67 Xu Miaofa, op. cit., p. 39.

68 Ibid.

69 For an analysis of the traditional systems of mutuality that the register fostered see Michael Dutton, 1991, chapters 2 and 3.

70 This figure becomes significant when compared with other countries. According to 1986 figures, Hong Kong has 68.1 police per 10,000 persons, Taiwan (1985 figures) has 26.3 per 10,000, Britain has 24.6, the United States has 27.8, France has 34 and the USSR has 36.4. Wang Zhongfang, op. cit., p. 486–7.

71 Already such structures had been established in certain places to control the birth rates of mobile traders. In Changzhi City, Shanxi, a system of landlord pacts has been established. Within these pacts, the landlord was charged with the responsibility of monitoring their tenants and making sure they abide by the birth control plan. Failure to do this would incur a fine of 1,000 yuan. *RMRB*, 23 August 1989.

72 Yang Shengxiao and Li Lianbao, 'Shixing zonghe zhili, shuli lianghao cunfeng' ('Implement comprehensive administration, establish good village practices'), *Fanzuixue Cankao Ziliao*, vol. 3, p. 76.

73 See 'Fujiansheng zai nongcun pubian tuixing zhixing zhi'an gongyue' ('The widespread adoption and implementation of security pacts in the rural areas of Fujian province'), *Fanzuixue Cankao Ziliao*, vol. 3, p. 79.

74 Some of the more successful model Public Security Committee's experiences have been collected into a classified study volume for Public Security workers. See *A Compilation of the Experiences of Public Security Committee Work* (*Zhi'an Baoweiyuanhui Gongzuo Jingyan Huibian*), Beijing, Qunzhong Chubanshe, 1984.

75 Dong Jianjin and Sun Guanghe, 'Qinian mei fasheng anjian de juminqu' ('A residential district which has been free from crime for seven years'), *Fanzuixue Cankao Ziliao*, vol. 3, p. 81.

76 Ibid., p. 83.

77 On the suspension of key sections of the criminal law and the increase in sentences metered out for particular crimes, see the regulations and commentary in section two of *Fanzuixue Cankao Ziliao*, vol. 3, pp. 94–145.

78 Zhao Mingzheng and Lan Jie, op. cit., p. 99. One may dispute the claim that this was a popular campaign and I can offer only anecdotal evidence to validate this assertion. I should add, however, that there was little sign of dissatisfaction with the campaign and certainly no public displays of dissent.

79 This figure is quoted by Shao-chuan Leng and Hungdah Chiu, op. cit., p. 137.

80 See Andrew Nathan, *Chinese Democracy*, London, I. B. Tauris and Co. Ltd, 1986, p. 230.

81 See the Amnesty International Report, *People's Republic of China: Preliminary Findings on Killings of Unarmed Civilians, Arbitrary Arrests and Summary Executions Since 3 June 1989*, London, Amnesty International, 1989, pp. 43–4. The 'flexibility' facilitated by the 1983 campaign is something not taken into account in the Shao-chuan Leng and Hungdah Chiu study. The fact that this campaign did not lead to a wholesale purge of intellectuals is taken by them as a sign of the new liberal attitude in post-reform China. While it is easy to look back now and say this was wrong, a more important error is the implicit rejection of street criminals' rights. See their comments in Shao-chuan Leng and Hungdah Chiu, op. cit., p. 149.

82 The 1982 legislation is entitled *Quanguo Renmin Daibiao Changwu Weiyuanhui Guanyu Yancheng Yanzhong Pohuai Jingji de Fanzui Jueding* (*Decision of the Standing Committee of the National People's Congress Concerning the Severe Punishment of Those Criminals Who Seriously Damage the Economy*), 8 March 1982. Even the title of the legislation is remarkably similar to the later set of legislation utilized against 'street criminals', *Quanguo Renmin Daibiao Changwu Weiyuanhui Guanyu Yancheng Yanzhong Weihai Shehui Zhi'an de Fanzuifenzi de Jueding* (*Decision of the Standing Committee of the National People's Congress Concerning the Severe Punishment of Those Criminal Elements Who Seriously Endanger Public Order*), 2 September 1983. Both sets of legislation can be found in *Zhonghua Renmin Gongheguo Changyong Falü Daquan* (*The People's Republic of China*

Compendium of Regularly Utilized Laws), Beijing, Falü Chubanshe, 1988, pp. 275-9. The 1988 legislation against corruption is also published in this volume and is entitled *Quanguo Renmin Daibiao Changwu Weiyuanhui Guanyu Chengzhi Tanwuzui Huiyinzui de Buchang Guiding (Supplementary Regulations of the Standing Committee of the National People's Congress Concerning the Punishment of Criminals Who Are Corrupt and Those Who Take Bribes)*, 21 January 1988, pp. 282–4.

83 *RMRB*, 20 August 1989.

84 Ibid.

85 Since 4 June 1989 a number of ethico-legal anti-crime campaigns have been launched, particularly targeting corruption and moral degeneracy. In May 1990, most of these campaigns were wed together to form the *Yanda* or severe attack campaign. This is reported to be the most severe crack-down on crime since 1983. See Amnesty International, 'Press Release', 13 September 1990.

86 Note, for example, the way the neighbourhood committee structure has been revamped in urban areas to help counter the deterioration in the social order. On 29 August 1989 the Standing Committee of the Seventh National People's Congress passed the 'Draft Law on the Organization of Neighbourhood Committees in Urban Areas'. This draft law not only laid stress on the traditional role of the committees but also noted their role in maintaining public security, helping with birth control work and in educating the young. See 'NPC Standing Committee brings new measures', *BR*, vol. 32, no. 37, 11–17 September, 1989, pp. 4–5.

87 For just one example of this see *RMRB*, 24 July 1989.

10

THE ROLE OF THE PEOPLE'S LIBERATION ARMY

Dennis Woodward

China's economic reform policies have had military modernization as one of their major goals. At the same time, however, a change in Chinese views concerning the strategic threats faced has also meant that military modernization has been seen as a less pressing task than that of other sectors. As a consequence defence expenditure has repeatedly declined as a percentage of the national budget. Meanwhile, the strategic doctrine of 'people's war' has been deemed inappropriate for 'modern conditions' and modified. Without the concomitant upgrading of military hardware, the PLA thus remains locked in a process of transition. Its ranks have been reduced by approximately one million, the number of military regions has been cut, many of its senior leaders have retired and there has been a shift to emphasizing educational standards and military training.

As well as these direct changes, the PLA has also been indirectly affected by economic reform policies. In particular, the greater rewards which can now be attained in the rural areas through sideline activities, rural industries and commerce has meant that an army career has lost much of its allure, and this traditional source of recruits has proved less fruitful. Similarly, opportunities for urban residents are now far greater in the civilian sphere. As a result, the PLA is confronted with problems in trying to conscript sufficient numbers of recruits of the required standard. This is symptomatic of a decline in its prestige which can be traced back to the 1970s and which has been heightened by revelations of corruption and arrogance on the part of certain military commanders. Inevitably, there is now evidence of low morale within the PLA as a result of these various processes.

Against this background, it is ironic that the PLA was to be drawn directly into the political process, with the declaration of martial law in Beijing in May 1989 and its subsequent role in savagely suppressing student protesters in Tiananmen Square. It was ironic for a number of reasons. Given that the PLA was suffering from low morale and a tarnished image, its involvement in the Beijing massacre could hardly be expected to improve the situation in the short term. In addition, the whole thrust of the reform movement has been to stress a more professional and streamlined PLA, which would concentrate its energies on military training divorced from the general populace and would play a lesser role in political affairs. Yet it has once again been placed in the forefront of political affairs. Moreover, the dislocations of the economic reforms were a direct cause of both student unrest and PLA dissatisfaction, yet they resulted in the two being, literally, on opposite sides of the barricades.

The events of June 1989 also, once again, highlight the importance of the PLA as an arbiter of power within the CCP leadership. Although it is difficult to disentangle the various linkages based on such things as family ties, personal loyalties, shared institutional position and shared policy views between senior military figures at the central level, between central and regional military commanders, and between military commanders and senior party figures, it is precisely these links (*guanxi*) which have played a crucial role in the leadership upheavals since the death of Mao. In this respect, it should be remembered that while it is convenient to talk of 'the PLA', it is by no means a monolithic body. There are different regional armies, main force units and local units, and different service arms. There is much potential for close relationships to develop between regional governments and regional armies and between different parts of the PLA and different sections of the party. It is also argued that only Deng Xiaoping has the guaranteed general support of the PLA. Other leaders are thought to face difficulty in obtaining secure army backing without Deng's aid. Events have borne out this view, as when Deng withdrew his support for Hu Yaobang and Zhao Ziyang in January 1987 and June 1989 respectively.[1] Despite Deng's resignation from the Military Affairs Committee at the Fifth Plenum of the Thirteenth Central Committee in November 1989, the real situation has not changed. Power is vested in individuals rather than formal positions and it still remains to be seen whether the currently designated successors to Deng will be able to secure PLA support (which now appears essential for the maintenance of power) after Deng's demise.

The fortunes of China's economic reforms and the PLA are thus inextricably bound together. On the one hand, the PLA is itself undergoing reform and modernization, while being directly affected by the repercussions of other aspects of economic reform. On the other hand, its leaders are playing a pivotal role in central leadership power struggles which will determine the direction and pace of policy changes. Indeed, antipathy towards aspects of economic reform on the part of senior PLA leaders could well spell their doom. For these reasons, an examination of the impact of reforms to date on the PLA is essential for measuring the likelihood of success of the reform programme as a whole. This chapter will first examine the new strategy under which the PLA is operating. It will then look at its changed military composition and capabilities, and briefly consider the economic impact on military industries. It will conclude by exploring some of the consequences of these developments for the role of the army in Chinese society.

PLA STRATEGIC DOCTRINE

Analysing precisely what constitutes the PLA's strategic doctrine is, as in the case of most other armies, a difficult task. Public pronouncements by Chinese military commanders cannot simply be taken at face value since they might well be designed to confuse potential enemies and to act as part of a general deterrence framework. For example, the 'people's war' strategic doctrine counted for little in the Sino-Indian border war of 1962. Similarly, the current official doctrine of 'people's war under modern conditions', which was first espoused in late 1977, can be seen variously as a compromise between those reluctant to discard totally past PLA traditions and those determined to develop a modernized, regularized, professional army, or as an interim measure adopted to provide a credible defence posture for the immediate future while the slow task of modernization is completed.[2]

It is possible, however, to draw inferences about the dominant strategic doctrine from such things as the priority given to defence expenditure, changes in the composition of the PLA and the types of military exercises practised, as well as from official statements. From an examination of these areas, it is apparent that senior Chinese leaders have decided that there is little likelihood of a major war in the near future and that it is safe to shift the PLA from its previous mobilized state to one of peacetime development. As the perceived threat of a large-scale war has receded, PLA training has changed to deal with frontier conflicts (such as with Vietnam), precipitated events and local wars.[3] While lip service may still be given to 'people's war', the emphasis is clearly on developing an ability to fight a positional war, to engage the enemy rather than to lure them deep into Chinese territory.[4] Increasingly, military exercises with a focus on combined arms operations and rapid deployment forces reflect this changed perspective.[5]

Similarly, other aspects of a 'people's war' orientation have become noticeable by their absence. For example, the militia which constitutes an important adjunct to the regular PLA forces in 'people's war', seems to have been given little emphasis since modernization of the PLA was undertaken. This corresponds with the shift within the regular forces away from large numbers of lightly armed troops in favour of a smaller more highly-trained and better-armed force. Likewise, the close integration of troops with the civilian community (including substantial army assistance for civilian economic tasks) which is an essential aspect of 'people's war', is largely incompatible with the demands of intensive military training carried out in isolated military barracks. In addition, political indoctrination within the army which is also a hallmark of 'people's war', has, until recently, been allowed to atrophy. On balance, therefore, it should be concluded that the PLA's ostensible strategic doctrine of 'people's war under modern conditions' masks a renunciation of 'people's war'. This would be more obvious if budgetary restraints were not acting as a major impediment to the upgrading of military hardware.

THE ECONOMIC ROLE OF THE PLA

In line with the apparent shift in strategic doctrine and linked with the programme for economic reform, the PLA has undergone a major process of restructuring in terms of its funding and economic role. Most obviously, military spending has consistently been given a lower priority as scarce resources (and particularly foreign exchange) have been devoted to importing technology for economic development. Defence expenditure as a percentage of the national budget declined from 17.5 per cent in 1979, to only 8.6 per cent in 1987.[6] Moreover, this represented a real decline in military expenditure. Taking 1978 military expenditure as 100, from a high of 130.1 in 1979 (coinciding with the border war with Vietnam), successive years saw defence spending of 106.8, 90.4, 93.1, 92.2, 91.5, 89.1, 88.1, 85.7, and down to 75.2 in 1988.[7] The first real increase after ten years of defence cuts came in 1990 when the defence budget was increased some 15 per cent from 25.1 billion yuan to 28.9 billion, representing 11.47 per cent of the total budget.[8]

The army (and in particular the defence industries) has also been encouraged to undertake entrepreneurial activities to raise some of their own income as well as to reduce costs. The *Jiefangjun Bao* (*Liberation Army Daily*) editorial for 1 January 1989, for example, stated:

> Carrying out production and management, broadening sources of income and reducing expenditure also constitute undeniably important aspects of strengthening army building.[9]

It went on to urge restraint and belt tightening for a few more years. This point was reiterated by Zhao Nanqi, head of the PLA General Logistics Department, who stated that the army would remain short of money and needed to reduce its expenditure and increase its income.[10]

It can be safely surmised that the cuts in military spending and the pressure to become entrepreneurial have contributed towards the evident lowering of morale within the PLA discussed below. Certainly, if a Hong Kong source is accurate in reporting a letter from a number of PLA officers to the Central Military Commission during the height of the 'Beijing democracy movement', a call for military leaders to set an example by sharing the cuts suggests that they had hitherto been more keenly felt at the lower ranks. The officers urged:

> Beginning with the armed forces, actively promote all reforms in the units, cut military spending, streamline the organs and reform the armed forces set-up. The armed forces leaders at all levels should take the lead in giving up their imported cars, share weal and woe with the masses, and spend on education the money thus saved, to accomplish the invigoration of the economy and culture of the whole nation.[11]

This reluctance to embrace the shift in economic priorities whole-heartedly has also been felt in the campaign to make defence industries enhance national economic construction by producing goods for civilian use. To address some of the problems in developing combined military–civilian production, a national work meeting on the operation of defence science, technology and industry for both military and civilian uses opened in Beijing on 7 October 1989.[12] Li Peng clearly expressed the views of the central leadership when he argued:

> Only after the defence industry developed products for civil use could it get better resources for carrying out research and the production of military items.[13]

This was a logical extension of the macro policy to devote more resources to economic development and less to military modernization applied at the micro level within the defence industries.

In January 1990 this position was reiterated by state councillor Zou Jiahua, who urged weapons manufacturers to 'follow unwaveringly' the principle of integrating the production of military and civilian goods. He stated:

> Making all-out efforts to serve battle needs in times of war and linking the production of military and civilian goods in times of relative peace are distinctive features of weapons production.[14]

Clearly, it was believed that this was a time of 'relative peace' and that more attention should be devoted to producing consumer goods. It was anticipated that by 1992 about two-thirds of China's arms manufacturers would be military–civilian producers.[15]

Considerable success has been claimed for this policy. For example, it has been said that the output value of civilian products constituted 66 per cent (two-thirds again) of gross industrial output value of military enterprises.[16] A similar figure ('over 60 per cent') was cited in early 1990 for the proportion of civilian products in the total output value of the nuclear, aeronautical, astronautical and weapons industries. This was contrasted with the lowly figure of 8.1 per cent which was said to have been the level in 1979.[17] One report even argued that 80 per cent of PLA manufactures were for civilian use and that this was valued at nearly 20 billion yuan.[18] In a related move, PLA hospitals have been opened to civilian patients during the last five years and such patients are claimed to account for two-thirds of the patients treated by these hospitals.[19] The frequency with which the figure of two-thirds crops up in these reports, however, suggests that it may have been a stipulated goal which sectors are keen to claim to have achieved.

Notwithstanding these reputed successes, however, this policy has met with difficulties. Apart from resistance caused by the likely operational inertia in shifting from military production to civilian production, products which are liable to be seen as less important in any case, converting from one line of output to another is no easy task. There have been complaints that some civilian products are unmarketable and hence have become seriously overstocked.[20] A common grievance is also that military enterprises are short of 'funds, energy and raw materials'.[21] If modernization of the PLA's weaponry is to be contingent on the defence industries' entrepreneurial efforts, it might prove to be a very long-term task indeed.

In fact, while some aspects of PLA restructuring have been quite dramatic, modernization of its military hardware has languished. Importing the latest weapons technology has been hampered by a lack of funds and by military trade embargoes – particularly in the wake of the Beijing massacre.[22] This could well be a cause for disgruntlement within the PLA, but there is little or no evidence of open conflict on this matter. Similarly, the reorganization of the PLA's eleven military regions into seven which took place in 1985, the forced official retirement of a number of senior military figures, and the reduction in troop numbers of roughly one million since 1985,[23] which could be expected to fuel disquiet within the PLA, also appear to have been accomplished with minimal opposition. It can be speculated that the reorganization of military regions in the mid-1980s and the reshuffling of six of the seven PLA military regional commanders in May 1990[24] were symptomatic of the dominant group within the party seeking to consolidate control of the army. Finding firm evidence of factional groupings within the PLA is, however, difficult. Overall, therefore, the changes in the economic position of the PLA reflect the changes that the reforms have brought to the relationship between military and civilian goals. And those changes have taken place against a background of internal problems and severely strained army–people relations.

PLA PROBLEMS

Despite the reduction in total troop number targets, the PLA has experienced acute recruitment problems in recent years.[25] In the past, peasants formed the vast bulk of recruits. For them, the army offered the chance of mobility, both in terms of social mobility to a higher paid, higher status job and equally importantly in terms of escaping from the countryside. Since the introduction of rural economic reforms, however, there are many alternative ways of getting out of the countryside and the army has lost much of its allure. Similarly, the salary paid to enlisted soldiers is only about one-quarter of urban civilian wages.[26] The result has been a fall in the quality of recruits, with the 'dregs' of society (unemployed youths and petty criminals) being conscripted.[27] There is ample evidence to support this claim. A Chinese report proclaimed:

> enlistment of young people who have committed acts of hooliganism, theft and affray, of bad ideological quality, and with a criminal record should be strictly prohibited[28]

A *Renmin Ribao* article listed offences such as fighting, gambling, theft and hooliganism among those often committed by such 'recruits'.[29]

Ironically, therefore, at a time when the needs of military modernization demand higher educational standards, there is a tendency for recruiting quotas to be filled with youths of a lower standard.[30] It was reported that 'in a minority of localities' conscripting such unqualified youths was creating problems for the services, and that tests revealed that educational qualifications had been greatly exaggerated.[31] While there were calls for seeking better educational standards and more stringent political qualifications,[32] the difficulty of attracting suitable recruits was reflected in changes to recruiting regulations. In early January 1989 the State Council and the Central Military Commission announced a change in the time for conscription from autumn to spring and relaxed some of the rules. The upper age limit for recruits was raised from 20 to 21, and enlisted urban youths could henceforth be senior middle school graduates of any year and not only the most recent year as before.[33] Given that these difficulties were being experienced in recruiting *before* the PLA became involved in the martial law crack-downs in Tibet, Beijing and elsewhere, it is hard to imagine that the situation has improved since those events.

Related to the difficulties in attracting suitable recruits has been the problem of declining morale within the PLA. Again, this was evident before the introduction of martial law. For example, an article in *Jiefangjun Bao* in January 1989 lamented that discipline in some army units was lax and that such units did not engage in military training and military activities because they saw no immediate military threat. It went on to state:

it is necessary to guide officers and servicemen to correctly treat their comparatively low remuneration and to understand that their work cannot be directly linked with material interests.[34]

Clearly, low levels of pay were at the heart of the problem. The need to ensure the rights and interests of servicemen, both during and after military service, was highlighted in the army press. Equal importance was given to the need to 'increase the sense of honour of the profession of servicemen'.[35] In the absence of a major injection of funds, the solution to problems of morale was, once again, seen in intensified political campaigns and, as discussed below, this was particularly the case in the aftermath of the Beijing massacre.

The continuation of poor conditions for troops was alluded to by Yang Baibing, Director of the General Political Department of the PLA, in March 1990. He stressed:

Leading organs must serve the grassroots level. We have emphasized this principle with our cadres at every level each year. But some leading organs have failed to implement this principle well enough. For example, such affairs as film shows, supply of drinking water, medical services and bathing facilities have been talked about at all levels for many years. But such problems still remain unsolved in many units.[36]

Moreover, while some blame for these conditions was placed on 'objective factors' such as the shortage of funds or the nature of the environment, a goodly portion of the blame was heaped on 'some leading organs' which failed to give sufficient importance to the grassroots level. In particular, those who 'lavishly decorated their offices and reception rooms' but showed no concern about the conditions in the nearby grassroots units were castigated.[37]

It would seem that the lower echelons of the army were shouldering a disproportionate share of the burden which cutbacks in military spending were imposing. It is against this background that the announcement of an increase in the military budget in 1990 needs to be seen. While it might be interpreted as a reward for services rendered during the martial law crack-down, it is probably more appropriate to view it as a necessary payment to still disquiet and to ensure future loyalty to the regime. Little wonder that the extra funds were designated for upgrading housing conditions in the army to lift declining morale.[38]

Doubtless, morale within the PLA would also have been adversely affected by the way in which it was treated by civilians. Indicative of a lack of respect for the PLA on the part of civilians are numerous reports of thefts and damage to military installations.[39] This became an item on the agenda of the Eleventh Session of the Standing Committee of the Seventh National People's Congress when it met in December 1989. It discussed a draft law on the protection of military installations, noting that they had suffered 'quite serious sabotage' in recent years.[40] It would appear that disputes over land and other resources between the army and civilians triggered this response. Occasional media reports provide an inkling of the nature of the problems. For example, in December 1989 it was reported that Hangzhou City had issued titles of building ownership to army units, giving their barracks 'protection under state law'.[41] This had obviously been a matter of contention. Similarly, the resolution of land disputes in the northeast provinces by the return to military units of 20,000 *mu* of military-purpose land which had been occupied by civilians was also reported.[42] The continued need to protect military property, however, was reflected in the passing of the draft law at the Twelfth Session of the Standing Committee of the Seventh National People's Congress in February 1990 as discussed above.[43]

Repairing strained civilian–army relations in the wake of the Beijing massacre has doubtless been a major problem calling for more than passing laws to protect army property. There has, of course, been a massive concerted propaganda campaign aimed at improving the army's image, as well as campaigns within the PLA to reform its behaviour. An emergency circular on supporting the military and giving preferential treatment to military dependants issued by the Ministry of Civil Affairs on 12 June 1989 is indicative of the thrust of the former campaign. It called for propaganda and education work, for extensive patriotic and 'support-the-army' activities, for the provision of special care for wounded soldiers and for preferential treatment for military dependents. It also argued:

> the vast number of people should fully understand and trust the people's army, consciously protect its lofty prestige, mobilize and organize people of all walks of life to warmly support the missions carried out by the martial law units and armed police force. . . . [44]

Clearly many citizens needed to be reminded of their duty towards the army. In a similar vein, the editorials which marked army day in 1989 pointedly stressed that the PLA was a 'benevolent and civilized army worthy of its name',[45] and a 'powerful, yet virtuous' army.[46] The people were exhorted to 'ardently love and learn from the PLA'.[47]

Yet, if a Hong Kong report is reliable, army–civilian tensions remained high enough for clashes to be sparked by something as seemingly trivial as a bicycle accident. In this instance, which is said to have occurred in Guangxi in November 1989, local peasants vented their anger by burning military vehicles and injuring some thirty-six sailors.[48] In this climate, therefore, it is little wonder that attempts to restore harmonious relations between the PLA and the people would not only encompass propaganda campaigns aimed at the people, but would also include efforts to revive PLA traditions of support for the people. For example, it was reported in *Renmin Ribao* in November 1989 that, beginning in 1990, every man in the army must contribute at least ten days' voluntary work in national economic construction each year.[49] This is an example of an attempt to revive an orthodox mechanism which no longer appears appropriate. It was also suggested that military installations which did not involve military secrets should be opened up for civilian use.[50]

As part of this attempt to restore elements of a 'people's army' orientation, a campaign to emulate the model soldier of the 1960s, Lei Feng, was launched once again.[51] His name was first invoked in connection with the posthumous awarding of the title of 'Guardian of the Republic' to ten PLA 'martyrs' from the Beijing massacre whose sacrifice was likened to that of Lei Feng.[52] The campaign, however, was not fully instigated until December 1989, when the PLA General Political Department distributed 300,000 deluxe copies of the *Selected Diaries of Lei Feng* to 'launch a new upsurge in learning from Lei Feng'.[53] It is interesting to note, however, that it was found necessary to assert that, 'facts have proved that the spirit of Lei Feng is not outmoded',[54] suggesting that there were those who held precisely that view. Nevertheless, learning from Lei Feng was one of the main goals featured in the PLA General Political Department's major document, *Some Questions Concerning the Strengthening and Improvement of Political Work in the Army Under the New Situation*, produced in November 1989.[55] And by March 1990 representatives from advanced 'Learn from Lei Feng' units were being fêted at a National Forum in the capital.[56] As in other institutions faced by a new situation as a result of the reforms, retreat to an orthodox approach designed for a different set of circumstances and therefore of dubious efficacy was being tried.

PLA–PARTY RELATIONS

The involvement of PLA forces in martial law operations in 1989 must have placed great strains on their loyalty to the dominant leadership group of the CCP and its goals. Prior to those events, there were already signs of less than wholehearted support for the policies of economic reform, as evidenced by a call in the *Jiefangjun Bao* for greater education among the troops on the current situation and the general principles and policies of reform.[57] It is not surprising, therefore, that the day after the declaration of martial law in Beijing, the paper's editorial stressed the need for:

> all cadres and soldiers of the army to rally closely around the party Central Committee and State Council and the Central Military Commission . . . to resolutely safeguard the authority of the party and the government.[58]

This was to be a constant theme during and after the turbulent events of the 'democracy movement'.

Indeed, in the aftermath of these events, the PLA seems to have been subjected to an intensified political campaign to ensure its unqualified acceptance of party leadership. While army personnel were again encouraged to help build a 'socialist spiritual civilization'[59] and the new party chairman, Jiang Zemin, told the Central Military Commission that the PLA had to become not only a 'mighty' army but also a 'civilized' one,[60] political strengthening, with its emphasis on party leadership over the army, was highlighted by Yang Shangkun, first Vice-Chairman of the Central Military Commission.[61] Critics of army involvement in politics were denounced in the army press:

> Some people who are in favour of bourgeois liberalization noisily advocated that the 'army should be depoliticized' and the 'army should not meddle in politics', trying in vain to separate the army from party leadership.[62]

This suggests that such views may well have had some currency within the army itself. In fact, the very intensity with which party leadership over the army was continually reiterated would indicate that it was under challenge from some quarters.

An All-Army Political Work Conference in late 1989, which produced the major document guiding political work, further took up this issue. It particularly took pains to refute the view that the army should be led by the state and not by the party:

> Thus leadership over the army by the party and leadership over the army by the state are identical, and we absolutely must not set one against the other, or try to dilute or weaken the party's leadership over the army by stressing that the army must be led by the state.[63]

It is interesting to note that this line of argument, by equating the party and the state, runs counter to the general thrust, which has been pursued in the economic sphere, of divorcing the two and regularizing state structures and procedures. It thus represents a step backwards towards an autocratic party in theory as well as practice.

Liu Huaqing, Vice-Chairman of the Central Military Commission, perhaps gave the definitive statement on the army's desired role *vis-à-vis* the party when he stated:

> The most important thing is to make sure that our army will steadfastly maintain its nature, guarantee the party's absolute leadership over the army, follow the party's command at any time, earnestly implement the party's line, principles and policies, keep in line with the party central committee and accomplish all the tasks entrusted by the party.[64]

He also emphasized the need for strengthening the 'political firmness' of cadres and fighters so that the 'gun barrels' were wielded by 'truly trustworthy' people. At issue here is the maintenance of general army support for the current leadership group within the party and its policies, as much as for the concept of party leadership.

Speaking at the same conference, Yang Baibing also reiterated the goal of further political construction to ensure that the army was 'up to the mark' politically. He significantly warned of the need to withstand the 'three tests' – the struggle against the view of 'peaceful evolution' (of socialism into capitalism), the dangers inherent in a period of reform and openness, and the perils of degeneration in an environment of peace.[65] This political work conference of November 1989 thus ushered in a renewed drive to raise the level of political indoctrination in the PLA. There had been a decline in the role played by political commissars within the army as a result of the moves for modernization and regularization,[66] and this was now to be redressed by promoting party building within the army. Study classes to this end were held in the last three weeks of 1989 by PLA general staff units, with unqualified party leadership over the army, once again, being the main preoccupation.[67]

By early 1990 it was announced that the General Political Department of the PLA had made arrangements for all army cadres to study Marxist theories and that there would soon be a 'new upsurge in studying Marxist philosophy' throughout the army.[68] One aspect of this was to increase the commitment towards socialism. It was revealed:

> Although all PLA units have paid attention to and achieved certain fruitful results in conducting the education on adhering to the socialist road in recent years, some comrades are still quite confused on such questions as the superiority and future of the socialist system.[69]

It is not clear whether this is a reference to dissatisfaction with an authoritarian variant of socialism rather than with socialism itself. Nevertheless, if disillusionment with the socialist system had crept into army ranks, as this implies, political education in the army had reached a low ebb. Hence the need for the campaign to conduct political work with its focus on opposing 'bourgeois liberalization' and maintaining party leadership.[70] The success of this campaign will, however, be able to be gauged only after Deng's demise, when general PLA support will be required not only of any group seeking leadership of the party but for the maintenance of the communist regime itself. Meanwhile it is ironic that the events of 1989 have led to a revival of the PLA's political role and of army politicization which runs counter to the direction set in train by the modernization drive.

THE ROLE OF THE PLA

The changed role for the PLA has been quite marked. While it has a long history of involvement in politics and has often been seen as playing a part in determining leadership issues, its progress after 1978 towards becoming a modern, highly trained, professional army saw it concentrating on purely military matters almost exclusively. This was clearly reflected in the goals set at the start of 1989. Primacy was given to raising combat effectiveness by strengthening military training and management.[71] Army training was to be carried out at

241

the individual unit level, to encompass combined tactical training and also operational training.[72] An all-army work conference of January 1989 proclaimed that military training was the central task for all military units in 1989.[73] It catalogued the areas in which training needed to be developed and also stressed the goal of army regularization. The chief of the general staff, Qi Haotian, also urged better quality in PLA training at that time.[74]

This focus on military training was, however, disrupted by the riots and declaration of martial law in Lhasa in March 1989, by the declaration of martial law in Beijing on 20 May 1989, and the subsequent violent suppression of demonstrators there in June.[75] While the lifting of martial law in Beijing on 11 January 1990 might have reduced this role in maintaining order, an uprising in Xinjiang in April 1990 again saw the PLA called upon to quell disturbances.[76] It is therefore unlikely that the PLA will be able to avoid such involvements in handling social and political unrest which may arise as a result of the new tensions introduced by the reforms.

The repercussions of this renewed political role have already been discussed. Among other things, it has seen the PLA drawn into conducting military and political training for students.[77] Such additional tasks, and the increased political indoctrination, can only lessen the time available for military training. The result may not be entirely welcome within the army, as an article in the army press in November 1989 attested. It cautioned against forgetting the development of the army's fighting capacity, and urged that military training should be the focus of the troop's routine rather than other things.[78] There is thus conflict between the goals of modernization and reform and the political role which the army is called upon to play.

By April 1990, there were indications of an attempt to return to the process of regularization and to give more attention to military training. At that time, Jiang Zemin (in his capacity as Chairman of the Central Military Commission) promulgated the *Interim Regulations for Legislative Procedures of the Chinese PLA* and the *Regulations on Military Training for the PLA*.[79] However, while military training was said to be the central task in peacetime, these regulations made clear that this included political training. Towards the end of 1990, the heavy emphasis on political training was continuing, with one report noting that up to 60 per cent of army time was devoted to that task.[80] It would appear that it may be quite some time before the PLA reverts to a role like it played before the dramatic events of 1989.

CONCLUSION

The goal of economic reform is to bring about China's modernization. One aspect of this is the belief that once economic modernization has been attained, it will provide the basis for producing the types of military hardware required for the army's complete modernization. In the meantime, modernization of the PLA has been sought as far as economic and budgetary constraints permit. A move away from a 'people's war' orientation has been evident and there has been greater emphasis on military training and the development of a regularized, professional army. In practice, however, this has been accompanied by cuts in military spending and encouragement for defence industries to shift production to goods for civilians and to become entrepreneurial.

Economic reform has also affected the PLA adversely in other ways. It has led to recruiting problems, a lowering of morale, and could be seen as contributing towards army–civilian disputes by providing an environment in which the fostering of self-interest has heightened tensions over the use of scarce resources. As well as being instrumental in causing dislocations within the PLA, economic reform has also created expectations and tensions within society which the army has been called upon to deal with forcefully. Declarations of martial law and the use of the army to crush protesters, therefore, can be seen, in part, as a by-product of economic reform. Clearly, the formation of the People's Armed Police in 1983, presumably specifically for such purposes as crowd control, demonstrated that the Chinese leadership was aware that the reforms would generate tensions which would require new methods of management. The fact that this force failed miserably in the face of the pro-democracy demonstrations necessitated army intervention. As a result, the People's Armed Police was reorganized in 1990, with its leadership replaced by new army generals and its forces strengthened by an injection of regular military units.[81]

PLA involvement in martial law operations has thus brought about a shift in its role. To an extent, some aspects of its modernization have been further slowed, or even reversed, as it has been called upon to devote more attention to political matters rather than to concentrate solely on military training. Politicization, typified by the revival of a 'learn from Lei Feng' campaign, which is perhaps more appropriate to a 'people's army', has taken precedence over other matters. And, above all, there has been a relentless campaign to ensure the total leadership of the party over the army. How successful this has been, has yet to be seen.

What is certain, however, is that PLA support (or at least acquiescence) will be essential for whoever seeks to cement their leadership in China after Deng dies. The PLA is also liable to be the main bulwark against major turmoil threatening the continued rule of the Communist Party. Since it is not without its own problems, its reliability may be sorely tested.

NOTES AND REFERENCES

1 The role of senior military figures in the dismissal of Hu Yaobang (and the scant regard shown for constitutional niceties) is discussed in Yang Zhongmei, *Hu Yaobang: A Chinese Biography*, trans. William Wycoff, Armonk, M. E. Sharpe, 1988, pp. 156 ff.
2 The doctrine of 'people's war under modern conditions' has been extensively analysed. For example, see Ngok Lee, *China's Defence – Modernisation and Military Leadership*, Sydney, Australian National University Press, 1989, chapter 5; Ellis Joffe, *The Chinese Army After Mao*, Cambridge, Harvard University Press, 1987, chapter 4, and Dennis Woodward,'The PLA: a people's army under modern conditions?' in Graham Young, ed., *China: Dilemmas of Modernisation*, London, Croom Helm, 1985, pp. 177 ff.
3 Zhongguo Tongxun She, 26 January 1989, in *SWB*, FE/0374/B2/5.
4 June Teuful Dreyer,'The reorganization and streamlining of the Chinese PLA', *Issues and Studies*, May 1987, p. 37.
5 Tai Ming Cheung, 'Goodbye people's war', *Far Eastern Economic Review*, 1 December 1988, p. 21, makes this point when discussing a week-long military exercise designed to counter a 'Soviet attack' carried out in the Lanzhou military region in October.
6 Chinese Academy of Social Sciences, *Information China*, vol. 2, Oxford, Pergamon Press, 1989, p. 817 and *SWB*, FE/0374/B2/5. Ellis Joffe, 'Civil–military relations in the PRC in 1987', in Richard Yang, ed., *SCPS Yearbook on PLA Affairs 1987*, Kaohsiung, Sun Yat-sen Center for Policy Studies, 1988, p. 128 cites figures of 20 per cent in 1979 to 'slightly over 8 per cent' in 1987.
7 Chen Bingfu, 'Economic analysis of changes in Chinese military expenditure over the last ten years', *JJYJ*, no. 6, 1990, p. 77.
8 T. M. Cheung,'Political payoff', *Far Eastern Economic Review*, 5 April 1990. The significance of this increased military expenditure is discussed further below.
9 *JFJB*, 1 January 1989, in *SWB*, FE/0357/B2/5.
10 *RMRB*, 9 January 1989, in *SWB*, FE/0361/B2/5.
11 Zhongguo Tongxun She, 18 May 1989, in *SWB*, FE/0462/B2/3. Later Chinese reports (discussed below) calling for greater concern for grass-roots units, suggest the reliability of this report.
12 *RMRB*, 8 October 1989, in *SWB*, FE/0587/B2/5.

13 *SWB*, FE/0589/B2/1.
14 Xinhua, 13 January 1990, in *SWB*, FE/0664.
15 Xinhua, 15 January 1990, in ibid.
16 *RMRB*, 8 October 1989, in *SWB*, FE/0587/B2/5.
17 Xinhua, 3 February 1990, in *SWB*, FE/0682/B2/1.
18 Cheung,'Political payoff' op. cit.
19 Xinhua, 5 February 1989, in *SWB*, FE/0379/B2/6.
20 *RMRB*, 8 October 1989, in *SWB*, FE/0587/B2/5.
21 Ibid. This was also acknowledged by Li Peng. See *SWB*, FE/0589/B2/1.
22 See Jane's Special Report, *China in Crisis: The Role of the Military*, Coulsdon, Jane's Information Group Ltd, 1989, pp. 117 ff., for a detailed inventory of PLA equipment. For a well balanced assessment of PLA modernization, see Hammond Rolph, 'The PLA in 1987: long road to modernisation' in Yang, ed., op. cit., pp. 58–62.
23 Bih-Rong Liu,'The organizational structure of the PLA' in Yang, ed., op. cit., pp. 32 ff.
24 Four newly appointed political commissars were also reassigned in 1990. See Tai Ming Cheung, 'Stars and bars', *Far Eastern Economic Review*, 14 June 1990, and *Ta Kung Pao*, 3 May 1990, in *SWB*, FE/0755/B2/1.
25 Tai Ming Cheung, 'Goodbye people's war', p. 21.
26 Tai Ming Cheung, 'Fish out of water', *Far Eastern Economic Review*, 18 August 1988, p. 31, quotes 24 and 100 yuan respectively.
27 Ibid.
28 Xinhua, 28 January 1990, in *SWB*, FE/0373/B2/4.
29 Luo Tongsong, 'Qualified young men are needed to defend the country', *RMRB*, 20 February 1990, in *SWB*, FE/0398/B2/1.
30 It should be noted, however, that this does not appear to apply to the officer corps.
31 Luo Tongsong, op. cit.
32 Xinhua, 28 January 1990, *SWB*, FE/0373/B2/4.
33 Ibid.
34 Zhang Zhanhui, 'Exploring the cure for laxity – round-up of forum held by some theoretical workers inside and outside the army in conjunction with the Hainan Military District', *JFJB*, 25 January 1989, in *SWB*, FE/0382/B2/3.
35 You Qianzhi, 'Thoughts on strengthening solidarity of the armed forces', *JFJB*, 14 February 1989, in *SWB*, FE/0399/B2/4.
36 *JFJB*, 31 March 1990, in *SWB*, FE/0743/B2/3.
37 Ibid.
38 T. M. Cheung, 'Political payoff,' op. cit.
39 See, for example, *JFJB*, 17 February 1989, in *SWB*, FE/0391/B2/5.
40 *SWB*, FE/0651/C1/1.
41 *SWB*, FE/0660/B2/6.
42 *JFJB*, 26 December 1989, in *SWB*, FE/0681/B2/4.
43 Xinhua, 23 February 1990, in *SWB*, FE/0699/B2/1. See also *SWB*, FE/0700/B2/1.
44 Xinhua, 14 June 1989, in *SWB*, FE/0484/B2/7.
45 *RMRB* editorial, 1 August 1989, in *SWB*, FE/0525/B2/2.

46 *GMRB* editorial, 1 August 1989, in *SWB*, FE/0530/B2/5.
47 Ibid.
48 *Ming Pao*, 6 December 1989, in *SWB*, FE/0634/B2/1.
49 *RMRB*, 11 November 1989, in *SWB*, FE/0616/B2/5.
50 *SWB*, FE/0651/C1/1.
51 Lei Feng was put forward as a model 'Maoist' soldier in the 1960s. See, *Lei Feng: Chairman Mao's Good Fighter*, Beijing, Foreign Languages Press, 1968. A similar campaign was launched in the early 1980s. See Woodward, op. cit., p. 190.
52 *SWB*, FE/0503/B2/14.
53 *SWB*, FE/0641/B2/1.
54 Ibid.
55 Xinhua, 27 February 1990, in *SWB*, FE/0701/B2/1.
56 Xinhua, 3 March 1990, in *SWB*, FE/0707/B2/2.
57 'Win new victories in the reform and building of our armed forces', *JFJB* editorial, 1 January 1989, in *SWB*, FE/0357/B2/3.
58 *JFJB* editorial, 21 May 1989, in *SWB*, FE/0464/B2/4.
59 Xinhua, 24 July 1989, in *SWB*, FE/0521/B2/8.
60 *SWB*, FE/0614/B2/1.
61 Ibid.
62 'Refuting the advocacy of "separating the army from the party"', *JFJB*, 21 November 1989, in *SWB*, FE/0640/B2/6.
63 *SWB*, FE/0644/B2/3.
64 Ibid.
65 *JFJB*, 19 December 1989, in *SWB*, FE/0672/B2/3.
66 Tai Ming Cheung, 'Fish out of water', p. 28.
67 *SWB*, FE/0660/B2/6.
68 Xinhua, 6 February 1990, in *SWB*, FE/0685/B2/5.
69 Xinhua, 10 February 1990, in *SWB*, FE/0687/B2/1.
70 Xinhua, 27 February 1990, in *SWB*, FE/0701/B2/1, and *RMRB*, 16 April 1990, in *SWB*, FE/0741/B2/1.
71 *JFJB* editorial, 1 January 1989, in *SWB*, FE/0357/B2/3.
72 *SWB*, FE/0358/B2/1.
73 *RMRB*, 15 January 1989, in *SWB*, FE/0364/B2/6.
74 *JFJB*, 15 January 1989, in *SWB*, FE/0368/B2/2.
75 For an account of PLA actions in the Beijing massacre, see Jane's Special Report, op. cit.
76 *SWB*, FE/0746/B2/1.
77 *SWB*, FE/0587/B2/4.
78 *JFJB*, 3 November 1989, in *SWB*, FE/0616/B2/5.
79 *SWB*, FE/0734/B2/1.
80 T. M. Cheung, 'Basic Marxist training', *Far Eastern Economic Review*, 23 August 1990.
81 The People's Armed Police commander, Li Lianxiu, one of his three deputies, Fan Zhilun, political commissar, Zhang Xiufu, and his deputy, Zhang Haitian, were all removed. The new commander, Major-General Zhou Yushu, was the PLA 24th Group commander. See T. M. Cheung, 'Security reshuffle', *Far Eastern Economic Review*, 1 March 1990.

11

CONCLUSION

Andrew Watson

The preceding chapters have, from a variety of perspectives, illustrated the complex interaction between economic reform and social change in China. They have shown that economic growth over the past ten years has transformed the behaviour of individuals and groups and, thereby, led to demands for further changes in social institutions and political relationships. They have also demonstrated that if further institutional and political change is not forthcoming, the nature of China's economic development will be increasingly constrained. Stresses and tensions will continue to grow, and the impact of those tensions will tug the economy in directions which will affect the speed and type of growth.

The efforts to slow down reform and reassert more centralized economic control by the party in the aftermath of June 1989 represented a clear attempt to re-establish the interests of those groups which had lost some of their privileges during the preceding ten years. These included the centralized bureaucracy, the political cadres of the party and the urban-based state enterprises. In economic terms, the changes were reflected by a cut-back in credit and money supply, protections for state urban industries, attacks on rural enterprises and criticisms of private enterprise. These economic policies were accompanied by a return to some of the familiar ideological and political discourses of the past, such as the revival of the campaign to learn from the model soldier, Lei Feng, the re-emphasis on political study and the calls for literature and intellectuals to serve the socialist cause. The cost of these economic and political efforts was a dramatic slump in the rate of economic growth, with the official figures for 1989 and 1990 dropping to 3.9 and 5 per cent respectively.[1] At the same time, fundamental features of the process of economic development taking place were also

247

halted or reversed. The growth of rural enterprises, for example, experienced an abrupt slow down, with a decline in the number of labourers employed and a drop in the real rate of growth of output. One of the major engines of economic change in China over the past ten years was thereby profoundly shaken, adversely affecting rural incomes, decelerating the rate of change in the structure of the rural economy, and altering the balance in the relationship between the rural and urban sectors.[2] The fact that the problems caused by such policies quickly led to a reversal of these conservative trends during late 1990 and to a reassertion of the push for economic growth demonstrated not only that the economic processes at work could not be stopped, but also that the new interest groups at work in society – the local governments, the private sector, the urban consumers and the peasant entrepreneurs – were able to make their interests felt despite a major political reversal. The cycle of policy change since June 1989 has thereby provided yet another clear illustration of the feedback mechanisms between economic and social development addressed in this book.

One of the central themes of this book has been that the reforms generated new sets of interests between different groups in society and that the evolution of these interests developed their own logic of political, social and economic change. The general case is argued by Findlay and Jiang and is borne out in all chapters. O'Leary shows how urban reform changed the economic environment for industrial workers and transformed the relationship between workers and management and between workers and the party. This in turn required a new approach to the role of trade unions. Chan shows how the emphasis on economic and technical modernization gave added status to the role of intellectuals, who set out to transform that status into economic and social power and to establish their critical and creative independence from the party. Young demonstrates the logic of development of the private economy, which, once rehabilitated, inevitably followed its own momentum of growth to compete with the planned economy, even though its nature and activities left it open to threat and forced it to adopt a short-term perspective and a defensive posture. Zhang describes the problems of teachers called upon to play a crucial role in the push for development yet constrained by officials unwilling to provide the resources required. The economic environment and the pressure to seek immediate gains meant that officials prefer to put their funds elsewhere and teachers are keen to work in higher-paid jobs. Dutton establishes how economic reform has changed the definition of crime and the nature of criminals. Private entrepreneurs, once criminals, have been rehabilitated, and the open nature of their activities has also required major changes to systems of household registration and social control to allow for the unpredictable behaviour of a much more mobile social group. Jacka shows how the reforms have changed employment opportunities for women but have not changed their social status and the underlying values which shape social behaviour. For example, while transforming the economic context, the assumptions and values which structure the division of labour between men and women remain unchanged. Woodward underlines how the commitment to transforming the army into a modernized military machine subject to a new strategic doctrine has not been matched by the provision of appropriate funds or a rebuilding of its social and political functions. The tension thus created has undermined the morale of the army and led to conflict between the quality of its recruits and the expectations for its role. Finally, my own study shows how the reforms led to a realignment of interests between rural cadres, local government and peasants, a realignment which has deep implications for the nature of rural administration and its role in the course of China's development.

Although these different social groups are loosely defined categories, all the contributors demonstrate that in the areas which they analyse, the reforms transformed established relationships and set new forces in motion. Those forces then produced tensions which began to drive the direction of reform and made it impossible to reverse the process.

A second theme of these studies is the inertia of institutions and procedures. Since the reforms were not a revolution which transformed both social institutions and personnel in one swoop, they have had to evolve by a gradual erosion of the established order. One might argue that this approach was the least-cost option available to reformers. It avoided open debate and confrontation, while generating the forces for change. Nevertheless, this approach brought conflict between the pressures unleashed by the realignment of social interests and the slowness of institutions to confront problems, to adapt quickly and to think outside existing norms and values. This issue is addressed directly by Dutton, who shows how the agenda for reform within policing was dominated by 'traditional' notions of political education, reform through labour and 'mass-line' tactics which in practice were no longer workable. My chapter also illustrates this by showing how the logic of territorially-based collective organization continues to influence both the nature of institutional adaptation within the countryside and the theoretical perceptions of those in China attempting to define what is happening and to prescribe what should be done. Similarly, Young provides evidence of how the administrative system has tended both to preserve negative attitudes towards private enterprise and to construct administrative mechanisms to fit it within previous patterns of social management. Woodward's example of the army demonstrates that enshrined concepts of 'people's war' and a social–political role for the army are not easily shrugged off. They continue to influence attitudes towards the place of the army in Chinese society, the moral training of soldiers and methods of military management. In much the same way, Chan describes the collapse of the special position of Marxism as a form of knowledge and the unwillingness of the party to accept the consequences of this for its relationship with intellectuals; Zhang illustrates how attitudes towards education shaped during the Cultural Revolution continue to impede educational development; O'Leary depicts how, despite the changes in the workplace, the party continues to see the trade unions as a 'transmission belt' whose role is to keep the workers aligned with party and management policies, and Findlay and Jiang stress the unwillingness of the urban population to forego the protections of the planned system, despite its desire for the freedoms of economic reform. As all of these studies show, this friction between established attitudes and procedures and the realities of the social forces emerging from the reforms has been a source of conflict which has continually forced the pace and set the agenda for institutional adaptation.

Ultimately, many of the issues discussed in this book have reflected the inherent contradictions within the reform process. The party set out to stimulate a more open society but was not prepared to relinquish its political and institutional control. It was prepared to countenance a private economy but wished to retain the primacy of the planned sector. It wished to stimulate greater incentives for productivity by removing some of the easy securities of the planned economy but it was not willing to bear the political costs of exposing some powerful social groups to greater risk. It wanted to adjust the balance in the division of social benefits between urban and rural areas but it was not prepared to enforce all the economic transfers implied by that aim. It wanted to call forth greater creativity from all groups in society but was not willing to surrender its managerial powers when that creativity made it necessary. While many of these conflicts were not envisaged or confronted when the reforms began, as the latter evolved and the social changes analysed in these studies emerged, they rapidly became central issues. They brought problems of social change and institutional adaptation to the fore. They also meant that future economic growth and development will in turn be shaped and constrained by how the conflicts are resolved. The events in Tiananmen Square in June 1989 were the product of these conflicts and contradictions. They demonstrated that such issues have profound consequences for the lives and deaths of China's citizens.

NOTES AND REFERENCES

1 *RMRB*, 21 February 1990, p. 2, and *SWB*, 25 February 1991, FE/1005/C1/1.
2 For a further discussion of the issues at stake and the factors involved, see Christopher Findlay and Andrew Watson, '"Surrounding the cities from the countryside": China's rural enterprises and their implications for growth, trade and economic reform', paper presented to the 19th Pacific Trade and Development Conference, Beijing, 27–30 May 1991.

INDEX

252